Critical Studies of the Asia-Pacific

Series Editor
Mark Beeson
University of Western Australia
Crawley, Australia

Critical Studies of the Asia Pacific showcases new research and scholarship on what is arguably the most important region in the world in the twenty-first century. The rise of China and the continuing strategic importance of this dynamic economic area to the United States mean that the Asia-Pacific will remain crucially important to policymakers and scholars alike. The unifying theme of the series is a desire to publish the best theoretically-informed, original research on the region. Titles in the series cover the politics, economics and security of the region, as well as focusing on its institutional processes, individual countries, issues and leaders.

More information about this series at
http://www.palgrave.com/gp/series/14940

Mohammad Zulfan Tadjoeddin
Anis Chowdhury

Employment and Re-Industrialisation in Post Soeharto Indonesia

palgrave
macmillan

Mohammad Zulfan Tadjoeddin
School of Social Sciences and Psychology
Western Sydney University
Sydney, Australia

Anis Chowdhury
School of Social Sciences and Psychology
Western Sydney University
Sydney, Australia

Critical Studies of the Asia-Pacific
ISBN 978-1-137-50565-1 ISBN 978-1-137-50566-8 (eBook)
https://doi.org/10.1057/978-1-137-50566-8

Library of Congress Control Number: 2018936531

Cover illustration: Cultura RM / Alamy Stock Photo

Printed on acid-free paper

This Palgrave Macmillan imprint is published by the registered company Macmillan Publishers Ltd. part of Springer Nature
The registered company address is: The Campus, 4 Crinan Street, London, N1 9XW, United Kingdom

Preface

This volume focuses on the challenge of re-industrialisation in post-Soeharto Indonesia to accelerate decent job creation for reversing rising inequality trend and growing productivity-wage growth gap. It argues that Indonesia cannot re-create the manufacturing miracle of the past based on repression of labour, when it has to respect human and labour rights, accommodate regional diversity and face increased competition from low-wage countries, especially within the Association of Southeast Asian Nations (ASEAN) Economic Community. Uncertainty and subdued recovery of the global economy following the global financial crisis (GFC) have also compounded Indonesia's past export-oriented development model.

Therefore, in this volume, we posit that Indonesia should not only transit to high value-added activities in order to move quickly up the regional flying geese of international division of labour but also develop its internal market by strengthening backward and forward linkages. In other words, for balanced regional development in an era of heightened global uncertainty, Indonesia also needs to develop internal flying geese of its manufacturing sector based on complementarities among diverse subnational entities in terms of their level of socio-economic development and resource endowments (human and natural). This is also necessary to address income inequality and inter-regional socio-economic disparity.

We also suggest that regional minimum wages can be a critical policy variable. Strict compliance with minimum wages closes the wage-productivity gap and hence addresses the rising inequality trend. Regional minimum wages can also accelerate industrial restructuring, including relocation. Thus, variation in regional minimum wages, reflecting regions' level of socio-economic development and resource endowments, is critical.

This volume draws on the findings of research conducted for the International Labour Organization (ILO) between 2011 and 2015. We remain grateful to ILO for its generous support, especially to Iyanatul Islam, Emma Allen, Nooman Majid, Aurelio Parissoto, Claire Harasty, Kazutoshi Chatani and Robert Kyloh.

Our research has benefited from comments at various conferences and seminars, especially at the Bappenas, Bank Indonesia, SMERU Research Institute, Indonesia Study Group (Australian National University), Andalas University (Padang, Indonesia), Indonesia Regional Science Association Conference (Makassar and Bali, Indonesia), Indonesia Employment Forum (Surabaya, Indonesia), ASEAN Inter-university Conference on Social Development (Brunei Darussalam), World Social Science Forum (Durban, South Africa) and Eurasia Business and Economic Society Conference (Madrid, Spain). We are thankful to the organisers and participants.

Professor Raja Junankar of Western Sydney University and the University of New South Wales, Dr Girija Mallik of Western Sydney University, Professor John Lodewijks of SP Jain School of Global Management, Dr Neven Knezevic (UNICEF Jakarta) and Dr Gazi Hassan of University of Waikato (New Zealand) kindly read different parts of the manuscript. We are grateful to them for their insightful comments.

We also thank our two very competent research assistants, Ilmiawan Auwalin and Alona Dwinata.

Some of our research findings were earlier published in the ILO Working Papers Series, ACDE Working Papers in Trade and Development (ANU Crawford School of Public Policy) and journals (*Economic and Labour Relations Review*, *Journal of the Asia Pacific Economy*, *Asian Journal of Social Science*, *Journal of Comparative Asian Development* and *European Journal of East Asian Studies*). However, where possible, we have updated the data and related analysis.

We dedicate this volume to our respective families who have supported our endeavour.

Western Sydney University, Sydney, Australia — Mohammad Zulfan Tadjoeddin
Western Sydney University, Sydney, Australia — Anis Chowdhury

Contents

1 Introduction 1

1.1 The Context 1

1.2 Contents of This Volume 6

1.3 Growth and Structural Transformation: The Rise and Fall of Manufacturing 12

1.3.1 Rise of Manufacturing 13

1.3.2 Fall of Manufacturing 14

1.3.3 Declining International Competitiveness 15

1.3.4 De-industrialisation 17

1.3.5 Missing Middle 19

1.4 Jobless Growth 20

1.5 Productivity, Earnings, Poverty and Inequality 22

1.6 From Shared Prosperity to Rising Disparities 25

1.7 Decentralisation: Unity and Diversity 26

1.7.1 Disparity of Welfare 29

1.7.2 Distribution of Manufacturing 30

1.7.3 Dispersion of Natural Resources 31

1.7.4 Variation of Human Resources 32

1.8 Concluding Remarks 33

References 34

2 An Overview of Employment Situation 39

2.1 Introduction 39

2.2 Employment and Unemployment 40

2.2.1 *Unemployment and Employment Rates: The Empowering Role of Education* 41
2.2.2 *Unemployment Rate: A Poor Indicator of Socio-Economic Progress* 45
2.3 *Employment Quality* 50
2.3.1 *Employment Status* 50
2.3.2 *Vulnerable Employment* 54
2.3.3 *Vulnerability and Social Security Coverage* 55
2.3.4 *Underemployment* 57
2.3.5 *Employment Quality and Poverty* 58
2.3.6 *Wage Inequality and Incidence of Low Pay* 61
2.3.7 *Youth NEET* 68
2.4 *Concluding Remarks: Employment Quality Matters* 69
References 70

3 Earnings, Productivity and Inequality 73
3.1 *Introduction* 73
3.2 *Trends in Real Wage Earnings* 74
3.2.1 *Trends Across Sectors* 77
3.2.2 *The Gender Dimension* 77
3.3 *Labour Productivity Trends* 79
3.4 *Productivity, Real Wages and Employment: Theoretical Perspectives* 81
3.4.1 *Productivity and Real Wages* 81
3.4.2 *Employment, Wages and Productivity* 82
3.5 *Disjoint Between Labour Earnings and Productivity in Indonesia* 86
3.5.1 *Delinking at the National and Sectoral Levels* 87
3.5.2 *Delinking at the Province Level* 88
3.6 *Wage-Earnings Inequality* 92
3.7 *Concluding Remarks: Attacking Inequality* 99
References 100

4 Wages, Employment, Productivity in the Manufacturing Sector 103
4.1 *Introduction* 103
4.2 *Employment, Productivity and Real Wage* 104

4.3 Wages and Productivity Trends in Manufacturing 106
4.3.1 Wage-Productivity Gaps Across Manufacturing Sub-sectors 107
4.3.2 Wage-Productivity Gaps in Large-Medium and Micro-Small Establishments 107
4.3.3 Wage-Productivity Gaps Within Manufacturing by Factor Intensity 111
4.4 Concluding Remarks: Implications for Re-industrialisation 119
References 120

5 Determinants of Employment, Wage and Productivity 123
5.1 Introduction 123
5.2 Wage and Productivity Functions 123
5.2.1 Large-Medium Firms 124
5.2.2 Micro and Small Firms 129
5.3 Employment Functions: Models and Empirics 134
5.3.1 Employment Function: Overall Economy and Nine Economic Sectors 137
5.3.2 Employment Function: Large-Medium Firms of the Manufacturing Sector 140
5.4 Concluding Remarks: Potential for Large-Medium Manufacturing 145
Appendices 146
References 150

6 Inequality, Employment and Manufacturing: Spatial Dimensions 153
6.1 Introduction 153
6.2 Indonesia's Spatial Inequality in Perspectives 153
6.3 Spatial Inequalities of Employment Outcomes 161
6.3.1 Unemployment Rate 161
6.3.2 Formal (Regular) Employment 166
6.3.3 Vulnerable Employment 168
6.4 Labour Force and Wage 177
6.5 Correlates of Formal Employment and Real Wage 178
6.6 Provincial Variation of the Manufacturing Sector 180
6.7 Concluding Remarks: Regional Dimensions Are Critical 186
References 187

7 Policy Perspectives 189
7.1 Introduction 189
7.2 Development Strategies to Turn a "Basket Case" to a Miracle Economy 190
7.2.1 Industrial Development Strategies 191
7.2.2 Regional Development Strategies 197
7.2.3 Employment, Industrial Relations and Manpower Policy 199
7.3 Post-AFC Strategies to Transform Indonesia into an Industrialised Economy 201
7.3.1 Industry and Regional Development Policies 202
7.3.2 Employment and Manpower Policies 206
7.3.3 Minimum Wage Policy 211
7.4 Concluding Remarks: Creating Internal Flying Geese and Avoiding Race to the Bottom 215
References 216

Index 219

List of Abbreviations

2SLS	Two-stage least squares
ADB	Asian Development Bank
AEC	ASEAN Economic Community
AFC	Asian financial crisis
APINDO	*Asosiasi Pengusaha Indonesia* (Indonesian Employers' Association)
Bappeda	*Badan Perencanaan Pembangunan Daerah* (Regional Development Planning Agency)
Bappenas	*Badan Perencanaan Pembangunan Nasional* (National Development Planning Agency)
BKPM	*Badan Koordinasi Penanaman Modal* (Investment Coordination Board)
BPJS	*Badan Penyelenggara Jaminan Sosial* (Social Security Implementing Agency)
BPS	*Badan Pusat Statistik* (Statistics Indonesia)
CV	Coefficient of variation
DPPD	*Dewan Penelitian Pengupahan Daerah* (Regional Wage Research Council)
DPPN	*Dewan Penelitian Pengupahan Nasional* (National Wage Research Council)
DPR	*Dewan Perwakilan Rakyat* (National Parliament)
GAPRI	*Gerakan Anti Pemiskinan Rakyat Indonesia* (Anti-impoverishment Movement for Indonesian Citizens)
GBHN	*Garis-Garis Besar Haluan Negara* (State Guidelines)
GDP	Gross domestic product

GFC	Global financial crisis
GOI	Government of Indonesia
HDI	Human Development Index
HRD	Human resource development
IDR	Indonesian Rupiah
IJP	Indonesia Job Pact
Inpres	*Instruksi Presiden* (Presidential Instruction)
ISIC	International Standard of Industrial Classifications
JALA PRT	Jaringan Nasional Advokasi Pembantu Rumah Tangga (National Network for Advocacy for Domestic Workers)
JAMSOSTEK	Jaminan Sosial Tenaga Kerja (Social Insurance for Private Sector Workers)
KFM	*Kebutuhan Fisik Minimum* (minimum physical needs)
KHL	*Kebutuhan Hidup Layak* (decent living needs)
KHM	*Kebutuhan Hidup Minimum* (minimum living needs)
MITI	Ministry of International Trade and Industry
MP3EI	*Master Plan Percepatan Pengembangan Pembangunan Ekonomi Indonesia* (Masterplan for Acceleration and Expansion of Indonesia's Economic Development)
MPR	*Majelis Permusyawaratan Rakyat* (*The* People's Consultative Assembly)
MVA	Manufacturing value added
NGOs	Non-government organisations
P4BM	*Pusat Pengelolaan Pembebasan dan Pengembalian Bea Masuk* (Agency for Import Duty Exemption and Restitution)
PDIP	Partai Demokrasi Indonesia Perjuangan (the Indonesian Democratic Party of Struggle)
PJP	*Pembangunan Jangka Panjang* (long-term development plan)
R&D	Research and development
RAPBN	*Rencana Anggaran Pendapatan dan Belanja Negara* (State budget)
REPELITA	*Rencana Pembangunan Lima Tahun* (five-year (medium-term) development plan)
RGDP	Regional gross domestic product
RIPIN	*Rencana Induk Pembangunan Industri Nasional* (Master Plan of National Industry Development)
RKP	*Rencana Kerja Pemerintah* (Government Work Plans)

RPJMD	*Rencana Pembangunan Jangka Menengah Daerah* (Regional Medium-Term Development Plans)
RPJMN	*Rencana Pembangunan Jangka Menengah Nasional* (Medium-Term National Development Plan)
RPJPN	*Rencana Pembangunan Jangka Panjang Nasional* (Long-Term National Development Plan)
Sakernas	*Survei Angkatan Kerja Nasional* (National Labour Force Survey)
SBY	Susilo Bambang Yudhoyono
SMEs	Small and medium enterprises
SOEs	State-owned enterprises
SPSI	*Serikat Pekerja Seluruh Indonesia* (All Indonesian Workers Union)
Susenas	*Survei Sosial Ekonomi Nasional* (National Socioeconomic Survey)
UN	United Nations
UNIDO	United Nations Industrial Development Organization

List of Boxes

Box 1.1	Key Policy Messages	10
Box 2.1	Paradox of Low Unemployment and High Poverty	49
Box 3.1	Minimum Wage Compliance and Inequality	95
Box 4.1	Problems Faced by Micro and Small Firms	118
Box 6.1	Studies on Indonesia's Spatial Inequality	159
Box 6.2	Employment and Regional Economic Progress	174
Box 7.1	Six Economic Corridors of MP3EI	203
Box 7.2	Provincial Minimum Wages	212

List of Figures

Fig. 1.1	Indonesia's annual GDP growth (%), 1961–2016. (Note: Average growth rates: 1961–1967 = 2%; 1968–1981 = 8.2%; 1982–1988 = 5.4%; 1989–1996 = 8.1%; 1999–2016 = 5.0%; Source: World Development Indicators (WDI))	12
Fig. 1.2	Structural change within non-oil/gas manufacturing post-AFC. (Source: Calculated from BPS data)	15
Fig. 1.3	Structural change within manufacturing pre-AFC. (Source: Aswicahyono et al. 2013)	16
Fig. 1.4	Export of goods and services by sector, share of total (%). (Source: World Bank data as quoted in Elias and Noone (2011, p. 38))	16
Fig. 1.5	Distribution of manufacturing firms by size (%), 2008. (Source: World Bank, Enterprise Survey 2008, quoted from World Bank (2012a, p. 8))	20
Fig. 1.6	Pre- and post-AFC employment growth (%). (Source: Aswicahyono et al. (2013, Table 6.7))	21
Fig. 1.7	Index of labour productivity, real average and median earnings, 2001–2016 (2001 = 100). (Note: Real average and median earnings are calculated using GDP deflators which are more appropriate for the purpose of this study since we are concerned with workers as part of the production process. Real earnings based on GDP deflator should reflect workers' productivity as earning is the reward for productivity. However, real earnings deflated by CPI—a better measure of worker's welfare—display similar trends; Source: Calculated from the Sakernas (National Labour Force Survey))	23

Fig. 1.8	Share of provincial manufacturing in national manufacturing GDP (%), 2015. (Source: BPS data)	30
Fig. 1.9	Share of provincial mining in national mining GDP (%), 2015. (Source: BPS data)	31
Fig. 1.10	Labour force distribution (%) across provinces, 2015. (Source: BPS data)	32
Fig. 1.11	Years of schooling of the labour force by provinces, 2015. (Source: BPS data)	33
Fig. 2.1	Employment and unemployment rate (%), 1990–2016. (Source: Calculated from Sakernas)	42
Fig. 2.2	Working age in poor households, 1993–2012 (employed, unemployed, economically inactive). (Source: Purnagunawan and Pirmana (2013: 8) based on Susenas data)	46
Fig. 2.3a	Unemployment rate and poverty (33 provinces, 2007–2011). (Source: BPS data (Sakernas and Susenas))	47
Fig. 2.3b	Unemployment rate and poverty (national level), 1990–2016. (Source: BPS data)	47
Fig. 2.4	Regular employment by sector, 2001–2016 (% of total employment). (Source: Calculated from Sakernas)	51
Fig. 2.5	Vulnerable employment by gender (% of total employment), 1996–2016. (Source: Calculated from Sakernas)	55
Fig. 2.6	Underemployment 1990–2016 (age 15–59, as % of total employment). (Note: Employment with zero working hours is excluded; Source: Calculated from Sakernas)	58
Fig. 2.7a	Poverty rate and regular employment in *agriculture*, 2001–2016. (Notes: Regular employment as per cent of total employment in each sector. Poverty head count is per cent population living below the national poverty line; Source: Calculated BPS data (Sakernas and National Account))	59
Fig. 2.7b	Poverty rate and regular employment in *services*, 2001–2016. (Notes: Regular employment as per cent of total employment in each sector. Poverty headcount is per cent population living below the national poverty line; Source: Calculated BPS data (Sakernas and National Account))	59
Fig. 2.7c	Poverty rate and regular employment in *industry*, 2001–2016. (Notes: Regular employment as per cent of total employment in each sector. Poverty headcount is per cent population living below the national poverty line; Source: Calculated BPS data (Sakernas and National Account))	60
Fig. 2.8	Incidence of poverty among underemployed (%), 1990–2016. (Source: Calculated from Sakernas)	61

Fig. 2.9	Real wage by employment status, 1990–2016 (IDR monthly, CPI deflated—base year 2001). (Source: Calculated from Sakernas)	62
Fig. 2.10	Gini index of earnings and consumption expenditure, 1990–2016. (Source: BPS data (Gini index of earnings is calculated from primary earning data of regular wage employment in Sakernas. Gini index of consumption expenditure is taken from BPS official calculations.))	63
Fig. 2.11	Low-pay incidence: National magnitude (%) by gender. (Source: Calculated from Sakernas)	65
Fig. 2.12	Low pay: National magnitude (%) in urban and rural areas. (Source: Calculated from Sakernas)	65
Fig. 2.13	Youth NEET (neither in employment nor in education or training) 1996–2016 by gender (%). (Source: Calculated from Sakernas)	69
Fig. 3.1	Real average and median earnings and real minimum wage by employment status, 2001–2016 (IDR, monthly, 2000 constant prices). (Source: Calculated from the Sakernas)	75
Fig. 3.2	Median to mean ratio of real earnings across employment status, 2001–2016. (Source: Calculated from the Sakernas)	76
Fig. 3.3	Declining real earnings in most sectors, 2001–2016 (Average yearly earning, IDR million per year, 2000 constant prices). (Source: Calculated from the Sakernas)	78
Fig. 3.4	Gender gap of real average earnings, 2001–2016 (IDR, monthly, 2000 constant prices). (Source: Calculated from the Sakernas)	79
Fig. 3.5	Productivity trend by economic sector, 2001–2016. (Source: Calculated from BPS data)	80
Fig. 3.6a	Marginal product and average product curves	84
Fig. 3.6b	Outright shift of marginal product and average product curves	84
Fig. 3.6c	Different supply responses to demand shift	85
Fig. 3.7	Wage earnings-productivity ratio (%) across sectors, 2001–2016. (Source: Calculated from the Sakernas)	88
Fig. 3.8	Labour productivity and real earnings, 2001–2016 (2001 = 100). (Source: Calculated from the Sakernas (annual: 2001–16) and the National Account (annual: 2001–16))	89
Fig. 3.9	Average earning-productivity ratio, average economic growth and average growth of GDP share for each provincial group (%). (Note: Ordinary least squares (OLS) regressions are used to estimate the trend lines; Source: Calculated from the BPS data (Sakernas and National Account))	91

Fig. 3.10 Gini coefficients of wage earnings across economic sectors, 2001–2016. (Source: Calculated the Sakernas) 93

Fig. 3.11 Wage-productivity ratio and Gini index, 33 provinces, 2001–2011. (Source: Calculated from BPS data) 94

Fig. 3.12 Percentage of workers earning less than provincial minimum wages, 2001–2014. (Source: Calculated from Sakernas and ILO database) 96

Fig. 3.13 Primary wage Gini, 2001–2014. (Source: Calculated from Sakernas) 97

Fig. 3.14 Gini index of wage earnings: *Regular wage employment*, 2001–2014. (Source: Calculated from Sakernas and ILO database) 98

Fig. 3.15 Gini index of wage earnings: *All employment*, 2001–2014. (Source: Calculated from Sakernas and ILO database) 99

Fig. 4.1 Real wage earnings, manufacturing ISIC 2, 2001–2015 (IDR million/year, 2000 constant prices). (Source: Calculated from the Sakernas) 107

Fig. 4.2 Wage-productivity ratio (%), manufacturing ISIC 2, 2001–2015. (Source: Calculated from BPS data) 108

Fig. 4.3 Manufacturing: ALL, large-medium (LM) and micro-small (MS), 2001–2014. (Source: Calculated from BPS data) 109

Fig. 4.4 Employment and value-added shares of LM and MS firms, 2001–2014. (Source: Calculated from BPS data) 110

Fig. 4.5 Wage-productivity ratio (%) across sub-sectors of LM industry, 2001–2014. (Source: Calculated from BPS data) 110

Fig. 4.6a Wage and productivity in large-medium firms manufacturing (IDR million/year, 2000 constant prices). (Source: Calculated from BPS data [microdata of Large and Medium Manufacturing Survey]) 113

Fig. 4.6b Wage-productivity ratio in large-medium firms (per cent). (Source: Calculated from BPS data [microdata of Large and Medium Manufacturing Survey]) 113

Fig. 4.7a Wage and productivity, manufacturing, 2010 (IDR million/year, 2000 constant prices). (Source: Calculated from BPS data) 116

Fig. 4.7b Wage-productivity ratio (per cent), 2010: firm sizes and factor intensity. (Source: Calculated from BPS data) 116

Fig. 4.8 Problems faced by micro and small manufacturing firms (per cent), 2009–2013. (Source: Calculated from BPS data [Micro and Small Manufacturing Survey]) 118

Fig. 4.9 Three main problems of micro and small manufacturing firms (per cent), 2009–2013. (Source: Calculated from BPS data [Micro and Small Manufacturing Survey]) 119

Fig. 6.1a	Theil (T) index of expenditure inequality, 2000–2015. (Source: Calculated from BPS data)	155
Fig. 6.1b	Share of *within*- and *between*-provinces inequalities, 2000–2015. (Source: Calculated from BPS data)	155
Fig. 6.2	Gini index of eight provinces with Gini index higher than national average in 2015. (Source: Calculated from BPS data)	156
Fig. 6.3a	Share of manufacturing (2000) and increase in Gini index (2000–2015). (Source: Calculated from BPS data)	158
Fig. 6.3b	Share of mining (2000) and increase in Gini index (2000–2015). (Source: Calculated from BPS data)	158
Fig. 6.3c	Mean years of schooling (2002) and increase in Gini index (2000–2015). (Source: Calculated from BPS data)	159
Fig. 6.4	Unemployment rates (2016) and per capita RGDP (2015) across provinces. (Source: Calculated from BPS data)	163
Fig. 6.5	Unemployment rate in selected provinces (%), 1996–2016. (Source: Calculated from Sakernas)	165
Fig. 6.6	Formal employment (2016) and share of manufacturing (2015). (Source: Calculated from BPS data)	170
Fig. 6.7	Vulnerable employment (2016) and per capita RGDP (2015). (Source: Calculated from BPS data)	174
Fig. 6.8	Investment growth exceeds GDP growth (%), 2001–2016 (aggregate Indonesia). (Source: Calculated from BPS data)	176
Fig. 6.9	Years of schooling of the labour force by provinces, 2015. (Source: BPS data)	177
Fig. 6.10	Wage earning across provinces, 2015 (IDR 000/month). (Source: Calculated from BPS data)	178
Fig. 6.11	Shares of manufacturing in provincial RGDP, 2000, 2005, 2010 and 2015. (Source: Calculated from BPS data)	180
Fig. 7.1	Map of MP3EI six economic corridors. (Source: GOI 2011, p. 46)	204
Fig. 7.2	Provincial minimum wage (IDR per month), 2015. (Source: BPS data)	213

List of Tables

Table 1.1	Share of total export by sector (%), 2000 and 2010	17
Table 1.2	Growth, employment, poverty and inequality, 2001–2016	24
Table 1.3	Diversity of Indonesian provinces	27
Table 2.1a	Categories of unemployment (% of total unemployment), 2001–2016	44
Table 2.1b	Average education (years) of the unemployed, 2001–2016	45
Table 2.2	Non-regular employment by sector, 2001–2016 (% of total employment)	52
Table 2.3	Vulnerable employment by employment status (% of total employment), 1996–2016	55
Table 2.4	Low-pay incidence with expanded coverage (2001, 2006, 2011 and 2016)	67
Table 3.1	Employment status (%), 2001, 2010 and 2016	74
Table 3.2	Functional distribution of income (%), 1975–2008	86
Table 3.3	Provinces grouping based on earnings-productivity slope	90
Table 4.1	Sectoral GDP, employment and productivity, 2001 and 2016	104
Table 4.2	Regular waged employment: sectoral share and wage index, 2001–2016	105
Table 4.3	The grouping of ISIC 2 manufacturing sub-sector based on factor intensity	112
Table 4.4a	Wage and productivity: Micro firms (IDR million/year, 2000 constant prices)	114
Table 4.4b	Wage and productivity: Small firms (IDR million/year, 2000 constant prices)	114
Table 4.4c	Paid employment at firm level (per cent)	115
Table 4.5	Shares of employment and value added (%), 2010	117

Table 5.1	Determinants of real wage (difference GMM regression)	126
Table 5.2	Determinants of labour productivity (difference GMM regression)	128
Table 5.3	Determinants of wage in micro and small firms (Heckman)	132
Table 5.4	Determinants of wage in micro and small firms (pseudo panel, difference GMM)	133
Table 5.5	Determinants of productivity in micro and small firms (Heckman)	134
Table 5.6	Determinants of productivity in micro and small firms (pseudo panel, difference GMM)	135
Table 5.7	Employment functions: endogenous versus exogenous wage earnings	139
Table 5.8	Employment function—manufacturing (overall and LM firms only)	141
Table 5.9	Employment function (2SLS regression, large-medium firms)	144
Table 6.1	The eight provinces driving national inequality	157
Table 6.2	Unemployment rates and RGDP per capita across provinces	162
Table 6.3	Open unemployment rate and regional variation, 1996–2016	164
Table 6.4	Employment status (%), 2001–2016	167
Table 6.5	Formal employment across provinces, 2001, 2010 and 2016	169
Table 6.6	Formal employment: magnitude at the national level (per cent of total employment), regional variation and gender gap, 1996–2016	171
Table 6.7	Vulnerable employment (per cent of total employment) and its regional variation (CV), 1996–2016	172
Table 6.8	Vulnerable employment by provinces (%), 2000, 2010 and 2016	173
Table 6.9	Correlations of formal and vulnerable employment with regional macroeconomic data (33 provinces, 2001–2011)	175
Table 6.10	Provincial variation (CV) and gender gap of wage earning, 2001–2016	177
Table 6.11	Correlates of formal employment and real wage, 2001–2011	179
Table 6.12	Decreasing and increasing shares of manufacturing, 2000–2015	182
Table 6.13	Provinces with a dominant role of manufacturing sector, 2015	183
Table 6.14	Manufacturing by sub-sectors in highly industrialised provinces (manufacturing share >30 per cent), 2015	184
Table 6.15	Manufacturing by sub-sectors in reasonably industrialised provinces (manufacturing share 15–30 per cent), 2015	185

CHAPTER 1

Introduction

1.1 The Context

Once characterised as "chronic dropout", and a country that "must surely be accounted the number one economic failure among the major underdeveloped countries" (Higgins 1968, p. 678),[1] Indonesia was one of the star performers in Southeast Asia until the Asian financial crisis (AFC) of 1997–1998. After recovering from the slump preceding the 1965 failed coup and take-over by President Soeharto, the Indonesian economy grew at an annual rate of around 8.1 per cent during 1968–1981 and 1989–1996.[2] Roughly three decades of high growth resulted in a rapid decline in the poverty rate (by national poverty line) from over 60 per cent in 1966 to around 11 per cent in 1996 and rising shared prosperity as inequality remained relatively low and stable.[3]

[1] Benjamin Higgins spent quite a bit of time in Indonesia in the early 1950s as an advisor from the World Bank.

[2] Nobel Prize Laureate Gunnar Myrdal also had a pessimistic assessment of the Indonesian economy "adversely affected by the turbulent and erratic course of national politics" (*Asian Drama*, 1967, p. 368). In the wake of the failed 1965 coup, he wrote, "the Indonesian economy, already near bankruptcy, was utterly destroyed" (p. 379). But he was almost prophetic and thought that only the army led by a "benevolent and enlightened" dictator would be able to restore "a minimum of order" … "stabilize and gradually develop the economy" (p. 380).

[3] The common measure of expenditure Gini remained stable around 0.31. However, there are disagreements about the extent to which expenditure Gini can capture the true nature of

M. Z. Tadjoeddin, A. Chowdhury, *Employment and Re-Industrialisation in Post Soeharto Indonesia*, Critical Studies of the Asia-Pacific, https://doi.org/10.1057/978-1-137-50566-8_1

This period also witnessed massive structural transformation of the economy. From being the largest rice importer in the world in the 1960s, Indonesia became self-sufficient in rice by the mid-1980s. The manufacturing sector's share in gross domestic product (GDP) nearly tripled, rising from just 9 per cent in 1966 to over a quarter in 1996 (Lankester 2004, p. 294), and manufactures became the principal driver of export growth during 1980–1995, with the share rising from an insignificant 2 per cent to more than 50 per cent (Aswicahyono et al. 2013, p. 185). Despite Indonesia having a considerably less developed manufacturing sector in the 1960s than India, its manufactured exports in absolute terms had outstripped India's by the mid-1990s (Lankester 2004, p. 204). The rapid growth and structural transformation led by labour-intensive manufacturing exports catapulted Indonesia into the league of eight "high-performing Asian economies" (World Bank 1993).

However, Indonesia was also hardest hit by the AFC. The annual GDP growth plummeted from 7.6 per cent in 1996 to −13.1 per cent in 1998—a staggering decline by over 20 percentage points! It not only took longer to recover but also failed to achieve its pre-crisis growth rate despite benefiting from a decade-long commodity price boom almost immediately following the AFC. Since 1999, Indonesia's average annual growth has been around 5 per cent—3 percentage points below the pre-crisis rate.

The manufacturing sector contracted in 1998 by roughly 13 per cent, about the same as for the economy as a whole. Although manufacturing growth recovered in 1999, as GDP, its growth rate remained below the pre-crisis level, and for first time since the 1960s, its growth rate fell below the economy-wide average. Furthermore, since the crisis, the share of manufacturing in GDP has tended to decline, triggering fears of a premature "de-industrialisation" (see, e.g., Tijaja and Faisal 2014, p. 2). Indonesia's manufacturing continued to lose its competitiveness since 2001 and hence the share of manufacturing in merchandise export also fell from the pre-crisis peak. Thus, the AFC marks a turning point for Indonesia's industrial sector (Aswicahyono et al. 2013, p. 185).

Indonesia seems to be the only Southeast Asian economy that has both benefited and suffered from the commodity price boom during the first decade of the 2000s. While the commodity price boom helped the economy to recover from the AFC and weathered the 2008–2009 global financial

inequality. Recent research reveals evidence of high wealth and earnings inequality in Indonesia. See Tadjoeddin (2013, 2016a).

crisis (GFC), it also "created a twenty-first century Dutch disease" (World Bank 2016). This seems to have aggravated Indonesia's tendency towards premature de-industrialisation.

Worryingly, the premature de-industrialisation has been accompanied by a growing disjoint between productivity and real earnings growth which has resulted in growing wage inequality. There has also been a disjoint between manufacturing growth and job growth, prompting the coinage of the term, "jobless growth". That is, employment growth in manufacturing has been far slower than the pre-crisis rate and lagged behind the growth (albeit slower) in manufacturing. Thus, the quality of employment, as measured by formal sector waged employment, has also stagnated. As a result, the average labour productivity in Indonesian manufacturing is far lower than in Malaysia, Thailand and China, and its unit labour cost is higher than that of the Philippines and Vietnam (Diop 2016).

Nevertheless, manufacturing still has the best potential to become the engine of growth once again. Its average labour productivity is about five times that of agriculture, and it has plenty of room to grow as only about 30 per cent of Indonesian firms are in the formal sector compared with 95 per cent in Brazil and 96 per cent in China (Diop 2016). The dramatic decline in commodity prices since 2012 and the consequent partial downward adjustments of real exchange rate have also created an opportunity for the manufacturing sector to regain the momentum. This has led to the call for re-industrialisation (see ADB 2013; World Bank 2016; Economic Intelligence Unit 2016).

The Government of Indonesia (GOI), too, has given priority to re-industrialisation. In 2007, the GOI introduced Law No. 27 on Long-Term National Development Plan (*Rencana Pembangunan Jangka Panjang Nasional* or RPJPN) for the period 2005–2025. RPJPN identified the industrial sector as the engine of growth for strengthening the economic structure. Thus, the 2008 Presidential Regulation on National Industrial Policy has set a long-term industrial development vision for Indonesia to be a strong industrialised nation by 2025. This vision was further elaborated in the Regulation of the Ministry of Industry issued in 2010,[4] which states that Indonesia will be a strong industrialised nation by 2025 through becoming a new industrially developed country by 2020 (Vision 2020).

[4] Regulation of the Minister of Industry No. 41/M-IND/PER/3/2010 on Strategy Mapping and Key Performance Indicators for the Ministry of Industry.

The priority to re-industrialise is further strengthened by the Government Regulation No. 14/2015 concerning Master Plan of National Industry Development (*Rencana Induk Pembangunan Industri Nasional* or RIPIN) 2015–2035. RIPIN is drafted to fulfil the mandate of Law No. 3/2014 concerning industry. Among the prescribed strategies include developing upstream and intermediate industries based on natural resources by controlling exports of raw materials and energy resources in the medium term and by improving the mastery of industrial technology and the quality of industrial human resources, and developing strategic industries in the longer term.

The discussion of re-industrialisation has centred mainly on the quality of regulatory reforms, infrastructure and labour (e.g., skills and education levels) as well as labour mobility (ADB 2013; World Bank 2016; EIU 2016). Of the regulatory reforms, labour cost—in particular, minimum wage and severance pay—received disproportionate attention. There is a significant view that high minimum wage and severance pay make labour market regulations tighter, and hence are serious obstacles to manufacturing's resurgence (Aswicahyono et al. 2013; World Bank 2014). They point to the existence of a large informal sector and "working poor" to argue in favour of further deregulating the labour market or reforming the legislations concerning minimum wage and severance pay.

This volume focuses on employment, wages and productivity but relates them to the challenge of re-industrialisation from a different perspective, especially in the context of rising inequality and a growing gap between productivity and wage growth. It argues that Indonesia cannot re-create the manufacturing miracle of the past based on repression of labour, at least for three reasons. *First*, Indonesia is no longer a centralised authoritarian state. It has to respect labour rights while it consolidates its democracy, and recognise regional differences in renegotiating a new social contract among the regions. In such a circumstance, growing earnings inequality and regional disparities in well-being can be politically explosive (see Tadjoeddin et al. 2016).

Second, the perpetuation of low wage and rising inequality constrains the domestic effective demand, resulting in prolonged growth stagnation in an uncertain global economic environment. On the other hand, if domestic demand is sustained by growing household debts, the economy becomes vulnerable to the balance of payments and banking crises. This may clash with the expectations of democratic dividend of higher prosperity and stability, ironically fuelling aspirations for reversal to an authoritarian inward-looking regime (see, e.g., Ostry et al. 2014; OECD 2015; ESCAP 2013, 2014 for the destabilising impacts of rising inequality).

Third, wage repression will trap Indonesia in a low-productivity economy, and hence it will not be able to compete with new comers such as Vietnam or Bangladesh. The manufacturing sector's higher unit labour cost in Indonesia than in the Philippines, Vietnam and Malaysia is "not because of how much workers were paid but because of how little they produced" (Diop 2016, p. 37). Therefore, it has to move up the ladder or take a forward position in the "flying-geese" formation of shifting international division of labour.

Finally, we believe that the recognition of Indonesia's regional diversity renders inappropriate any analysis that treats Indonesia as a homogeneous economic unit. For example, while industrially advanced regions, such as Java and Batam (Riau Islands), have to move towards high skilled, high value-added activities to remain internationally competitive, industrially backward regions, such as Lampung and Nusa Tenggara, may need to focus on labour-intensive manufacturing. Thus, Indonesia can have a mix of high- and low-end manufacturing, creating an internal flying-geese formation. Likewise, given its resource diversity, Indonesia should have a mix of resource- and non-resource-intensive manufacturing.

The above is broadly in line with the 2005–2025 RPJPN and the 2015–2035 RIPIN both of which aim to promote local and international competitiveness, and strengthen the national industrial base by integrating small and medium enterprises (SMEs) into the value chains for stronger forward and backward linkages and more balanced economic development outside the most populated island of Java. In other words, both the 2005–2025 RPJPN and the 2015–2035 RIPIN underscore the need to strengthen *horizontal* inter-industry relations among supporting and complementary industries and *vertical* integration through product processing and diversification (downstream development) as well as structural deepening (upstream development). They also commit to eliminate monopolistic behaviour and other market distortions, especially to improve domestic market integration.

Thus, while we advocate active industry policy where exchange rates, minimum wages, and public investment in research and development (R&D), human resource development (HRD) and infrastructure can play critical roles in propelling the economy into a high productivity-high wage trajectory, we also recognise that there cannot be a monolithic approach.

Wages, HRD and industry policies, in particular, have to take into account regional variations in resource (both human and natural) endowments and level of industrial development. This also means a high degree of coordination among regional and central policy makers. This is particularly important to create backward and forward linkages not only among industries but also among the regions for balanced development. High-degree centre-region coordination is also needed to prevent race to the bottom competition among the regions to attract investment and fragmentation of a national market with distortionary or discriminatory regional policy barriers.

1.2 Contents of This Volume

In Chap. 2, we provide an in-depth analysis of Indonesia's employment situation, with particular emphasis on the quality of employment, as proxied by formal employment, underemployment, the incidence of low pay, vulnerability, wage inequality and youth NEET (neither in employment or education and training). We find significant variations in the employment situation between pre- and post-AFC periods. For example, the unemployment rate declined only slightly during 1999–2001 but rose again reaching its highest point at 11.2 per cent in 2005—more than twice the pre-crisis unemployment rate—even after economic recovery. The unemployment rate of 5.6 per cent in August 2016 was higher than the pre-crisis unemployment rate of 5.4 per cent. The share of regular employment stagnated or decreased during 2001–2009, even when the economy grew at an average of 5 per cent annually. More disturbingly, industry is the only sector that experienced a sharp drop in the share of regular employment during this period. Although the industrial sector has the highest proportion of regular employment, in 2016 it remained below the 2001 level. The relationship between the unemployment and employment rates also seems to have changed since 2011—both declining at the same time, instead of moving in the opposite directions. Growing underemployment may explain this. We also find a significant rise in wage inequality and the incidence of low pay together with increased casualisation, especially in the industrial sector. This is also reflected in the rise in vulnerable employment and working poverty. The dominance of working poor among the employed indicates the dominance of low-wage or poor quality jobs, such as casual or informal employment.

In Chap. 3, we examine wage-earnings and productivity trends in Indonesia during post-AFC period. We find that both average and median real wage earnings across the sectors are relatively stagnant, increasing during 2001–2004 and 2009–2016, but declining between 2004 and 2008. Till 2015, they remained below the peak reached during the early part of the previous decade. This trend is also observable for all categories of employment. However, there is a clear declining trend in the median to average real earnings ratio, pointing to the rise of wage-earnings inequality. We also find that labour productivity across four dominant economic sectors accounting for 85 per cent of total employment experienced continuous productivity increase during 2001–2016. Manufacturing was the most productive sector and recorded the highest labour productivity growth during the post-AFC period, highlighting the importance of the manufacturing sector in the Indonesian economy. The service sector's productivity was marginally above the lowest productivity agricultural sector, indicating low-level service activities. The mining sector, which enjoyed a boom during the post-AFC period, experienced a steep fall in labour productivity. We also find that there has been a growing disjoint between productivity and real wage-earnings growth both across the sectors and provinces, resulting in a growing earnings inequality. This disjoint is most prominent during 2001–2008, but converged in the manufacturing sector since 2008. The productivity-earnings disjoint is more pronounced in the provinces with higher growth rates of provincial real GDP, indicating that better economic performance did not benefit the labour. Interestingly, we find that compliance of minimum wage has an equalising effect. That is, wage-earnings inequality declines with the increase in the minimum wage compliance rate, as this improves labour's bargaining power.

In Chap. 4, we extend the analysis of productivity, wages and employment trends during the post-AFC period with a case study of the manufacturing sector. We find that the trends of real earning across manufacturing sub-sectors at the International Standard of Industrial Classifications (ISIC) 2 digit level are similar to the general trend of real earnings in the overall manufacturing sector. The trend of delinking between wages and productivity was also apparent across manufacturing sub-sectors, as the wage-productivity ratios declined in most of sub-sectors until 2008. The same is observable in large-medium (LM) regardless of their factor intensity (capital, resource and labour); but since 2008, wage-productivity ratio in LM firms began increasing. LM firms also performed better than (micro-small) MS firms; productivity of LM firms increased at a much faster rate than productivity of MS firms. But the value-added share of LM firms in overall manufacturing industry stagnated at 54 per cent, and their employment share declined from 36 per cent to 32 per cent. This observation is consistent with the overall finding on the process of de-industrialisation in the Indonesian economy. We also find, as expected, that levels of wage and productivity are the highest among capital-intensive firms, followed by resource-intensive and labour-intensive categories. Productivity gaps are larger than wage gaps across factor intensity. One key observation is the increase in levels of both wage and productivity with the firm size. That is, both wages and productivity are higher in larger firms than in smaller firms.

In Chap. 5, we econometrically investigate the determinants of real wage, productivity and employment in the manufacturing sector by firm size and factor intensity. We find that productivity is the most important determinant of real wages for both LM and MS firms. As expected, we also find that capital intensity has a positive and significant effect on real wage levels, but the elasticity coefficients are very small and have no significant effect in the resource-intensive manufacturing. Surprisingly, no significant impact of export orientation and foreign ownership on real wage levels across firm size and factor intensity is found. We find similar results in relation to the effects of real wages on productivity, but the impacts are generally smaller compared to the impacts of productivity on real wages. Estimation results for the overall economy as well as the nine economic sectors support the delinking hypotheses between real wage earnings and productivity. In most cases, productivity has no meaningful relationship with real wage earnings, pointing to a situation where the two are not moving in the same direction or do very marginally. However, an examination of variations across sub-sectors of LM firms at the ISIC 3 level produces a different delinking story. We find a significantly positive real wage and productivity relationship. This is consistent with the observed rising wage-productivity ratio in the manufacturing sub-sectors, especially in the LM firms, as reported in Chap. 4. While real wage is found to affect employment negatively in a static setting, both productivity and real wage positively affect employment in a dynamic setting. The modern and dynamic LM section of manufacturing industry displays an ideal outcome where wages and employment increase when the overall economy (GDP) expands. This finding across firm size and factor intensity should affirm the call for re-industrialisation to reverse the trend of premature de-industrialisation since the 1997–1998 AFC.

In Chap. 6, we provide a regional perspective on the broad trends in employment, wages and productivity. We begin with a short discussion of the context and an overview of spatial inequalities in Indonesia. We find the rise in inequality in all Indonesian provinces; however, the rates of increased inequality vary considerably. The decomposition analysis shows that within-province inequality is driving the overall increase in inequality in Indonesia, whereas there has been some reduction in between-province inequality. We also find that there are negative associations between increase in inequality and provinces' initial conditions, such as the shares of manufacturing and mining in 2000, and mean years of schooling in 2002. We also found a negative correlation between wage-productivity ratios and Gini indices across provinces. These findings have clear policy implications. For example, improving educational attainment and productivity-led re-industrialisation that creates decent jobs can contribute to reductions in inequality. We also present results of an empirical exercise relating formal employment, real wage, productivity and Human Development Index (HDI) at the regional level. We find that provinces with higher shares of formal employment (as a percentage of total employment) tend to have higher shares of physical capital investment (as a percentage of regional GDP [RGDP]), higher HDI and higher labour productivity. Without implying any causality, these findings indicate the importance of formal employment and investment in terms of both physical and human capital for labour productivity. The negative correlation between HDI and real wage is quite unusual as it indicates that provinces with better stock of human capital (represented by HDI) do not enjoy higher real wage. This could be explained by the missing link between real wage and labour productivity, as discussed in Chap. 3. Finally, the chapter provides a snapshot of regional diversity of Indonesia's manufacturing sector. It reveals some interesting facts, such as high concentration of manufacturing in few provinces and a diverse pattern of industrialisation. Interestingly, while there have been declines in manufacturing in a good number of provinces, a few experienced growth in manufacturing, indicating industrial relocations. For example, it seems labour-intensive activities are moving from Jakarta to Central Java. Government policies can accelerate such relocations to create a flying geese of internal division of labour and complementarities. Most resource-rich provinces (except West Papua) suffered significant drops in manufacturing, indicating the importance of policies to revitalise resource-based industrial activities. These findings highlight the importance of regional dimensions in policy-making related to employment creation, inequality reduction and re-industrialisation in such a large and diverse country.

In Chap. 7, we review government policies with regard to industrialisation, regional development, employment and minimum wages. While the focus is on the post-Soeharto period, we also briefly review policy framework of the Soeharto regime. It reveals a great deal of continuity in terms of broad nationalistic policy thrust. However, given the systemic change that occurred following the fall of Soeharto, the approach has changed from a highly centralised to a radically decentralised decision-making process. The successive governments seemed to have recognised the challenge and designed strategies to accelerate industrial development; but unlike the previous authoritarian regime, the emphasis is more on spreading industrial activities across the regions based on their characteristics and resource endowments. The decentralised decision-making is also extended to industrial relations, especially with regard to minimum wages. This has essentially created an element of labour market flexibility in terms of regional variations. Thus, labour-intensive activities can potentially relocate to regions with lower minimum wages while industrially advanced regions with higher minimum wages can specialise in high value-added activities. While such industrial relocation is key to balanced regional development, its facilitation would require increased investment in reliable infrastructure and HRD. More importantly, governments at both centre and regions need to coordinate their strategies in order to prevent fragmentation of the national economy and race to the bottom. The ultimate aim should be to strengthen backward and forward linkages within the industrial sector and among regions, and thereby create internal dynamics within Indonesia's development path.

Box 1.1 Key Policy Messages

The volume's key policy messages can be summarised as follows:

First, the policy framework to achieve *penghidupan yang layak bagi kemanusiaan* (decent life for humanity), as mandated by the 1945 Constitution, should emphasise improving employment quality instead of quantity. In other words, the focus should shift from the objective of mere unemployment reduction to increasing the share of formal employment. Enlarging the coverage of decent jobs in the form of formal employment is in line with improving workers' productivity and, in turn, their earnings, culminating in higher living standards.

(*continued*)

Box 1.1 (continued)

Second, minimum wage policies can play a useful role in addressing the rising inequality trend by reversing the widening gap between productivity and wage earnings, found across the major economic sectors and provinces during the post-Soeharto period. Strictly enforced compliance with minimum wage helps improve workers' bargaining power, especially when trade unions are weak. This should, therefore, increase workers' earnings and labour shares of income, and thereby reduce inequality.

Third, the dynamic and modern manufacturing sector, represented by the large and medium establishments, provides an ideal platform for enhancing formal employment and realigning productivity and wages. The supposed trade-off between wage and employment does not manifest in large and medium establishments, where improving productivity and wage positively affect each other, resulting in higher employment. Thus, policies to facilitate graduation of small and micro manufacturing establishments into large and medium becomes critical.

Fourth, the diversity of Indonesia's regions in terms of stages of socio-economic development and resource endowments is an asset as they should complement each other in creating internal dynamism to expand domestic market and flexibility to compete internationally, especially within the ASEAN Economic Community (AEC). Diversity in regional minimum wages is critical in facilitating industrial relocation in line with regional comparative advantage. As a matter of fact, wages policy can be an important neutral industry policy tool to avoid the pitfalls of "picking the winners".

Finally, complementary policies to improve communication and transport infrastructure and human resources are also important. More significantly, national-level coordination is essential to ensure proper facilitations of industrial relocation, prevent fragmentation of the national economy and avoid race to the bottom among the regions. National dialogue to articulate long-term vision and strategies can be useful.

In this introductory chapter, we provide the macroeconomic background of Indonesia's industrialisation question within the context of rising inequality and employment challenges in a decentralised setting.

1.3 Growth and Structural Transformation: The Rise and Fall of Manufacturing[5]

Since stabilising the economy and politics in the late 1960s, the Indonesian economy grew at an average annual rate of 8.2 per cent during 1968–1981 (Fig. 1.1), mainly aided by the oil price boom. The economy decelerated significantly in 1982 with the annual growth rate dropping to 1.1 per cent from around 8.5 per cent in 1980–1981. It grew by 5.4 per cent during 1982–1988, as oil prices first tapered off and then fell sharply. Oil, gas and related minerals provided about two-thirds of government revenue and almost three-quarters of merchandise exports (Aswicahyono et al. 2013, p. 187). Thus, the economy needed to adjust to the changing oil and resource fortunes in the 1980s, and Indonesia decisively adopted an export-oriented industrialisation strategy based on the availability of its vast surplus labour.

Fig. 1.1 Indonesia's annual GDP growth (%), 1961–2016. (Note: Average growth rates: 1961–1967 = 2%; 1968–1981 = 8.2%; 1982–1988 = 5.4%; 1989–1996 = 8.1%; 1999–2016 = 5.0%; Source: World Development Indicators (WDI))

[5] More details can be found in Booth (2016) and Hill (2000).

Policy reforms in the 1980s and the reorientation of the economy produced rapid growth and structural transformation. During 1989–1996, the economy grew at an annual average rate of 8.1 per cent. Although the annual average growth rate was about the same as in the 1970s, it was qualitatively different. During the 1970s, the share of manufacturing value added (MVA) in GDP barely rose and remained stagnant at around 10 per cent. However, the rapid growth during 1989–1996 was accompanied by a dramatic rise in the share of MVA in GDP from around 15 per cent in 1988 to 25 per cent in 1996—a 10-percentage point rise in only 8 years! Thus, manufacturing became truly the engine of Indonesia's growth. The shares of manufacturing in merchandise exports rose from a minuscule 2 per cent in 1980 to over 50 per cent by 1996, and Indonesia became a significant industrial exporter from the mid-1980s (Hill 2000).

1.3.1 Rise of Manufacturing

Indonesia barely had manufacturing or modern industries until about the mid-1960s, except a few large state-owned enterprises (SOEs).[6] Industrialisation began in earnest since the late 1960s, with annual industrial growth of at least 9 per cent during 1970–1996, excluding only two years—1971 and 1982—when the annual growth rate dropped to around 2 per cent (Hill 1997). This burst of industrial growth was mainly a catch-up factor aided by oil fortunes and import-substitution strategy (Aswicahyono et al. 2013). However, as noted earlier, the share of MVA in GDP remained low at around 10–11 per cent. Manufacturing share began to rise rapidly since 1983 with the switch towards export orientation from around 12 per cent reaching the peak of around 30 per cent in 2001.

The manufacturing sector itself undergone significant changes and became more diversified, away from the earlier dominance of simple consumer goods and resource processing. The switch towards export orientation resulted in rapid growth of labour-intensive industries, such as textiles, garments and footwear, since the mid-1980s. Wood products also expanded fast in response to the prohibition on the export of unprocessed timber, before encountering environmental constraints in the 1990s. Electronics, too, became increasingly important and export oriented but was

[6] In most cases, established by Dutch commercial interests before World War II, and subsequently taken over by the state as part of the 1957–1958 nationalisations.

never as significant as in other neighbouring Southeast Asian countries, such as Malaysia or Thailand. Heavy industry, such as automotive, grew quickly until the mid-1980s assisted by protection and major state investments.

The rise of manufacturing and changes within it were reflected in Indonesia's merchandise exports. Initially, resource-based products (especially plywood) dominated manufacturing exports, reflecting the country's natural resource endowments aided by the ban against exporting unprocessed commodities. Since the mid-1980s, the manufacturing export structure changed significantly with the rapid growth of labour-intensive textiles, garments, footwear, electronics, furniture, sporting goods and toys. The share of labour-intensive products in total manufactured exports increased from about 44 per cent in 1980 to 70 per cent by 1990 (Aswicahyono et al. 2013).

1.3.2 Fall of Manufacturing

As noted earlier, the AFC marks a turning point for Indonesia's manufacturing. The average annual GDP growth rate remained significantly below the pre-crisis level since recovering from the AFC. During 1999–1916, the economy grew at an average annual rate of 5 per cent, peaking only to 6.3 per cent in 2007.

MVA grew at a much slower rate, between 5 and 2 per cent. The slower growth of MVA resulted in a decline in its share in GDP from a peak of 30 per cent in 2001 to around 25 per cent in 2014. The share of manufacturing in merchandise exports also declined from its highest of around 57 per cent in 2001 to around 40 per cent in 2014.

In the post-AFC era, neither the labour-intensive nor the seemingly high-tech (but mostly labour-intensive electronics) manufactures performed well in exports. The fastest growing manufacturing exports have been medium-technology manufactures (Aswicahyono et al. 2013). This has been reflected in the decline of labour-intensive manufacturing's share in non-oil/gas MVA from 51 per cent in 2000 to 43 per cent in 2014.[7] During the same period, the share of capital-intensive manufacturing rose from 34 per cent to 50 per cent (Fig. 1.2).[8] The transport equipment,

[7] Labour-intensive manufacturing includes food, beverages and tobacco; textiles, leather products and footwear; wood and wood products; and paper and printing.

[8] Capital-intensive manufacturing includes fertilisers, chemicals and rubber; cement and non-metallic minerals; iron and basic steel; and transport equipment, machinery and apparatus.

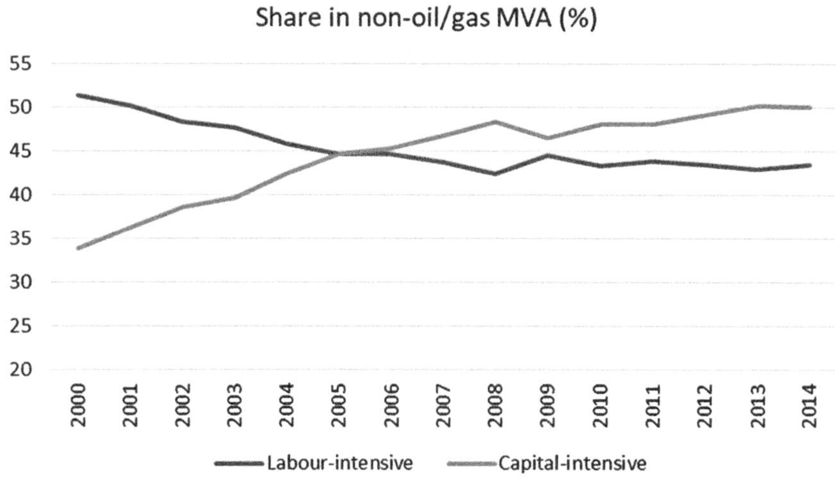

Fig. 1.2 Structural change within non-oil/gas manufacturing post-AFC. (Source: Calculated from BPS data)

machinery and apparatus sector's share doubled from around 17 per cent to 34.3 per cent.

Thus, Indonesia's labour-intensive manufacturing and exports lost steam since the 1997–1998 AFC as other countries chipped away its comparative advantage in these activities, and the trend of industrialisation stalled during the post-crisis period. As documented by Dhanani (2000), the decline in traditional manufacturing competitiveness started even few years before the onset of the crisis. As a matter of fact, the decline in labour-intensive manufacturing's share in MVA accelerated from 1990 (Fig. 1.3).

1.3.3 Declining International Competitiveness

The manufacturing sector's share in total export dropped significantly after 2000 (Fig. 1.4). On the other hand, the role of natural resource-based commodities was on the rise, both in absolute term and as a share of total export, taking advantage of global commodity booms (Table 1.1). It has to be noted that the good old days of the manufacturing export in the 1980s and 1990s was driven by labour-intensive and resource-based

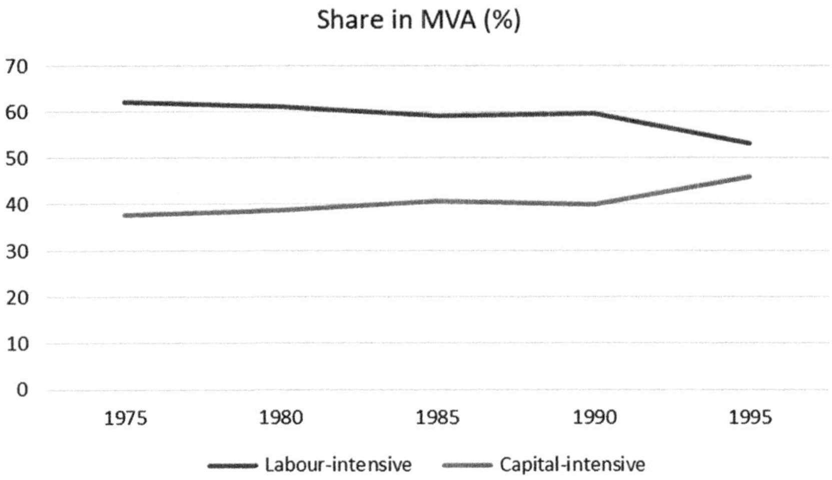

Fig. 1.3 Structural change within manufacturing pre-AFC. (Source: Aswicahyono et al. 2013)

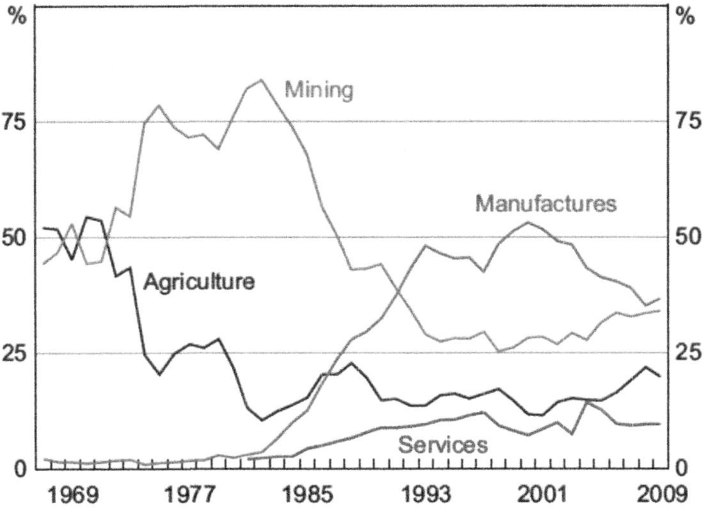

Fig. 1.4 Export of goods and services by sector, share of total (%). (Source: World Bank data as quoted in Elias and Noone (2011, p. 38))

Table 1.1 Share of total export by sector (%), 2000 and 2010

	2000	*2010*
Oil and gas	23	18
Agriculture commodities	10	20
Mining and mineral commodities	8	22
Forestry products	11	5
Textiles and footwear	16	9
Electronics and computers	15	8
Furniture	2	1
Machinery	2	2
Chemical materials	5	5
Other manufactured	9	9

Source: World Bank (2012b, p. 2)

industries with limited markets. According to a major report by the United Nations Industrial Development Organization (UNIDO), four categories of manufacturing product (plywood, garments, textiles and footwear) accounted for half of the manufactured exports, while three countries (the USA, Japan and Singapore) bought nearly half of Indonesia's exports (Dhanani 2000). The situation has changed since the AFC. The labour-intensive and resource-based manufacturing products have been losing their competitiveness against Asian competitors, most notably China (World Bank 2012a); however, this trend became visible a few years before the Asian crisis (Dhanani 2000).

1.3.4 De-industrialisation

As noted earlier, the decline in relative importance of the manufacturing has promoted the fear of premature de-industrialisation.[9] De-industrialisation refers to manufacturing sector's declining share of either output or employment or both. De-industrialisation is a natural process of development, however. Rowthorn and Ramaswamy (1997) argued that de-industrialisa-

[9] See Naudé (2013) and Raz (2013). Concerns on the de-industrialisation have also been featured in popular media, among others, see *Bisnis Indonesia*, 4 February 2015 (Pertumbuhan Industri Gagal Capai Target, Gejala Deindustrialisasi?), *Bisnis Indonesia*, 7 May 2014 (Deindustrialisasi Kembali Intai Indonesia), *Koran Tempo*, 7 November 2013 (Indef: Indonesia Terjebak Deindustrialisasi), *Kompas*, 22 December 2010 (LIPI: Indonesia Menuju Deindustrialisasi).

tion in advanced economies is not a negative phenomenon but a natural consequence of further growth. The main reason for de-industrialisation is the faster growth of productivity in manufacturing than in services, labelled as positive de-industrialisation.

The distinction between positive and negative de-industrialisation was developed by Rowthorn and Wells (1987). Positive de-industrialisation is:

> regarded as ... the normal result of sustained economic growth in a fully employed, and already highly developed, economy. It occurs because productivity growth in the manufacturing sector is so rapid that, despite increasing output, employment in this sector is reduced, either absolutely or as a share of total employment. However, this does not lead to unemployment, because new jobs are created in the service sector on a scale sufficient to absorb any workers displaced from manufacturing. Paradoxically, this kind of de-industrialisation is a symptom of economic success. (Rowthorn and Wells 1987, p. 5)

On the other hand, negative de-industrialisation is "a product of economic failure and occurs when industry is in severe difficulties ... labour shed from the manufacturing sector—because of falling output or rising productivity—will not be reabsorbed into the service sector. Unemployment will therefore rise" (Rowthorn and Wells 1987, p. 5).

In advanced economies, the peak of manufacturing sector's contributions to GDP—achieved in the 1960s—was around 36 per cent in Japan, 32 per cent in the European Union and 30 per cent in industrial countries (Rowthorn and Ramaswamy 1997), before declining. But in Indonesia, the share of manufacturing in GDP began falling much earlier—after reaching around 28 per cent.

More importantly, at the peak of industrialisation in the advanced economies, the employment share of the manufacturing sector was more or less comparable to the sector's share in GDP. In Indonesia, employment share in the manufacturing sector is far below (around 13.5 per cent) its share in GDP indicating the failure of this sector in absorbing surplus labour from the agricultural sector. Thus, Indonesia seems to be experiencing a "premature" or negative de-industrialisation process (Priyarsono et al. 2010). Additionally, the service sector's slow productivity growth (1.7 per cent) indicates that post-crisis Indonesia has aborted the historical path of structural transformation (a la Chenery 1960 and Kuznets 1971) that advanced countries, including the newly industrialised ones, followed, where the high-productivity services sector took over the dynamism from the manufacturing sector.

However, Aswicahyono et al. (2013) disagree and believe that Indonesia was actually "over-industrialised" prior to the AFC. Its manufacturing share has been higher than the international average since 1986, when the income per capita at constant 2000 dollars was about $500. Thus, the manufacturing sector's declining share in MVA in the case of Indonesia could reflect returning to the average trend.

It is further argued that sectoral shares in any economy are not of great normative significance. An individual country's sectoral shares can vary from the average shares of countries in Chenery's original formulation of a relationship between the shares of the agriculture, mining and service sectors and per capita income, depending on a range of country-specific factors, including natural resource endowments, size, degree of export orientation and industry policies.

Nevertheless, Aswicahyono et al. (2013) believe that the industrial slowdown and manufacturing's declining sectoral share is a cause for concern, to the extent that it is linked to declining competitiveness and regulatory obstacles. But to them, the slowdown in manufacturing growth, from well above the economy-wide average to just below it, is most puzzling. The manufacturing sector should have benefited from the competitive boost of a depreciating exchange rate in the wake of the AFC. It also did not face significant demand-side constraints until the GFC. However, the World Bank (2016) attributed the decline in manufacturing to "twenty-first century Dutch disease", caused by appreciating currency due to resources boom that followed the AFC.

1.3.5 Missing Middle

The Indonesian manufacturing sector evolved with a severe imbalance. It has a disproportionately large presence of small firms, relative to other developing countries (Fig. 1.5). This phenomenon is referred to as the "missing middle" with a large portion of small firms and a comparatively small number of middle-sized firms transitioning from small to large category. Anas (2013) finds that the "missing middle" situation is also observable in the Indonesian manufacturing exports.

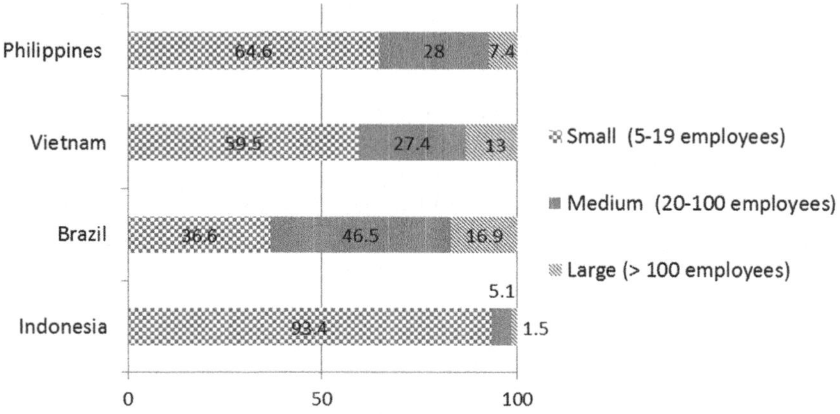

Fig. 1.5 Distribution of manufacturing firms by size (%), 2008. (Source: World Bank, Enterprise Survey 2008, quoted from World Bank (2012a, p. 8))

1.4 Jobless Growth

The rapid growth of labour-intensive manufacturing since the early 1980s obviously had an impact on employment growth. However, structural transformation of employment has not been as impressive as in the case of GDP or exports. The share of manufacturing in total employment rose from around 7 per cent in 1971 to only 13 per cent prior to the AFC, despite manufacturing employment growing at 10.1 per cent during 1986–1996.

The post-AFC manufacturing employment story is even less impressive. The subdued growth in manufacturing has not produced commensurate job growth to absorb surplus labour in the agriculture sector as was during the early period and hence is termed as "jobless". The output-employment elasticity—percentage change in employment due to 1 per cent change in output—in manufacturing declined from 0.67 during 1988–1996 to 0.2 during 2000–2008 (Aswicahyono et al. 2013, p. 218). That is, the manufacturing sector has become less labour absorbing.

However, employment growth in the post-AFC period declined across the board, except in agriculture (Fig. 1.6). The economy-wide employment growth was about three-quarters of that in the pre-crisis period. Moreover, despite a consistent declining trend of the unemployment rate

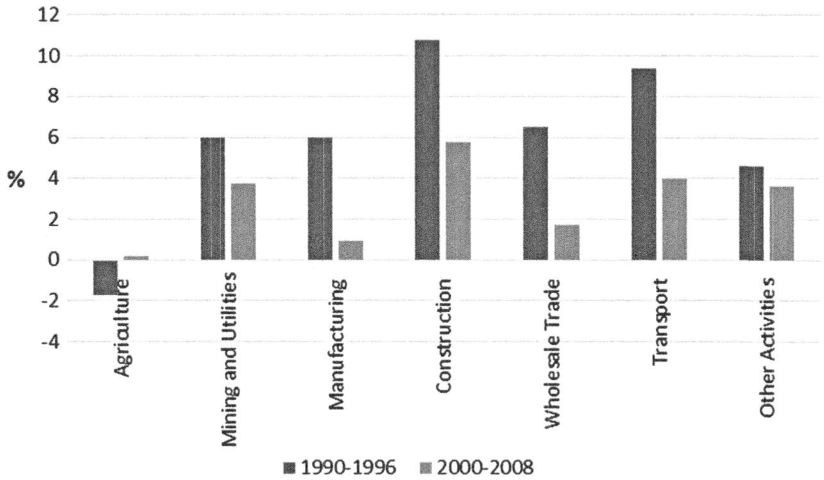

Fig. 1.6 Pre- and post-AFC employment growth (%). (Source: Aswicahyono et al. (2013, Table 6.7))

since 2005, the size of formal employment,[10] the main proxy for employment quality, had been virtually stagnant during the first decade of democratisation and decentralisation, and increased only since 2010.

According to Aswicahyono et al. (2013), the decline in employment elasticity in manufacturing cannot be explained by changing technology; "the explanation has to lie elsewhere, in the commercial environment and factors affecting the willingness of employers to hire labour" (p. 217). They also doubt that the country's tighter labour market regulation since 2000 is the principal explanation for the sharp drop in output-employment elasticity as is widely believed in Indonesia, citing a similar decline in Thailand, where the labour market is not as heavily regulated.

As a matter of fact, manufacturing employment growth has been declining even before the AFC with the declines in Indonesia's competitiveness in traditional manufacturing as mentioned earlier. However, the decline during the post-AFC period (2000–2006) has been more marked, from 10.1 per cent (during 1986–1996) to just 4.6 per cent. By examining

[10] Formal employment consists of employer and regular wage employment referring to the Sakenas' employment status 3 and 4 respectively.

manufacturing employment growth according to the firm size,[11] Aswicahyono et al. (2013) found that the medium-sized firms led the decline even prior to the AFC. The share of medium-sized firms' employment declined throughout 1986–2006, whereas employment in both large and small firms grew rapidly during the post-AFC period (1986–1996), by 10.3 and 11.4 per cent, respectively. During 1996–2006, employment in large firms barely increased, at just 1 per cent per annum, whereas small firm employment continued to expand rapidly by 8.8 per cent, and medium-sized firms with 20-plus workers, virtually stopped hiring.

While tighter labour market regulations likely to have affected labour-intensive manufacturing, other factors, such as corporate debt work-out, tighter access to finance and uncertainty caused by the democratisation and decentralisation process may have played a major role in the substantial slowdown of manufacturing employment growth during the post-AFC period. As noted earlier, significant real appreciation of the real exchange rate due to commodity boom did not help the situation.

As highlighted by Aswicahyono et al. (2013), and others, for example, World Bank (2016), EIU (2016) and Tadjoeddin (2016b), the decline in manufacturing employment is a concern as it weakens a major link in the transmission mechanism from growth to poverty. Fewer workers are now absorbed into the relatively better-paid jobs in the manufacturing sector. Furthermore, most of the manufacturing jobs now being created are in small firms, where employment conditions are generally inferior and productivity is low. Therefore, revitalisation of large and medium firms is crucial.

1.5 Productivity, Earnings, Poverty and Inequality

One of the consequences of jobless growth is the rise in measured labour productivity as can be seen in Fig. 1.7. However, both real median and average earnings declined until 2008. More disturbingly, the gaps between labour productivity and real earnings (both median and average) widened during the post-AFC period. Real median and average earnings also diverged since 2005, and the gap tended to widen until recently.

[11] To investigate the impacts across firms of different size, establishments are classified into three groups:

"large" (100+ employees), "medium" (20–99) and "small" (5–19).

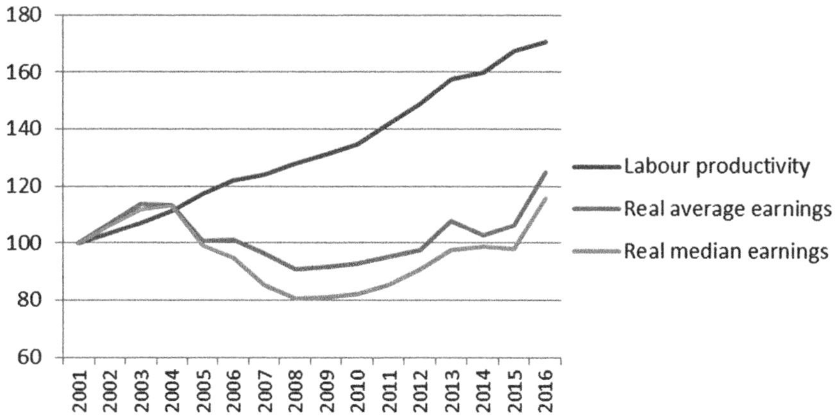

Fig. 1.7 Index of labour productivity, real average and median earnings, 2001–2016 (2001 = 100). (Note: Real average and median earnings are calculated using GDP deflators which are more appropriate for the purpose of this study since we are concerned with workers as part of the production process. Real earnings based on GDP deflator should reflect workers' productivity as earning is the reward for productivity. However, real earnings deflated by CPI—a better measure of worker's welfare—display similar trends; Source: Calculated from the Sakernas (National Labour Force Survey))

Although the poverty head count continues to decline, the overall inequality measured by the Gini index of per capita household expenditure is on the rise, reaching its peak at 0.41 in 2001, a level that was never seen before.[12] The diverging trend of the median real earnings from average real earnings indicates an increasing trend of the overall earnings inequality.

Moreover, despite economic recovery, a large segment of population remains highly vulnerable to the changing poverty lines or economic shocks. For example, the poverty head count in 2001 rises by a factor of 2.1 if the poverty line is shifted from $1.90 Purchasing Power Parity (PPP) to $3.10 PPP—a more appropriate poverty line for a middle-income country. A little over a decade later in 2014, the multiplication factor increased to 4.4 (Table 1.2).

[12] Gini index measures the overall level of inequality ranging from 0 representing perfect equality when everyone has the same level of income and 1 denotes perfect inequality when one person has all the income. The discussion of overall (vertical) inequality in Indonesia, so far, is primarily driven by the evolution of the Gini coefficient of per capita household expenditure derived from the National Socioeconomic Survey (Survei Sosial Ekonomi Nasional—Susenas).

Table 1.2 Growth, employment, poverty and inequality, 2001–2016

	2001	*2002*	*2003*	*2004*	*2005*	*2006*	*2007*	*2008*	*2009*	*2010*	*2011*	*2012*	*2013*	*2014*	*2015*	*2016*
GDP growth (%)	3.8	4.4	4.9	5.0	5.7	5.5	6.3	6.0	4.6	6.1	6.2	6.0	5.6	5.0	4.9	5.0
Unemployment rate (%)	8.1	9.1	9.5	9.9	11.2	10.3	9.1	8.4	7.9	7.1	6.6	6.1	6.3	5.9	6.2	5.6
Formal employment (%)	32.4	30.4	28.9	30.4	30.7	31.1	31.0	30.4	30.7	33.1	37.8	39.9	40.4	40.6	42.3	42.4
Gini (HH expenditure)	0.3	0.3	0.3	0.3	0.3	0.3	0.4	0.4	0.4	0.4	0.4	0.4	0.4	0.4	0.4	0.4
Poverty HCR (%, national)	18.4	18.2	17.4	16.7	16.0	17.7	16.6	15.4	14.1	13.3	12.5	12.0	11.4	11.3	11.2	10.9
Poverty HCR (%, $1.90 PPP)	36.0	23.4	23.3	24.4	21.6	28.0	22.8	21.6	18.4	16.0	13.6	11.8	9.8	8.3		
Poverty HCR (%, $1.90 PPP)	76.0	63.4	61.2	61.5	59.5	64.2	56.8	54.8	52.7	46.4	43.3	41.7	39.4	36.4		

Source: BPS (Susenas and Sakernas) and World Bank

1.6 From Shared Prosperity to Rising Disparities

It is widely claimed that the Indonesian economy during the pre-AFC (or the East Asian miracle period) did not follow Kuznets' predicted trade-off between income and equality (see, e.g., Asra 2000). The three decades of sustained high growth was achieved while maintaining a relatively constant overall inequality level measured by the Gini coefficient (around 0.33) of household expenditure (World Bank 1993).

However, as noted earlier, the story is different in the post-crisis Indonesia. While the economy recovered fairly quickly from the AFC and the growth has been quite reasonable amid the 2008–2009, the overall inequality has increased. During 2000–2011, the Gini index of expenditure inequality increased by 32 per cent reaching the record high of 0.41 and remained at that level till 2014.[13] According to the Palma ratio, inequality has increased by 66 per cent (Yusuf 2014).[14] The rising inequality in Indonesia is due to the increase in inequality within the provinces and within the economic sectors rather than inequality between regions or sectors (Tadjoeddin et al. 2017).

The sharp rise in inequality amid democratisation and decentralisation reform is against public expectations, and such unfulfilled public expectations can be socially explosive (Tadjoeddin et al. 2016). The growing concern about rising inequality in Indonesia is fully acknowledged in a recent World Bank report (World Bank 2015, p. 2): "Growth over the past decade has primarily benefitted the richest 20 percent and left the remaining 80 percent of the population behind." The World Bank report identified four drivers of rising inequality: (1) inequality of opportunity, (2) unequal jobs, (3) high wealth concentration and (4) low resiliency. On unequal jobs, the report underlines the widening wage gap between few skilled workers and the unskilled majority as one of the main drivers of increasing inequality. This also refers to the divisions between regular and non-regular employment. The report then suggests promoting better jobs and skill training opportunities for the workforce that could expand the coverage of higher productivity and higher-wage regular employment.

[13] A Gini coefficient of 0.4 is regarded as the warning threshold for dangerous levels of inequality. See, for example, Chen (2013) and Yang (2013).

[14] Palma index is the ratio of the income share of the richest 10 per cent population to the income share of the poorest 40 per cent population (Palma 2011). Palma index has been assessed to be more relevant for policymaking as it concerns with the particular income segments where inequality is actually located (Cobham and Sumner 2013).

Previous studies on earnings in Indonesia have tended to focus on wage and income determinants. For example, Comola and de Mello (2013) concentrated on explaining the effect of individual characteristics on earnings of salaried workers only in a single 2004 Sakernas. Pirmana (2006) used four Sakernas between 1996 and 2004 to estimate earning differentials among groups of workers. Other studies have focused on the impact of minimum wage on earnings and employment. The exercise in this volume is different from the previous studies on earnings or wages as it examines earnings inequality within the dynamics of relationships among earnings, productivity and employment across economic sectors.

1.7 Decentralisation: Unity and Diversity[15]

Understanding regional variations is important in a large and highly diverse country, Indonesia. No national policy can yield expected results unless it takes into account regional variations. As noted by Aswicahyono et al. (2013, p. 202), "Indonesia is the world's largest archipelagic state, and therefore any review of its Industrialisation patterns needs to include the spatial dimension." This is also important for regional policymakers trying to address employment and labour market issues in their respective regions, especially in the context of rising inequality and growing disjoint between productivity and real earnings.

Indonesia is the world's largest archipelagic state, with more than 17,500 islands covering land and sea area of 1.9 million square miles stretching from the Indian Ocean to the Pacific Ocean. Around 60 per cent of Indonesia's population lives on the island of Java, which accounts for only 7 per cent of the nation's land area. The country is administratively divided into 34 provinces and 524 districts (sub-provincial units). In 2001, Indonesia embarked on a radical decentralisation programme, transferring most of administrative and fiscal functions to the district level, leaving the central government with only six key functions (defence, police, monetary, justice, foreign affairs and religious affairs), while the provinces act more as regional coordinators representing the central government. Table 1.3 shows the disparity of Indonesian provinces regarding population size, income and human development.

As can be seen, provinces vary widely in terms of population size and sub-provincial units (districts). Furthermore, there does not seem to be

[15] The title of the pioneering volume, Hill (1991), on Indonesia's regions.

Table 1.3 Diversity of Indonesian provinces

Provinces	*No of districts*	*Population 2015 (million)*	*RGDP per capita (current prices, IDR million, 2016)*	*Human Development Index (HDI), 2016*	*Key economic characteristics*
11. Aceh	23	5.0	26.9	70.0	
12. North Sumatera	33	13.9	44.6	70.0	
13. West Sumatera	19	5.2	37.2	70.7	
14. Riau	12	6.3	105.0	71.2	Oil, gas
15. Jambi	11	3.4	49.6	69.6	
16. South Sumatera	17	8.1	43.6	68.2	
17. Bengkulu	10	1.9	29.1	69.3	
18. Lampung	15	8.1	34.3	67.7	
19. Bangka Belitung	7	1.4	46.5	69.6	
21. Riau Islands	7	2.0	106.8	74.0	Oil, gas, manufacturing
31. Jakarta	6	10.2	211.8	79.6	National capital
32. West Java	27	46.7	34.9	70.1	
33. Central Java	35	33.8	32.1	70.0	
34. Yogyakarta	5	3.7	29.6	78.4	
35. East Java	38	38.8	47.5	69.7	
36. Banten	8	12.0	42.3	71.0	
51. Bali	9	4.2	46.5	73.7	
52. West Nusa Tenggara	10	4.8	23.7	65.8	
53. East Nusa Tenggara	22	5.1	16.2	63.1	
61. West Kalimantan	14	4.8	33.2	65.9	
62. Central Kalimantan	14	2.5	44.1	69.1	
63. South Kalimantan	13	4.0	36.1	69.1	
64. East Kalimantan	10	3.4	144.8	74.6	Oil, gas
65. North Kalimantan	5	0.6	100.2	69.2	Oil, gas

(*continued*)

Table 1.3 (continued)

Provinces	*No of districts*	*Population 2015 (million)*	*RGDP per capita (current prices, IDR million, 2016)*	*Human Development Index (HDI), 2016*	*Key economic characteristics*
71. North Sulawesi	15	2.4	41.3	71.1	
72. Central Sulawesi	13	2.9	41.2	67.5	
73. South Sulawesi	24	8.5	44.1	69.8	
74. Southeast Sulawesi	17	2.5	38.0	69.3	
75. Gorontalo	6	1.1	27.7	66.3	
76. West Sulawesi	6	1.3	27.5	63.6	
81. Maluku	11	1.7	21.6	67.6	
82. North Maluku	10	1.2	24.6	66.6	
91. West Papua	13	0.9	74.6	62.2	Gas
94. Papua	29	3.1	55.6	58.1	Copper mining
Indonesia	514	255.5	48.0	70.2	

Source: BPS data

any correspondence between population size and the number of districts within a province. For example, West Papua's 0.9 million are spread over 13 districts, while Banten's 12 million people are concentrated in only 8 districts. Therefore, it seems geography or size has played a role in creating districts—that is, geographically larger provinces have more districts. However, this may have impacts on the cost and efficiency of service delivery. For instance, reaching thinly spread population over a large area divided in too many administrative units can be costly.

There are also substantial differences among provinces in terms of human welfare levels, measured by HDI and productive capacity, proxied by per capita regional GDP (RGDP). Existence of natural resources, especially oil and gas, generally has a significant influence on a province's productive capacity or RGDP. Resource-rich provinces also have higher HDI. However, in the case of both Papua and West Papua, HDI is much below the national figure, despite having natural resources (gas and copper); their RGDP is also relatively low.

1.7.1 *Disparity of Welfare*

Two main groups of indicators dominate the discussion of spatial inequality in Indonesia. The *first* group relates to regional income, primarily reflecting the productive capacity of a region as an economic entity. The *second* one concerns social development indicators closely attached to human development, such as household expenditure, poverty, health, education and gender gap.

Studies on spatial inequality in Indonesia have been disproportionally dominated by inter-provincial analyses on regional income,[16] with extensions to also cover household consumption as another proxy for income.[17] These studies have found a sharp increase in spatial inequality of per capita regional GDP (RGDP) in the early years of Soeharto, which remained stable during the later period, but at a considerably high level primarily due to significant differences in resource endowments across provinces. However, the magnitude of regional expenditure inequality was found to be much lower than regional inequality of per capita RGDP.

Spatial inequality analysis on human development-related indicators was pioneered by Tadjoeddin et al. (2001). In addition to regional income and household expenditure, they measured inter-district spatial inequality of life expectancy, schooling, literacy, purchasing power and the overall Human Development Index. As expenditure, regional inequalities with respect to measures of community welfare (health, education, purchasing power and the overall HDI) were also found to be much lower than the relatively high degree of regional inequality of per capita RGDP. There is also a clearer trend of regional convergence with respect to the overall HDI during the post-AFC democratic and decentralised era.

Focus on the two groups of indicators, namely regional income as a proxy for economic activity and human development outcomes, is well founded as the two do not necessarily move consistently. Higher regional economic productive capacity might not be automatically translated into better human development status of people living in the region (Tadjoeddin et al. 2001; Tadjoeddin 2011). Furthermore, higher regional income inequality due to differences in resource endowments can be offset by policy interventions, as seen in the case of both lower expenditure and

[16] See Esmara (1975), Uppal and Handoko (1986), Akita (1988), Akita and Lukman (1995), Garcia and Soelistianingsih (1998), Vidyattama (2013) and Hill and Vidyattama (2014).

[17] See Hughes and Islam (1981), Islam and Khan (1986) and Akita and Lukman (1999).

community welfare inequality. In this regard, where people work for a living or location of employment could be the most important factor in bridging economic activities (growth) and human development outcomes. However, higher level of employment or growth may not necessarily trickle down to higher levels of living. It is the quality of job that is likely to ensure that growth is translated into improved social development.

1.7.2 Distribution of Manufacturing

Figure 1.8 is a snapshot of the role of regional manufacturing in the national MVA as in 2015. The salient features can be summarised as follows.

First, all provinces of Java island (West Java, East Java, Central Java, Jakarta and Banten) are among most industrialised in Indonesia. Outside Java, significant manufacturing activities are found in Riau Islands (mainly Batam) and North Sumatra. In 2015, Java accounted for 73.4 per cent of national MVA, while the combined contribution of Java plus Riau Islands and North Sumatra national MVA was 82.3 per cent. Other provinces contributed very marginally to national MVA.

Second, the next largest contributor, after Java plus Riau Islands and North Sumatra, to national MVA is East Kalimantan with 4.2 per cent share, mainly due to the existence of oil and gas manufacturing. However, the share of manufacturing in East Kalimantan economy significantly

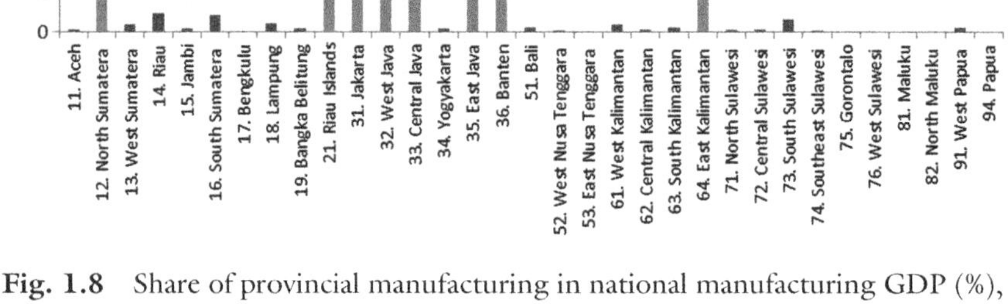

Fig. 1.8 Share of provincial manufacturing in national manufacturing GDP (%), 2015. (Source: BPS data)

declined during 2000–2015, due to the declines in oil and gas manufacturing. Other provinces barely contributed to the national MVA.

The uneven spatial patterns of Indonesia's manufacturing reflect uneven distribution of its population and resource endowments. Aswicahyono et al. (2013) identified that three broad sets of factors have shaped the spatial patterns of industrialisation in Indonesia: (1) proximity to the local market; (2) location in relation to export facilities—harbours, airports, export zones; and (3) natural resource endowments. The availability of energy supplies, principally coal and gas, has also been a factor in the location of some heavy industries, such as fertiliser and mineral processing.

1.7.3 Dispersion of Natural Resources

Figure 1.9 presents the distribution of mining GDP across provinces. As can be seen, mining GDP concentrates in few provinces outside Java. They are Riau, South Sumatra, West Nusa Tenggara, South Kalimantan, East Kalimantan and Papua. In these provinces, the mining sector plays an important role in their provincial economy with a contribution of more than 20 per cent. There is some degree of overlap between the provinces with manufacturing and those with natural resources. For example, East

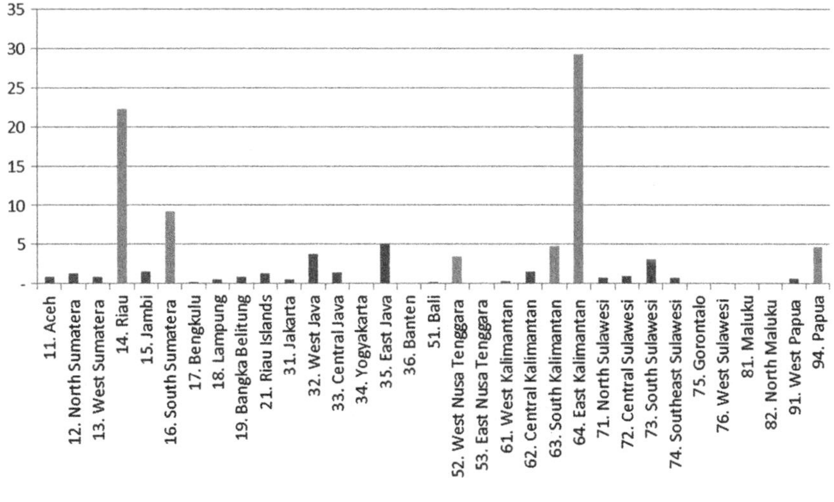

Fig. 1.9 Share of provincial mining in national mining GDP (%), 2015. (Source: BPS data)

Kalimantan and Riau are both resource rich and industrialised, indicating that most of the industrial activities in these provinces are resource based. On the other hand, in Java provinces where manufacturing is highly concentrated, the mining sector plays a minor role, contributing around 2 per cent to the provincial GDP.

1.7.4 Variation of Human Resources

Although Indonesia as a country is regarded as labour surplus, not all provinces share this characteristic. Four Java provinces (West Java, Central Java, East Java and Jakarta) accounting for over half the Indonesian labour force can be regarded as labour surplus (Fig. 1.10). This is, however, consistent with Indonesia's population distribution—nearly 60 per cent of Indonesia's population lives on the Java Island.

Although Indonesia can be broadly divided into two regions in terms of labour force, Java Island as labour surplus and the rest as labour scarce, Fig. 1.11 shows that the regional distribution of quality of labour force by education level or schooling is more even.

Notwithstanding uneven resource endowments across provinces affecting regional productive capacity, there has been regional convergence of per capita RGDP across provinces. As Hill (2000, p. 235) notes, "there is no case of a high-income province growing much faster than the national average, or conversely of a poor province falling sharply behind." There was a

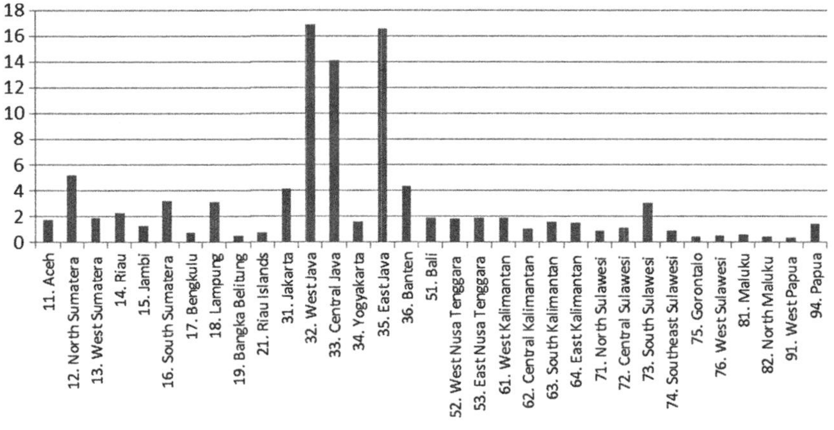

Fig. 1.10 Labour force distribution (%) across provinces, 2015. (Source: BPS data)

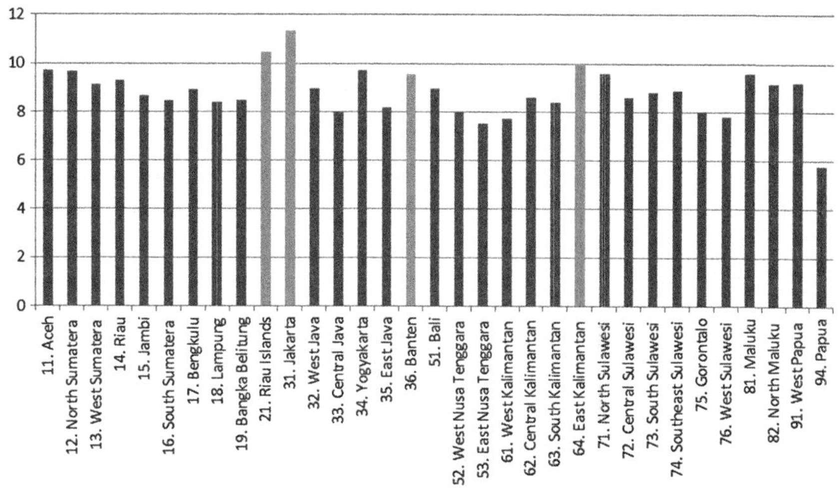

Fig. 1.11 Years of schooling of the labour force by provinces, 2015. (Source: BPS data)

concern for possible widening of regional disparity in the early periods of decentralisation because of the nature of fiscal decentralisation (Suharyo 2002). But the regional income convergence continued after the late 1990s' democratisation and decentralisation, but at a much slower speed, termed as weak convergence (Vidyattama 2013; Hill and Vidyattama 2014).

1.8 Concluding Remarks

Besides summarising the main findings of the chapters contained in this volume, the purpose of this introductory chapter is two-fold: to highlight Indonesia's changed economic challenges during the post-Soeharto period and to emphasise that going forward, Indonesia needs to take into consideration its wide regional diversity. Indonesia is not a homogeneous country, often described as unity in diversity (*Bhinneka Tunggal Ika*).[18] The challenge is how to harness its regional diversity to propel it to a

[18] *Bhinneka Tunggal Ika* is the official national motto of Indonesia. The phrase is Old Javanese translated as "Unity in Diversity" (different but one). It is a quotation from an Old Javanese poem *Kakawin Sutasoma*, written by Mpu Tantular during the reign of the Majapahit Empire sometime in the fourteenth century, under the reign of Hayam Wuruk.

dynamic path of balanced industrialisation and development. Regional diversity, while challenging, also offers the opportunity for flexibility in designing development strategies. Indonesia needs to abandon monolithic strategies such as import substitution or labour-intensive export orientation. It can have a mix of activities, based on its regional characteristics, geared to both internal and external markets. Radical decentralisation of administration and policymaking, while advantageous for local initiatives, can be challenging for coordination and coherence.

References

ADB 2013. *Asia's economic transformation: Where to, how, and how fast? – Key indicators for Asia and the Pacific 2013 special chapter.* Manila: Asian Development Bank.

Akita, T. 1988. "Regional development and income disparities in Indonesia." *Asian Economic Journal* 2(2): 165–91.

Akita, T. and R.A. Lukman 1995. "Interregional inequalities in Indonesia: A sectoral decomposition analysis for 1975–92." *Bulletin of Indonesian Economic Studies* 31(2): 61–81.

Akita, T. and R.A. Lukman 1999. "Spatial patterns of expenditure inequalities in Indonesia." *Bulletin of Indonesian Economic Studies* 32(2): 67–90.

Anas, T. 2013. "Missing middle in the Indonesian manufacturing exports." Paper for 23rd *Pacific Conference of the Regional Science Association International* (RSAI), Bandung, 2–4 July.

Asra, A. 2000. "Poverty and inequality in Indonesia: estimates, decomposition and key issues." *Journal of the Asia Pacific Economy* 5(1–2): 91–111.

Aswicahyono, H., H. Hill and D. Narjoko 2013. "Industrialization: Patterns, issues, and constraints." In H. Hill, M.E. Khan and J. Zhuang (eds.). *Diagnosing the Indonesian economy: Toward inclusive and green growth.* Manila: Asian Development Bank.

Booth, Anne 2016. *Economic change in modern Indonesia: Colonial and post-colonial comparisons.* Cambridge: Cambridge University Press.

Chen, Y. 2013. "China's "above warning level" income gap shows inequality." *Global Times*, January 19. Retrieved from http://www.globaltimes.cn/content/756786.shtml.

Chenery, H.B. 1960. "Patterns of industrial growth". *American Economic Review* 50(4): 624–54.

Cobham, A. and A. Sumner 2013. "Putting the Gini back in the bottle? 'The Palma' as a policy-relevant measure of Inequality." Available at: https://www.kcl.ac.uk/aboutkings/worldwide/initiatives/global/intdev/people/Sumner/Cobham-Sumner-15March2013.pdf. Accessed on 1 January 2016.

Comola, M. and L. de Mello 2013. "Salaried employment and earnings in Indonesia: New evidence on the selection bias." *Applied Economics* 45(19): 2808–16.

Dhanani, S. 2000. *Indonesia: Strategy for manufacturing competitiveness.* Jakarta: UNIDO.

Diop, N. 2016. "Making Indonesian manufacturing an engine of growth again: Now or never?" In EIU, *Hopes and doubts perspectives on the long road to Indonesia's economic development.* London: The Economist Intelligence Unit.

EIU 2016. *Hopes and doubts perspectives on the long road to Indonesia's economic development.* London: The Economist Intelligence Unit.

Elias, S. and C. Noone 2011. "The growth and development of the Indonesian economy." *Bulletin December Quarter 2011.* Reserve Bank of Australia.

ESCAP 2013. *Economic and social survey of Asia and the Pacific 2013: Forward-looking macroeconomic policies for inclusive and sustainable development.* Bangkok: ESCAP.

ESCAP 2014. *Economic and social survey of Asia and the Pacific 2014: Regional connectivity for shared prosperity.* Bangkok: ESCAP.

Esmara, H. 1975. "Regional income disparities." *Bulletin of Indonesian Economic Studies* 11(1): 41–57.

Garcia, J.G. and L. Soelistianingsih 1998. "Why do differences in provincial incomes persist in Indonesia?" *Bulletin of Indonesian Economic Studies* 34(1): 95–120.

Higgins, B. 1968. *Economic development principles, problems, and policies.* London: Constable.

Hill, H. 1997. *Indonesia's industrial transformation.* Singapore: Institute of Southeast Asian Studies.

Hill, H. 2000. *The Indonesian economy, 2nd edition.* Cambridge: Cambridge University Press.

Hill, H. and Y. Vidyattama 2014. "Hares and tortoises: Regional development dynamics in Indonesia." In H. Hill (Ed.), *Regional dynamics in a decentralized Indonesia* (pp. 68–97). Singapore: ISEAS.

Hill, H. ed. 1991. *Unity and diversity: Regional economic development in Indonesia since 1970.* Oxford. Oxford University Press.

Hughes, G.A. and I. Islam 1981. "Inequality in Indonesia: A decomposition analysis." *Bulletin of Indonesian Economic Studies* 17(2): 42–71.

Islam, I. and H. Khan 1986. "Spatial patterns of inequality and poverty in Indonesia." *Bulletin of Indonesian Economic Studies* 22(2): 80–102.

Kuznets, S. 1971. "Modern economic growth: Findings and reflections". *Nobel Memorial Lecture.*

Lankester, T. 2004. "Asian drama: The pursuit of modernisation in India and Indonesia." *Asian Affairs* 35(3): 291–304

Naudé, W. 2013. "Why Indonesia needs a more innovative industrial policy." *ASEAN Journal of Economics, Management and Accounting* 1(1): 48–65.

OECD 2015. *In it together: Why less inequality benefits all.* Paris: OECD

Ostry, J.D., A. Berg and C.G. Tsangarides 2014. "Redistribution, inequality and growth." *IMF Staff Discussion Note* 14/02. Washington, DC: International Monetary Fund.

Palma J.G. 2011. "Homogeneous middles vs. heterogeneous tails, and the end of the 'inverted-U': It's all about the share of the rich." *Development and Change* 42(1): 87–153.

Pirmana V. 2006. Earnings differential between male-female in Indonesia: Evidence from Sakernas data. *Working Paper in Economics and Development Studies (WoPEDS)* No. 2006–08. Bandung: Padjadjaran University.

Priyarsono, D.S., T.K. Lestari and D.A. Dewi 2010. "Industrialization and de-industrialization in Indonesia 1983–2008: A Kaldorian approach." *Journal of Indonesian Economy and Business* 25(2): 143–54.

Raz, A.F. 2013. "In search of better industrial policy in Indonesia." *Jakarta Post*, 13 August.

Rowthorn, R. and J. Wells 1987. "*De-industrialization and foreign trade.*" Cambridge, UK: Cambridge University Press.

Rowthorn, R. and R. Ramaswamy 1997. "Deindustrialization: Causes and implications." *IMF Working Paper* 97/42. Washington, DC: International Monetary Fund.

Suharyo, W.I. 2002. "Indonesia's fiscal decentralization: A preliminary assessment of the first year experience." *UNSFIR Working Paper* No. 02/07. Jakarta: UNSFIR.

Tadjoeddin M.Z., A. Zuhdi and R. Izzati 2017. "Economic inequality in post-crisis Indonesia: Does structural change matter." SMERU Research Institute, mimeo.

Tadjoeddin, M.Z. 2011. "The economic origins of Indonesia's secessionist conflicts." *Civil Wars* 13(3): 312–32.

Tadjoeddin, M.Z. 2013. "Miracle that never was: Disaggregated level of inequality in Indonesia." *International Journal of Development Issues* 12(1): 22–35.

Tadjoeddin, M.Z. 2016a. "Earnings, productivity and inequality in Indonesia." *Economic and Labour Relations Review* 27(2): 248–71.

Tadjoeddin, M.Z. 2016b. "Productivity, wages and employment: Evidence from the Indonesia's manufacturing sector." *Journal of the Asia Pacific Economy* 21(4): 489–512.

Tadjoeddin, M.Z., A. Yumna, S.E. Gultom, M.F. Rakhmadi, M.F. Hidayat and A. Suryahadi (2016). "Inequality and stability in democratic and decentralized Indonesia." *SMERU Working Paper*. Jakarta.

Tadjoeddin, M.Z., W. Suharyo and S. Mishra 2001. "Regional disparity and vertical conflicts in Indonesia." *Journal of the Asia Pacific Economy* 6(3): 283–304.

Tijaja, J. and M. Faisal 2014. "Industrial policy in Indonesia: A global value chain perspective." *Asian Development Bank Economics Working Paper Series* No. 411.

Uppal, J.S. and B.S. Handoko 1986. "Regional income disparities in Indonesia." *Ekonomi Keuangan Indonesia* 34(3): 287–304.

Vidyattama, Y. 2013. "Regional convergence and the role of neighbourhood effects in a decentralised Indonesia." *Bulletin of Indonesian Economic Studies* 49(3): 193–211.

World Bank 2012a. *Picking up the pace: Reviving growth in Indonesia's manufacturing sector.* Jakarta: World Bank

World Bank 2012b. *Policy Note 1: Why the manufacturing sector still matters for growth and development in Indonesia.* Jakarta: World Bank.

World Bank 2014. *Development policy review 2014 (Indonesia: Avoiding the trap).* Jakarta: World Bank.

World Bank 2016. *Indonesian economic transformation and employment: Policy input for an Indonesia jobs strategy.* Jakarta: World Bank.

World Bank 1993. The East Asian miracle: Economic growth and public policy. Washington, DC: World Bank and Oxford University Press.

World Bank 2015 *Indonesia's rising divide: Why inequality is rising, why it matters and what can be done.* Washington, DC: World Bank.

Yang, L. 2013. "Gini coefficient release highlights China's resolve to bridge wealth gap. Xinhuanet." January 21. Retrieved from http://news.xinhuanet.com/english/china/2013-01/21/c_132116852.htm.

Yusuf, A.A. 2014. *Has prosperity been for all? Revisiting the trend of various dimension of inequality in Indonesia.* Jakarta: INFID.

CHAPTER 2

An Overview of Employment Situation

2.1 Introduction

This chapter provides an in-depth analysis of employment situation in Indonesia, with particular emphasis on the quality of employment in line with the global discussion on decent work. Thus, in addition to conventional unemployment and employment data, this chapter examines a range of indicators representing the quality of employment. They include, among others, formal employment, underemployment, the incidence of low pay, wage inequality, youth NEET (neither in employment nor in education or training) and social security coverage. The chapter argues that policymakers should focus more on improving the quality of employment rather than the traditional concern of unemployment reduction.

This chapter covers (1) the high-growth last decade of Soeharto era, (2) the volatile period of subsequent democratic and decentralisation reform and (3) the last decade of democratic consolidation era, which also includes global financial crisis (GFC) of 2008–2009. This chapter proceeds in three parts. The first part concerns with the basic employment and unemployment data; the second part looks at the quality of employment and the last part examines wage growth and wage inequality.

The main data source for the employment-related indicators is the August series of the Indonesian National Labour Force Survey (Sakernas). The survey was initiated in 1976 to cover national labour market characteristics of all working-age individuals within sampled households.

M. Z. Tadjoeddin, A. Chowdhury, *Employment and Re-Industrialisation in Post Soeharto Indonesia*, Critical Studies of the Asia-Pacific, https://doi.org/10.1057/978-1-137-50566-8_2

However, it was conducted on a regular basis only since 1986: quarterly (1986–1993), annually (1994–2004), biannually (2005–2010) and again quarterly (2011 onwards). The August Sakernas has the largest sample size of around 200,000 households. Furthermore, the survey quality has constantly improved.

The methodology used for Sakernas during the period covered in this chapter has undergone several changes. There are two important differences between Sakernas before 2001 and since. The current Sakernas methodology since 2001 follows the expanded International Labour Organization (ILO) definition of unemployment using 15 years as the starting point of working age, and the category of unemployed now includes those who are not working, but (a) actively looking for jobs, (b) not actively looking for jobs, (c) have jobs to start later or (d) preparing a business. Sakernas since 2001 also includes earnings of (1) self-employed, (2) regular wage employment and (3) casual employment. Before 2001, Sakernas used working age as ten years and did not include categories (b), (c) and (d). It only recorded earnings for regular wage employment.

2.2 Employment and Unemployment

This section specifically examines the trend of employment and unemployment rates and the merit of using these indicators for monitoring development progress. Employment and unemployment numbers essentially represent two sides of the same coin as both will form the total number of labour force. However, it is not the case with employment rate and unemployment rate, as they are defined differently. While the unemployment rate is the proportion of unemployed people to the total number of labour force, the employment rate is a measure of the extent to which available labour resources (i.e., all working-age population) are being used. The employment rate is calculated as the ratio of the employed to the entire working-age population. The employment rate is also often referred to as employment-to-population ratio. The ratio is useful for examining trends in employment over time as it allows for fluctuations in the size of the population. Due to differing methods in calculating the unemployment rate, the employment rate can be used as an alternate method of comparison when describing labour market conditions across countries, regions or within populations. It is often used to assess employment by socio-demographic characteristics, such as gender, age or educational attainment.

The unemployment rate is generally treated as one of the few key macroeconomic or socio-economic variables and hence is usually monitored on a regular basis. But it does not reflect the true picture of employment situation, especially in a country like Indonesia with a large informal sector and where employment, such as in agriculture, is affected by seasonal variations. Moreover, the measured unemployment rate does not capture situations of some significant groups, such as the underemployed—part-time or full-time workers who would prefer to work more hours—who are also counted among the employed. As a result, a decline in the unemployment rate may not necessarily imply an improvement in other socio-economic variables such as poverty. Additionally, due to high sensitivity to seasonality as well as to the participation rate, it is difficult to discern long-term impacts of government policies from changes in unemployment rates.

On the other hand, employment rates are not affected by the participation rate as they include all available working-age population regardless of their labour force status. The employment rate measures the proportion of the adult population in work, unaffected by the proportion of those not working who choose to define themselves as unemployed. Thus, a decline in the unemployment rate does not automatically reflect an increase in the employment rate. Although employment rates are sensitive to economic cycles, they are significantly affected in the longer term by government policies, especially in the areas of higher education, vocational training, special employment programmes for disadvantaged groups such as youth and women, as well as income supports.

2.2.1 Unemployment and Employment Rates: The Empowering Role of Education

Assessing the long-term trend of unemployment rates in Indonesia is tricky because the official definitions of unemployment used by the BPS (*Badan Pusat Statistik*—Statistics Indonesia) were drastically revised in 1994 and 2001 (Dhanani, Islam and Chowdhury 2009). When the Sakernas was initiated in 1976, BPS adopted the ILO definition of unemployment as those who are not working and looking for work during one week prior to the survey. According to BPS official calculation, unemployment rates were stable around 2 per cent between 1976 and 1982 and around 3 per cent during 1983–1993. The jump of the unemployment rate in 1994 was due to the expansion of definition of unemployment from the narrow question "currently looking for work in the previous

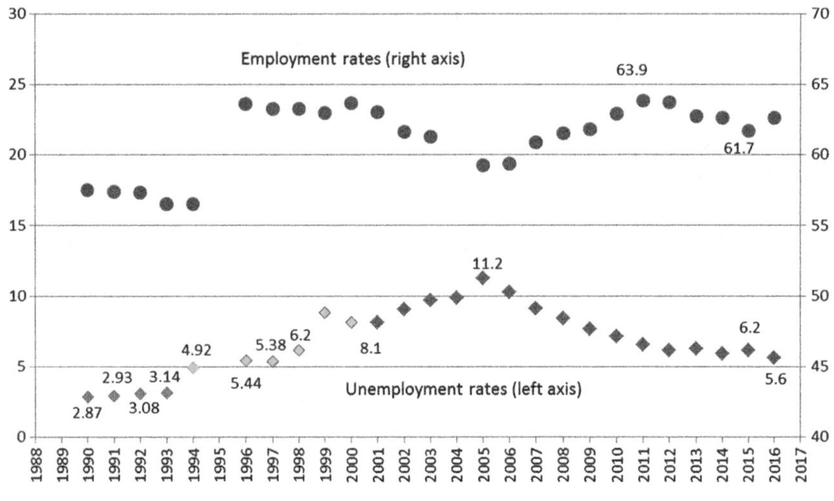

Fig. 2.1 Employment and unemployment rate (%), 1990–2016. (Source: Calculated from Sakernas)

week" to the broader question of "currently looking for work" (Dhanani, Islam and Chowdhury 2009).

Figure 2.1 depicts trends of employment and unemployment rates in Indonesia since the late 1980s. As the Sakernas methodology changed during the period covered in Fig. 2.1, the data prior to 2001 are adjusted using 15 years to define working age for the sake of comparability. Yet, they should be interpreted with cautions as the figures are not adjusted for the expanded definition of unemployment used in the Sakernas since 2001.

With this caveat in mind, the following trends are noticeable. *First*, unemployment rates were on the rise towards the end of the stable high growth period 1990–1993 and 1994–1997 of the Soeharto era when the economy grew at 7 per cent on average. The jump in the unemployment rate in 1994 was primarily due to the definitional change. *Second*, there was a significant impact of the late 1990s' crisis, when the unemployment rate jumped from 6.18 per cent in 1998 to 8.83 per cent in 1999. A 2.7 percentage point increase means that the unemployment rate worsened by 43 per cent in a single year as the direct effect of the 13.1 per cent economic contraction at the peak of the 1998 crisis.

Third, even though the economy recovered relatively quickly from its worst situation in 1998, the unemployment rate declined only slightly during 1999–2001, but rose again reaching its highest point at 11.2 per cent in 2005. This is more than twice the pre-crisis unemployment rate. Since then, the declining trend of unemployment rates has continued, but the rate of reduction has been slowing in the past few years. Eighteen years after the crisis, the unemployment rate of 5.6 per cent in August 2016 remains higher than the pre-crisis unemployment rate of 5.4 per cent.

Fourth, the relationship between the unemployment rate and employment rate seems to have changed since 2011. While they were moving in opposite directions as generally expected, the employment rate has been declining from its peak at 63.9 per cent in 2011 when the unemployment rate was also declining. This may be due to growing underemployment, which will have implications for other socio-economic variables such as working poor[1] and inequality as well as productivity growth.

Thus, it will be interesting to disaggregate the unemployment figures according to the four categories of unemployment (actively looking for work, not actively looking for work/discouraged, have jobs to start later and preparing a business) as presented in Table 2.1a. Two observations stand out. *First*, the proportion of the four unemployment categories fluctuates over time, but their rankings are unchanged (Table 2.1a). Two categories of unemployed (those actively looking for work and the discouraged workers) dominate the overall figure. These two categories move in opposite directions as expected, and their changing proportions should reflect macroeconomic cycles. For example, the proportion of discouraged workers should rise during downswings as the prospects for jobs become gloomy.

Thus, the proportion of the discouraged workers increased between 2001 and 2003 due to the lingering effect of the 1999–1998 Asian financial crisis (AFC). It began declining with the economy gaining momentum since 2003 and reached its lowest point in 2007 when economic growth peaked at 6.3 per cent coming out of the AFC. At the same time,

[1] The term was coined by Hans Singer and Richard Jolly in their 1972 ILO mission report on Kenya, *Employment, Income and Equality*. A related terminology introduced in the report was "informal sector". Singer and Jolly rightly stated that the main problem of the informal sector is that its income tends to be below the subsistence minimum, creating working poor—those who are fully employed but badly paid. Working poor replaced Arthur Lewis' concept of disguised unemployment.

Table 2.1a Categories of unemployment (% of total unemployment), 2001–2016

	2001	*2003*	*2005*	*2007*	*2010*	*2011*	*2012*	*2013*	*2014*	*2015*	*2016*
1. Actively looking for work	66.6	57.9	63.5	82.8	77.2	59.4	64.0	74.3	75.8	81.5	76.3
2. Not actively looking for work/ discouraged	26.5	33.4	31.9	12.5	15.2	34.9	31.2	19.9	17.8	11.8	18.1
3. Have jobs to start later	4.9	7.5	4.0	3.4	5.7	3.4	3.1	4.2	4.6	4.5	3.0
4. Preparing a business	2.0	1.2	0.6	1.4	1.8	2.3	1.8	1.6	1.8	2.2	2.7
Total unemployment (%)	100	100	100	100	100	100	100	100	100	100	100
Total unemployment (million persons)	8.0	9.9	11.9	10.0	8.3	7.7	7.2	7.4	7.2	7.6	7.0

Source: Calculated from Sakernas

the proportion of those actively looking for work increased, as economic growth improved during 2003–2007. Since then, the proportion of discouraged workers increased again, as economic growth dipped to 4.5 per cent in 2009 in the wake of the 2008–2009 GFC. Although the economy turned around and grew at 6.1 per cent in 2010, the proportion of discouraged workers continued to rise until 2011 when it peaked, showing the lagged impact of a slowing economy on the perception of job prospects. Since 2011, the situation seemed to have improved as the economic recovery consolidated with the growth rate maintaining above 6 per cent, and hence the proportion of discouraged workers among the unemployed began declining.

Second, among the unemployed, those who actively look for work are the most educated (Table 2.1b). In contrast, as expected, the discouraged workers are the least educated among the unemployed. These observations imply that education has an empowerment effect among the unemployed. This is consistent with the finding (as reported later) that the majority of working poor are poorly educated or do not have much formal education, beyond the primary level.

Table 2.1b Average education (years) of the unemployed, 2001–2016

	2001	*2003*	*2005*	*2007*	*2010*	*2011*	*2012*	*2013*	*2014*	*2015*	*2016*
1. Actively looking for work	10.2	10.1	10.3	10.2	10.4	10.3	10.4	10.4	10.7	10.9	10.9
2. Not actively looking for work/ discouraged	6.6	7.0	7.4	7.6	8.0	8.4	8.2	7.8	7.6	8.1	8.4
3. Have jobs to start later	7.2	6.8	7.1	8.5	9.8	10.0	9.6	9.3	9.6	10.1	9.8
4. Preparing a business	9.0	8.8	8.3	9.4	10.2	10.3	10.0	9.7	10.4	10.8	10.2
All unemployed	9.1	8.8	9.3	9.8	10.0	9.6	9.7	9.8	10.1	10.6	10.4

Source: Calculated from Sakernas

2.2.2 Unemployment Rate: A Poor Indicator of Socio-Economic Progress

It has to be noted that reduction of the open unemployment rate is not a good indicator of development progress in poor or developing countries (Majid 2012; Tadjoeddin 2014, 2015). This is because the poor or the vulnerable simply cannot afford to be unemployed in the absence of social security provisions. Another reason concerns with the technical definition of employment as the Sakernas classifies a working-age person as employed if s/he worked for at least one hour during the last week prior to the survey. This "work" does not consider the quality of work as the person could be severely underemployed, without decent wage/income or engaged in vulnerable/non-standard employment. To shed further lights on this, we need to look at a range of variables representing the quality of employment. To begin with, however, the most important variable is probably the phenomenon of working poor.

Working poor is defined as working individuals who are living below the poverty line (ILO 2011). Using the National Socioeconomic Survey (*Survei Sosial Ekonomi Nasional*—Susenas) data, Purnagunawan and Pirmana (2013) estimated the incidence of working poor in Indonesia during 1993–2012. They found that the majority of working-age cohort of the poor are, in fact, employed (around 63 per cent), followed by around 34 per cent of non-economically active working-age poor (not in labour force), while the remaining 3 per cent are unemployed poor

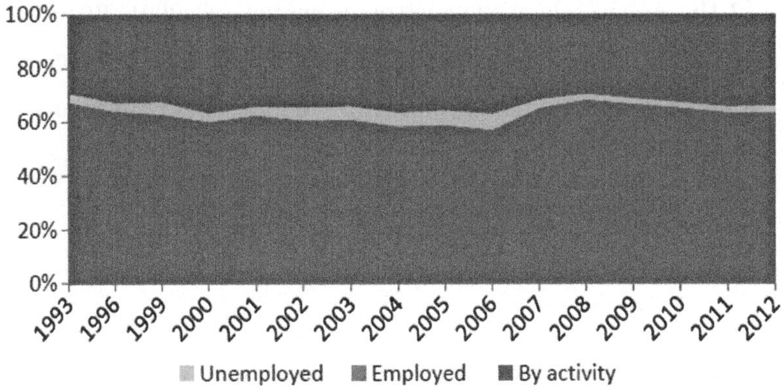

Fig. 2.2 Working age in poor households, 1993–2012 (employed, unemployed, economically inactive). (Source: Purnagunawan and Pirmana (2013: 8) based on Susenas data)

(Fig. 2.2). The incidence of working poor in rural areas is higher than in urban areas, pointing to a strong association between the agricultural sector and working poor. As many as 61 per cent of the working poor work in the agricultural sector, and 78 per cent are engaged in the informal economy. Furthermore, the majority of the working poor are poorly educated, where around 90 per cent of them have only primary education or less (Purnagunawan and Pirmana 2013). These findings are quite within expectations.

The dominance of working poor among the employed indicates the dominance of low-wage or poor-quality jobs, such as casual or informal employment. This also means that the poor simply cannot afford to be unemployed in the absence of adequate social security provisions, which is a typical characteristic of developing countries; they have to accept whatever is available. This is in contrast with the situation in developed countries. In Australia, for example, 61 per cent of people living below the poverty line (relative poverty measure) relied upon social security as their main income and 33 per cent relied upon wages as their main income (ACOSS 2015).

To shed further light on the unemployment rate as an indicator of socio-economic progress, Figs. 2.3a and 2.3b present scatter plots between unemployment and poverty rates at the province and national levels. A priori one can expect a positive correlation between unemployment and

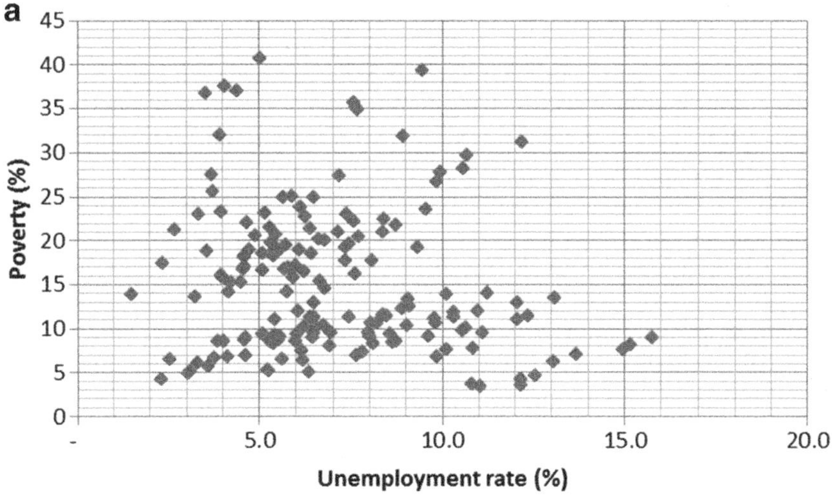

Fig. 2.3a Unemployment rate and poverty (33 provinces, 2007–2011). (Source: BPS data (Sakernas and Susenas))

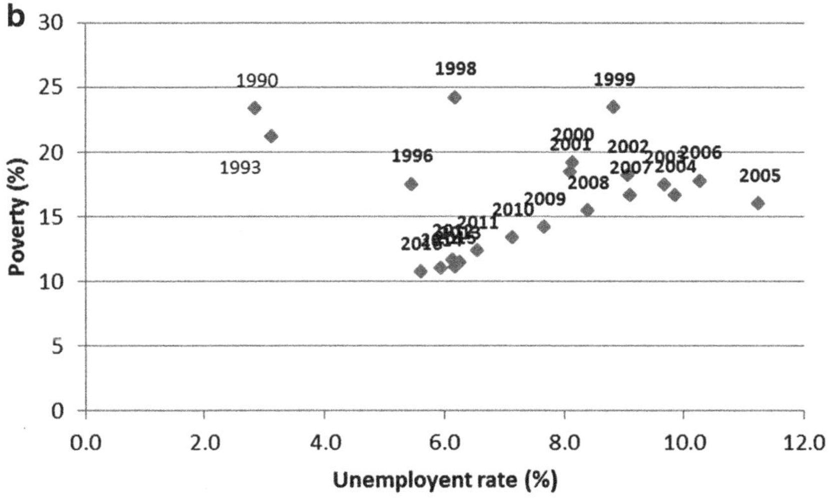

Fig. 2.3b Unemployment rate and poverty (national level), 1990–2016. (Source: BPS data)

poverty. That is, poverty should decline as the unemployment rate falls. However, as can be seen from Fig. 2.3a, there is no clear relationship between provincial unemployment and poverty rates. Similarly, there was no relation between national unemployment and poverty rates during 1990–2000 (Fig. 2.3b). This is despite witnessing rapid economic growth and declines in poverty until 1997 when the financial crisis hit.

Figures 2.3a and 2.3b display some other interesting features. *First*, provincial poverty rates below 15 per cent co-exist with any level of provincial unemployment rates. *Second*, a positive relationship between provincial unemployment and poverty rates seems to appear when the provincial poverty rate is between 10 and 25 per cent. *Third*, at the national level, there is a strong positive relationship between unemployment and poverty rates when the incidence of poverty is below 18 per cent; that is, the poverty rate rises with the unemployment rate. *Fourth*, this relationship at the national level breaks down when the incidence of poverty is above 18 per cent; that is, other factors contribute more to poverty when the incidence is very high.

Thus, it seems that reduction of unemployment may impact poverty reduction when the incidence of poverty is in the range of 10–25 per cent. That is, reduction of unemployment may not impact on hard-core poverty (below 10 per cent) or when the incidence of poverty is very high (above 25 per cent). In other words, the potency of unemployment reduction as an instrument for poverty reduction disappears at both low and high ends of poverty—when the poverty rate is below 10 per cent or above 25 per cent. When the poverty rate is less than 10 per cent, we are talking about the hard-core poverty with structural problem of low education and lack of skills. In this case addressing structural problems is far more important than mere unemployment reduction from the point of view of poverty alleviation. That is, the hard-core poor should be empowered with education and skills so that they can productively engage in either self-employment or better-paid employment. When poverty rate is above 25 per cent, the focus should shift to quality of employment, such as addressing the issue of low-pay incidence, instead of reducing unemployment by expanding any kind of job.

The above observations, together with the fact that a large proportion of working poor are economically active in low-paying jobs and have low level of formal education, suggest that policymakers should focus more on employment quality as well as education and training than unemployment reduction as a pathway for socio-economic progress.

Box 2.1 Paradox of Low Unemployment and High Poverty

Figure 2.3a displays seemingly paradoxical facts—co-existence of lower provincial unemployment rates with higher provincial incidences of poverty. Within-country labour mobility, *a la* Harris-Todaro (1970) model, seems to be causing this apparent paradox. The following comparative cases of Banten and East Nusa Tenggara can help explain this paradox.

The province of Banten: This non-resource province is one of the most industrialised regions of Indonesia, with a 50 per cent share of manufacturing in its economy; its share of formal employment is among the highest at 55.2 per cent. The non-oil and gas per capita regional gross domestic product (RGDP) of this province is just about the same as the national average. Its economy grew at around 5 per cent annually during 2000–2011, similar to the national average. In 2011, the poverty rate in Banten was 6.3 per cent, less than half of national poverty rate at 12.5 per cent. The province is relatively well connected with Sumatra and the rest of Java. It also has much better infrastructure than, for example, those in remote Eastern Indonesia. Yet, the province has recorded the highest unemployment rate since 2006. In 2011, its unemployment rate was 13.1 per cent, reduced from the peak of 18.9 per cent in 2006.

The province of East Nusa Tenggara: Located in remote Eastern Indonesia bordering with East Timor, East Nusa Tenggara is the poorest province in the country. In 2011, 21 per cent of its population lived below the poverty line, nearly twice the national poverty rate. Its per capita RGDP is only 31 per cent of the national average, and its economy grew only at the rate of 3.3 per cent annually during 2000–2011. Manufacturing sector is nearly non-existent, accounting for only 1.4 per cent of its RGDP. The share of formal sector employment is among the lowest, only 20.5 per cent, where government employments play an important role. Employees of the government bureaucracy and the educational sector (mostly teachers) account for more than half of regular wage employment. Despite these unfavourable features, the province's unemployment rate was very low at 2.7 per cent in 2011, among the lowest in the country.

The paradoxical relationship between unemployment and poverty rates is perhaps due to pull and push factors for internal migration

(*continued*)

Box 2.1 (continued)

(*a la* Harris-Todaro). Banten's more modern, industrialised and dynamic economy creates a perception of better job prospects or economic opportunities. On the other hand, East Nusa Tenggara's high level of poverty and lack of economic opportunities or a large informal sector act as push factors, resulting in out-migration. Better transportation also helps internal migration.

2.3 Employment Quality

Moving beyond the unemployment rate, there are several variables to look at for gauging the quality of employment. They include employment status differentiating types of employment, underemployment and earnings.

2.3.1 Employment Status

Since 2001, the Sakernas has listed seven employment statuses: (1) self-employed workers, (2) employer assisted by temporary workers/unpaid workers, (3) employer assisted by permanent worker/paid worker, (4) regular wage employee, (5) casual employee in agriculture,[2] (6) casual employee not in agriculture and (7) unpaid family worker.

Based on these categories, we can broadly classify the overall employment into (1) regular employment, covering statuses 3 and 4; and (2) non-regular employment, covering statuses 1, 2, 5, 6 and 7. Furthermore, statuses 1, 2 and 7 could be grouped into "self-employed" and statuses 5 and 6 into "casual employment". Figure 2.4 plots data on regular employment, while Table 2.2 presents data on non-regular employment and its breakdown for the overall economy as well as three broad economic sectors: agriculture, industry and services.

These three broad economic sectors are formed by aggregating the nine economic sectors—(1) agriculture, (2) mining, (3) manufacturing, (4) electricity, (5) construction, (6) trade, (7) transportation, (8) finance

[2] BPS defines a casual employee as someone who worked for more than one employer in the past one month. In the agricultural sector, landless farmers are likely to work as casual employees, while farmers with a very limited land holding (near landless) may shift their status between casual employees and self-employed, or combine the two, depending on their situation at the time of the survey.

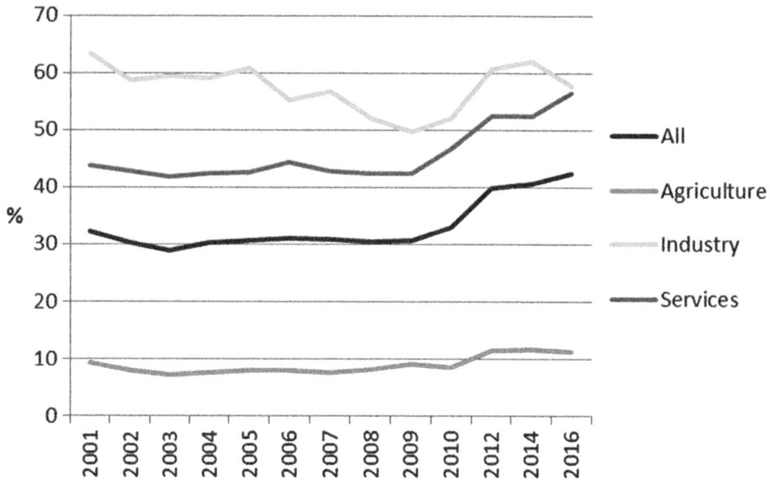

Fig. 2.4 Regular employment by sector, 2001–2016 (% of total employment). (Source: Calculated from Sakernas)

and (9) services: *Agriculture* covers sector 1; *industry* covers sectors 2, 3 and 5; and *services* covers sectors 4, 6, 7, 8 and 9.

While regular employment (usually called formal employment) can be inferred as good quality employment, non-regular employment (usually referred to as informal employment) can be associated with low-quality employment. Thus, the change in the proportions of regular and non-regular employment becomes important. In this regard, Majid (2014) argues that a large amount of surplus labour exists in the non-regular employment (unorganised employment), creating underemployment that manifests itself in a range of forms of employment. In this case, the headcount of the employed overestimates economy-wide employment, and the headcount of the unemployed seriously underestimates economy-wide unemployment.

Indonesia's development progress in the last one and a half decades (post-AFC) reveals that the reduction in the unemployment rate has not been followed by equivalent improvements in terms of employment quality. The following three observations are in order. *First*, overall, the share of regular employment stagnated or decreased during 2001–2009, despite the economy growing at an average of 5 per cent annually. Industry is the only sector that experienced a sharp drop in the share of

Table 2.2 Non-regular employment by sector, 2001–2016 (% of total employment)

ALL	2001	2002	2003	2004	2005	2006	2007	2008	2009	2010	2012	2014	2016
Self-employed (1+2+7)	61.0	60.8	62.6	60.9	58.8	58.3	58.7	58.6	58.3	56.8	49.7	49.4	47.1
Casual employment (5+6)	6.7	8.8	8.5	8.7	10.5	10.6	10.4	11.0	11.0	10.1	10.4	10.0	10.5
Non-regular (1+2+5+6+7)	67.7	69.6	71.1	69.7	69.3	68.9	69.1	69.6	69.4	66.9	60.1	59.4	57.6
AGRICULTURE (1)	2001	2002	2003	2004	2005	2006	2007	2008	2009	2010	2012	2014	2016
Self-employed (1+2+7)	81.5	80.8	82.0	81.3	78.6	78.1	78.0	77.2	76.6	77.4	74.6	75.1	74.0
Casual employment (5+6)	9.1	11.1	10.7	11.0	13.4	13.8	14.4	14.5	14.2	14.0	13.7	13.1	14.6
Non-regular (1+2+5+6+7)	90.7	91.9	92.7	92.3	92.0	92.0	92.3	91.7	90.7	91.4	88.4	88.2	88.6
INDUSTRY (2,3,5)	2001	2002	2003	2004	2005	2006	2007	2008	2009	2010	2012	2014	2016
Self-employed (1+2+7)	27.1	26.8	26.7	25.5	22.4	26.9	26.3	28.2	29.1	30.2	19.8	18.4	21.6
Casual employment (5+6)	9.5	14.5	13.9	15.4	16.8	18.0	17.1	19.7	21.2	17.9	19.5	19.7	20.8
Non-regular (1+2+5+6+7)	36.6	41.3	40.6	40.9	39.2	44.9	43.4	47.9	50.3	48.1	39.3	38.1	42.3
SERVICES (4,6,7,8,9)	2001	2002	2003	2004	2005	2006	2007	2008	2009	2010	2012	2014	2016
Self-employed (1+2+7)	53.8	53.9	55.1	54.4	53.4	51.7	53.9	54.0	54.0	50.2	44.3	44.3	40.2
Casual employment (5+6)	2.5	3.2	3.1	3.2	4.0	3.9	3.2	3.6	3.6	3.1	3.3	3.3	3.2
Non-regular (1+2+5+6+7)	56.2	57.2	58.2	57.6	57.4	55.6	57.1	57.7	57.6	53.3	47.6	47.6	43.4

Source: Calculated from Sakernas

regular employment during this period. This also coincided with a sharp rise in inequality.

Non-tradable sectors became the main engine of growth after the 1997–1998 AFC, when labour-intensive tradable sectors grew at a moderate pace. The capital-intensive nature of the non-tradable sectors meant that high growth was not followed by increased employment. Given the moderate growth in labour-intensive tradable sectors, only limited new formal sector employment was created. The situation improved markedly since 2010, and the proportion of formal sector employment rose from around 30 per cent in 2009 to around 33 per cent in 2010.[3] It reached 42.4 per cent in 2016. The improvement was led by the industrial sector, followed by the service sector.

Second, while the unemployment rate fell from the peak of 11.2 per cent in 2005 to its lowest point of 5.6 per cent in 2016 representing an overall 50 per cent reduction or a cut by a half, the percentage of non-regular employment declined from 69.3 per cent to only 57.6 per cent registering a mere 17 per cent improvement (Table 2.2). It is worth noting that the improvement was led by the service sector where the percentage of non-regular employment declined by 24.6 per cent from 57.6 per cent in 2009 to 23.4 per cent in 2016. In the industrial sector, it fell from 50.3 per cent in 2009 to 42.3 per cent in 2016, an improvement of 16 per cent. The less impressive performance of the industrial sector vis-à-vis the service sector is due to higher prevalence of casual employment as noted below.

Third, the percentage of casual employment was on the rise during 2001–2016, increasing from 6.7 per cent to 10.5 per cent. The industrial sector recorded the worst casualisation rate with the figures jumping from 9.5 per cent to 20.8 per cent during the period (Table 2.2). The casualisation rate in the agricultural sector increased from 9.1 per cent to 14.6 during the period, while it remained at around 3 per cent in the service sector.

To summarise, in the *agriculture sector*, the bulk of employment is categorised as non-regular. The regular and non-regular split is around 10 per cent and 90 per cent, and the proportions barely changed during 2001–2016. The proportion of self-employment in the agriculture sector slightly declined, while the casualisation rate was also on the rise. The *industrial sector* has the largest proportion of regular employment; how-

[3] 2010 Economic Report on Indonesia, Bank of Indonesia, p. 29.

ever, in 2016, it remained below the 2001 level despite improvements since 2010. Furthermore, the casualisation rate increased dramatically during 2001–2016, implying that employment quality in the industrial sector has been deteriorating. In the *service sector*, the proportion of regular employment was only slightly larger than that of non-regular employment with some improvement in employment quality. The casualisation rate was much smaller than that in the agriculture and industrial sectors, and remained stable at around 3 per cent.

2.3.2 Vulnerable Employment

If formal employment is a good or better type of employment, then vulnerable employment is located at the other end of the spectrum. We follow the ILO's standard definition of vulnerable employment, which includes own account workers and unpaid family workers, referring to employment status numbers 1 and 7 in Sakernas. This definition of vulnerable employment is different from that of the BPS, which defines vulnerable employment as workers belonging to status numbers 1, 2, 5, 6 and 7 (BPS 2011). This means that in addition to own account workers and unpaid family workers, BPS also regards own account workers assisted by temporary workers and casual employees as vulnerable. In fact, the BPS definition of vulnerable employment is similar to our definition of informal employment. The definition of vulnerable employment used in this chapter is similar to how formal employment is defined, but more focused on the most vulnerable types of employment.

Comparing the 1996 and 2001 figures, it seems that the AFC had no impact on the size of overall vulnerable employment. However, the figure worsened among female workers. The crisis mainly affected women who took refuge in vulnerable employment. But since 2001, the figure has continuously declined, albeit only slightly. The gender gap of vulnerable employment was prominent, and improvement of the gap was not noticeable. In 2016, the incidence of vulnerable employment among women was 90 per cent higher than that of male, and this gender gap is worse than the respective figure in 1996 (Fig. 2.5). The burgeoning gender gap of vulnerable employment can be explained by the gender gap of unpaid family workers as this category is dominated by women, while that of own account workers is slightly dominated by men (see Table 2.3).

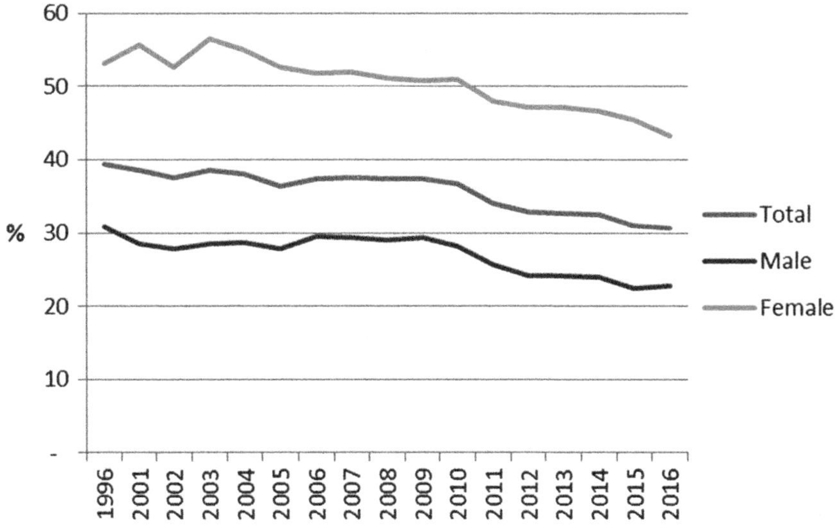

Fig. 2.5 Vulnerable employment by gender (% of total employment), 1996–2016. (Source: Calculated from Sakernas)

Table 2.3 Vulnerable employment by employment status (% of total employment), 1996–2016

	1996	*2001*	*2006*	*2011*	*2016*
Own account worker					
Total	21.8	19.2	20.4	17.7	16.9
Male	23.0	20.5	21.9	18.3	16.8
Female	19.7	17.0	17.8	16.7	17.2
Unpaid family worker					
Total	17.5	19.4	16.9	16.4	13.7
Male	7.7	8.1	7.7	7.3	6.0
Female	33.4	38.6	34.1	31.2	26.2

Source: Calculated from Sakernas

2.3.3 *Vulnerability and Social Security Coverage*

On the vulnerability of employment, the following may be highlighted: migrant and domestic worker, and child labour. There are around 4.5 million documented Indonesian migrant workers working overseas, while the undocumented figures are estimated to be two–four times larger.

Approximately 75 per cent of them are women, and the majority work as domestic workers. Overseas migrant domestic workers are vulnerable, lacking in legal protection both in Indonesia and abroad. They are exposed to trafficking and forced labour practices throughout the entire migration cycle. Furthermore, inside the country, there are approximately 10.7 million Indonesians, predominantly women, who are engaged as domestic workers.[4] They work long hours with low pay, mostly without appropriate days off, and are prone to abuse without any access to complaints and mediation mechanisms. Although Indonesia has ratified the United Nations (UN) Convention on the Protection of the Rights of All Migrant Workers and Members of Their Families (1990), the law on the Placement and Protection of Migrant Worker (2004) has been strongly criticised for being weak in protecting Indonesian migrant workers, and the much-needed revision has not been materialised. Although a law on domestic workers has also been initiated, Indonesia has not ratified the 2011 UN Convention on Decent Work for Domestic Workers.

In 2001, the Government of Indonesia (GOI) established a National Action Committee on the Elimination of the Worst Forms of Child Labour, which prepared a National Action Plan. The first survey on child labour was conducted in 2009 as part of the Susenas. It was found that out of the total number of 58.8 million children aged 5–17, about 4.05 million or 6.9 per cent were considered working children. Out of the total working children, 1.8 million or 43.3 per cent were child labour, defined as all persons aged 5–17 years who, during a specified time period, were engaged in one or more of the following categories of activities: (1) worst forms of child labour and (2) employment below the minimum age for employment or work (BPS and ILO 2010). The RPJMN (*Rencana Pembangunan Jangka Menengah Nasional* or National Medium-Term Development Plan) 2010–2014 has a target of pulling out 28,000 children from the worst forms of work by 2014. The RPJMN 2014–2019 re-emphasises the aim of abolishing child labour.

One important element of decent work is social security of the workers, and Indonesia is very much behind. In 2008, the ILO reported that, out of 36 million formal sector workers, only 16.8 million workers or 47 per cent

[4] The figure is a recent estimate by the National Network of Domestic Worker Advocates (JALA PRT) in 2009. The figure is much higher than the ILO's previous estimate of 2.6 million domestic workers in 2002 (ILO 2004).

are actually contributing to *Jamsostek*, *Taspen* and *Asabri* schemes.[5] This means that only about 17 per cent of the employed population is covered by formal social security schemes. This percentage has been declining as employment has shifted towards the informal economy or due to non-compliant small business enterprises, especially during economic downturns. The social security coverage is unlikely to change dramatically in coming years as the shift from informal to formal sectors has been very slow or stagnant. This means that the formal (or proper) social security coverage of the employed population would remain unchanged at a very low level.[6] This is confirmed by the latest available data from the 2016 Sakernas; only 48.3 per cent of regular wage employment is covered by any sort of health insurance and pension.[7]

In addition to the formal social security scheme, the government has been providing targeted social assistances to the poor. The most notable progress in social assistance is related to two new initiatives: health insurance and the cash transfer scheme for the poor. These new initiatives took place against a background of the inflation shock in 2005, following fuel price increases due to significant removal of fuel subsidies.

2.3.4 Underemployment

Based on a quarter century of data presented in Fig. 2.6, one can see that the reduction in the proportion of underemployment among the core working age (15–59) was very slow. In 2016, around 40 per cent of the total employment was underemployed at different levels of underemployment. This magnitude was barely different from the pre-1998 Asian crisis. Figure 2.6 also disaggregates underemployment into four types according to its severity. Underemployment is persistently higher when more hours are considered.

[5] There were four social security schemes available in Indonesia. (1) *Jamsostek* is the social insurance fund for private sector employers and their employees. It provides four programmes: employment injury, death, health insurance, and a provident fund-type old age benefit. (2) *Taspen* is the fund for civil servants. It provides a retirement lump-sum and a pension programme. (3) *Askes* provides health insurance cover for public sector employees and some others. (4) *Asabri* is the counterpart fund for the armed forces and police. It provides similar lump-sum retirement benefits and pensions. The armed forces also have some hospitals of their own (ILO 2008).

[6] ILO (2008: 14) assessed that "there has been little visible progress in respect of social insurance for workers in the formal employment sector."

[7] Authors' calculation from Sakernas 2016 (August).

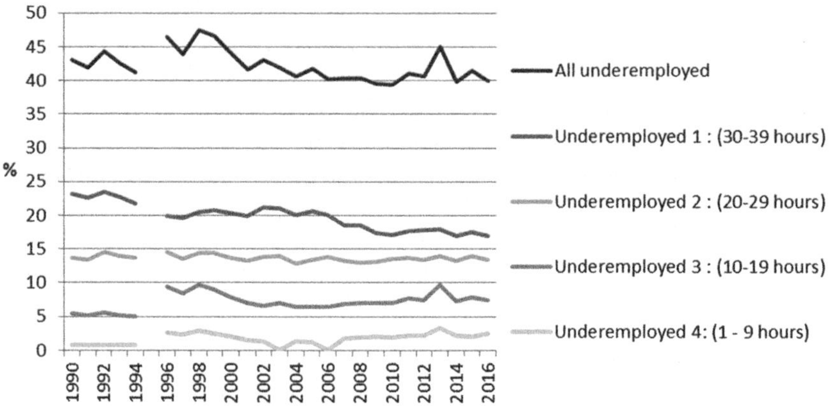

Fig. 2.6 Underemployment 1990–2016 (age 15–59, as % of total employment). (Note: Employment with zero working hours is excluded; Source: Calculated from Sakernas)

2.3.5 Employment Quality and Poverty

It will be interesting to see the correlates between indicators of employment quality with other development variables. *First*, we examine the link between regular employment across economic sectors and poverty reduction. It has to be borne in mind that, while employment can be disaggregated into economic sectors, poverty is not. In this case, we want to see what sector plays a more important role in poverty reduction. Therefore, we correlate the relative size of regular employment in each sector and national poverty rate based on the national poverty line measure.

It is found that poverty reduction is strongly correlated with increased relative size of regular employment in agricultural and service sectors as in Figs. 2.7a and 2.7b. This means that the largest contributor to poverty reduction is the improvement of employment quality in the agricultural sector followed by that in the service sector. This is expected as poverty is concentrated in rural areas and in the informal economy.

The scatter plot between poverty and regular employment in the industrial sector, however, shows a U-shaped relationship (Fig. 2.7c), which is very interesting. The negative relationship is in line with our expectation as in the case of the agriculture and services sectors; poverty should decline as formal sector employment increases. The positive relationship, however, deserves a close scrutiny. When the year of each scatter point is added

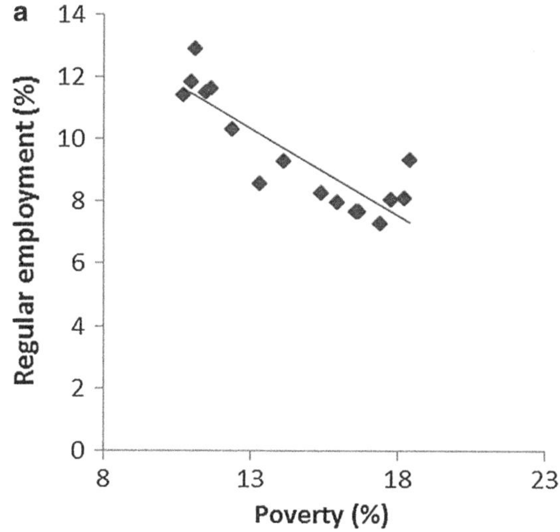

Fig. 2.7a Poverty rate and regular employment in *agriculture*, 2001–2016. (Notes: Regular employment as per cent of total employment in each sector. Poverty head count is per cent population living below the national poverty line; Source: Calculated BPS data (Sakernas and National Account))

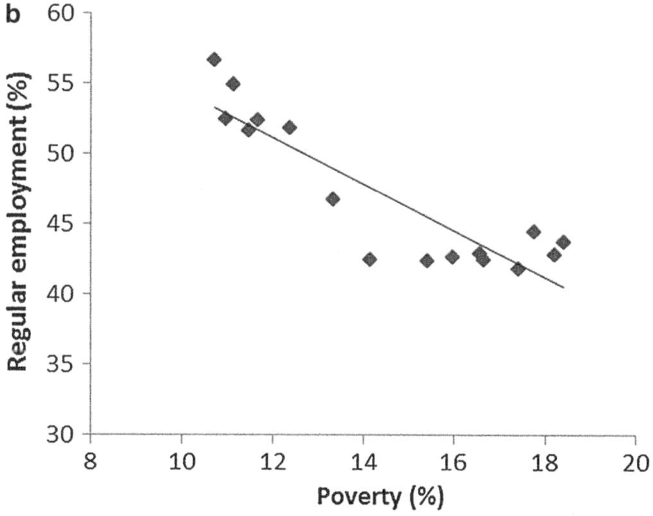

Fig. 2.7b Poverty rate and regular employment in *services*, 2001–2016. (Notes: Regular employment as per cent of total employment in each sector. Poverty head-count is per cent population living below the national poverty line; Source: Calculated BPS data (Sakernas and National Account))

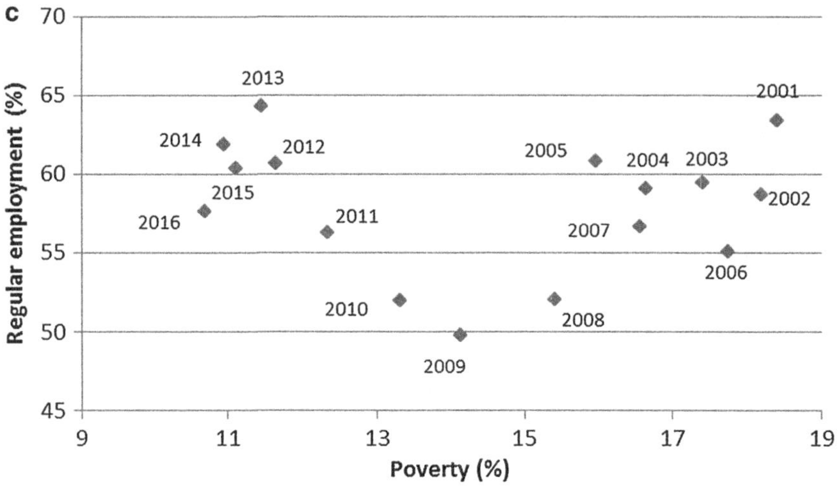

Fig. 2.7c Poverty rate and regular employment in *industry*, 2001–2016. (Notes: Regular employment as per cent of total employment in each sector. Poverty headcount is per cent population living below the national poverty line; Source: Calculated BPS data (Sakernas and National Account))

to Fig. 2.7c, a clear pattern emerges for the industry sector. The expected negative relationship between the share of regular employment and poverty emerges after 2009 when the unemployment rate has been much lower, manufacturing productivity started to rise and the share of regular employment began to improve. The apparent paradoxical positive relationship between regular employment and poverty existed before 2009, coinciding with the period of declining share of regular employment in the industry sector, rising inequality and declining real wage. This also indicates that regular employment may not necessarily pay good wages. As will be seen later in the chapter, the incidence of low pay is quite high among regular employment. This, again, emphasises the importance of improving the quality of employment, especially in the industry sector as the main driver of economic growth.

Second, we examine poverty among the underemployed and the severity of underemployment. As expected, we find that the incidence of poverty among the underemployed positively correlates with the severity of underemployment (Fig. 2.8). During 2001–2012, there was virtually no improvement of poverty incidence among the underemployed. The

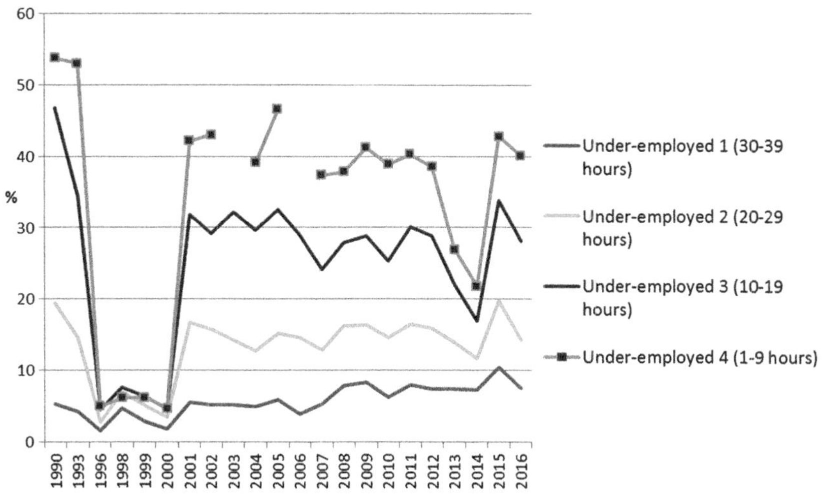

Fig. 2.8 Incidence of poverty among underemployed (%), 1990–2016. (Source: Calculated from Sakernas)

poverty rates declined during 2012–2014, especially among the severely underemployed, and the national elections year 2014 saw the steepest decline. But poverty incidence among the underemployed increased again in 2015 and 2016. This temporary dip in poverty among the underemployed was likely due to cash handouts by political parties, engaged in political mobilisation leading up to the presidential and parliamentary elections.[8]

2.3.6 *Wage Inequality and Incidence of Low Pay*

Real Wage

A long-term trend of real wage earnings covering a quarter century is presented in Fig. 2.9. The longer time series data of real wage earnings are available only for regular wage employment. A few observations stand out. Real wage was on steady rise prior to the 1997–1998 AFC. Then it fell sharply by 32 per cent in 1998 due to the crisis but recovered fairly quickly.

[8] Cash handouts were used as the main method of attracting votes (Aspinall and Sukmajati 2016).

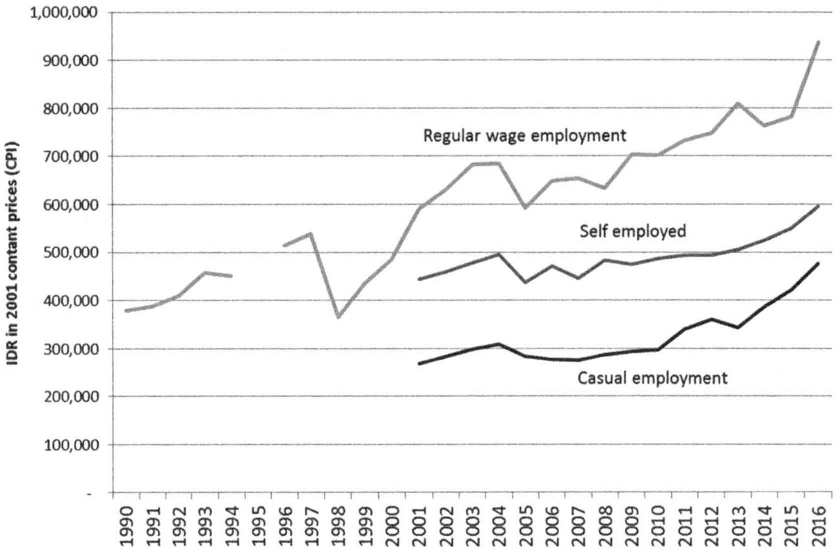

Fig. 2.9 Real wage by employment status, 1990–2016 (IDR monthly, CPI deflated—base year 2001). (Source: Calculated from Sakernas)

Ironically, real wage of regular wage employment stagnated during 2003–2010, a period associated with the resource boom. In general, the AFC did not seem to have affected the long-term pattern of real wage in a significant way, except a temporary but sharp dip.

Since 2001, the Sakernas has also collected earnings data for self-employed and casual employment. Since they are part of non-regular employment with a much lower job quality than regular wage employment, earning levels of self-employed and casual employment are also much lower. Significantly low level of earnings among casual employment is likely due to very low wages of casual workers in the agricultural sector.

Wage Inequality

Figure 2.10 presents probably the longest series of wage inequality so far available. The figure displays two lines. The longer one since 1990 is for Gini index of earnings of regular wage employment only accounting for less than 40 per cent of total employment. The shorter one since 2001 is for earnings Gini of all employment for which earnings data are available (self-employed, regular wage employment and casual employment),

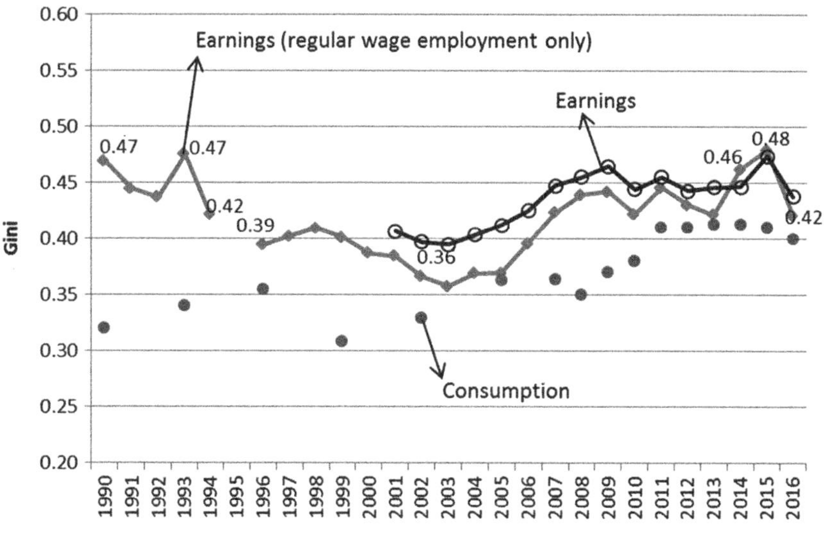

Fig. 2.10 Gini index of earnings and consumption expenditure, 1990–2016. (Source: BPS data (Gini index of earnings is calculated from primary earning data of regular wage employment in Sakernas. Gini index of consumption expenditure is taken from BPS official calculations.))

covering around two-thirds of total employment. For comparison, Gini index of consumption expenditure from the Susenas is also presented as dots in the figure.

The Gini measure of earnings inequality among regular wage employment declined during 1990–2003, then it has shown an increasing trend since its lowest point in 2003 and was at 0.48 in 2015, then declined to 0.42 in 2016. The latter trend, before 2016, is consistent with the common understanding that economic inequality in Indonesia has been on the rise during the last decade (Yusuf 2014). Based on household consumption expenditure data, it is commonly believed that economic inequality was relatively low during the high growth period of the New Order era. But our data on wage inequality reveal that the level of wage inequality in the last few years of the New Order era before the 1997–1998 AFC was in fact very high with a magnitude comparable to the current level of wage inequality. This lends an additional support to Tadjoeddin's (2013) study that rejects the common perception that high growth during the authoritarian New Order development period that propelled Indonesia to the league of high-performing Asian economies was accompanied by low level of inequality (World Bank 1993).[9]

Incidence of Low Pay

By low-pay employment we refer to those in the regular wage employment earning less than two-thirds of the national median monthly wage income. The two-thirds median wage is close to the minimum wage. However, the two-thirds median wage is preferable as the benchmark rather than the minimum wage because it provides a consistent benchmark across regions. Minimum wages significantly vary across regions depending on the bargaining process that is highly influenced by the strength of labour activism in each region. Therefore, unlike the minimum wage, the low-pay incidence is more consistently comparable across regions.

The incidence of low pay among regular wage employment is essentially another indicator to gauge the level of wage inequality. It represents the most deprived segment of wage employment. As indicated earlier in Fig. 2.7c, the period of rising inequality coincides with the paradoxical positive relation between poverty and the share of regular employment in the industry sector. Overall, the incidence of low pay has been constant since 1996 (Fig. 2.11); that is, there has been no improvement since the pre-crisis period. The incidence of low pay in 2016, which equalled 31 per cent, was similar to its value in 1996. The low-pay incidence was more acute among women, twice as much as men; although the gap has narrowed during 1996–2011, it widened slightly during 2011–2016. In 2016, the incidence of low pay among women was 79 per cent higher than that of men, increased from 63 per cent in 2011. Furthermore, based on urban-rural differentiation, the increasing trend of low-pay incidence is much clearer in urban areas, where the majority of wage employees are located (Fig. 2.12).

[9] According to the measure of household consumption expenditure, it has been well established that during the three decades of high-growth New Order era, Indonesia was successful in maintaining a relatively low level of economic inequality at the Gini index of around 0.32–0.35. Then the inequality of consumption expenditure has continued to rise from its lowest point in 2000 since the Asian crisis and reached a record high at 0.41 in 2011 and has remained at that level until now. The debate surrounding the issue of wage inequality is further elaborated in Chap. 3.

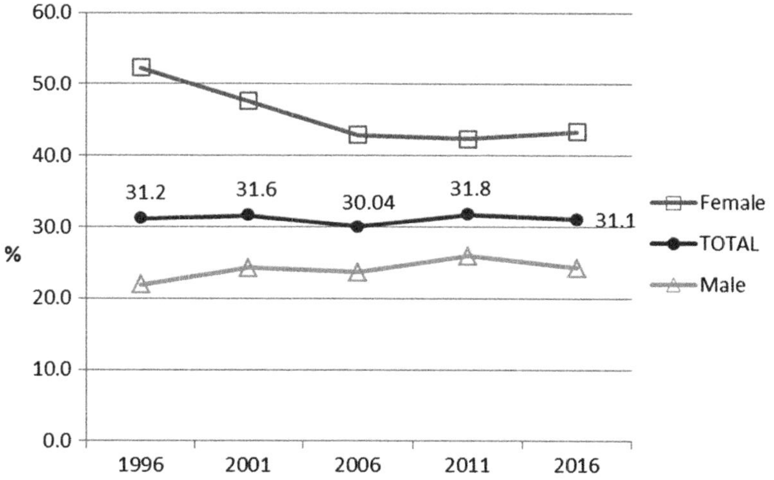

Fig. 2.11 Low-pay incidence: National magnitude (%) by gender. (Source: Calculated from Sakernas)

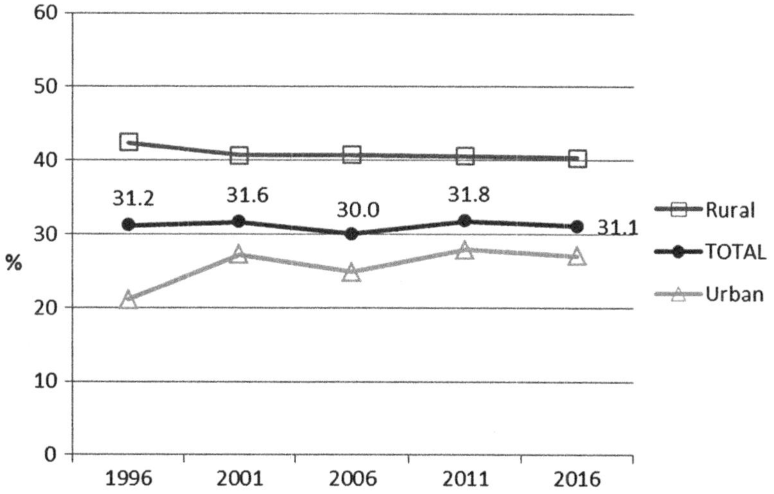

Fig. 2.12 Low pay: National magnitude (%) in urban and rural areas. (Source: Calculated from Sakernas)

The low-pay incidence equalling 31 per cent among regular wage employment (in 2016) can be considered very high. Regular wage employment accounts for 39 per cent of total employment and forms the bulk of formal sector that is considered "decent" according to the RPJMN. If we apply the two-thirds median wage benchmark to other employment status such as self-employed workers and casual employees, the incidence of work with low earnings would be much higher.

The data allow us to extend the analysis of low-pay incidence to other employment status, as the Sakernas also had a question on the average monthly income for employment status numbers 1, 5 and 6 (self-employed workers, casual employees in agriculture and casual employees in non-agriculture). By combining this question with the question on wage for wage employment (status no. 4), we gathered the income/earnings data for the four employment statuses.

Table 2.4 reports the extended coverage of low-pay incidence. As discussed earlier, the benchmark for calculating the low-pay rate is the two-thirds median wage of regular wage employment. The overall low-pay incidence with the extended coverage was much higher, at 41 per cent in 2016. The low-pay incidence was the highest among casual employees in agriculture, followed by casual employees in non-agriculture and self-employed workers.

Interestingly, there is a negative correlation (−0.2), between the low-pay incidence and the unemployment rate, indicating that lower unemployment rate correlates with higher incidence of low pay. At the same time, the lower unemployment rate also negatively correlates (−0.3) with vulnerable employment. These facts may suggest that the reduction in unemployment rate is achieved at the expense of higher incidence of low pay in the formal sector and higher proportion of vulnerable employment. This is consistent with the fact that poverty positively correlated with the size of formal employment in the industry sector before 2009 when inequality was on the rise as highlighted earlier. It seems that the previously unemployed workers are now employed, but they enter into either low-paid formal sector employment or vulnerable employment. This is yet another vindication of the proposition that the unemployment rate is not a good measure of socio-economic progress in developing countries. Unemployment reduction does not automatically correlate with an improvement in the quality of employment or reduction of poverty.

Table 2.4 Low-pay incidence with expanded coverage (2001, 2006, 2011 and 2016)

	2001		*2006*		*2011*		*2016*	
Employment status	*Employment share (%)*	*Lowpay incidence*	*Employment share (%)*	*Lowpay incidence*	*Employment share (%)*	*Lowpay incidence*	*Employment share (%)*	*Lowpay incidence*
1	19.2	46.5	20.4	48.4	17.7	51.11	16.9	53.39
2	22.4		20.9		17.9		16.4	
3	3.1		3.0		3.4		3.7	
4	29.3	31.64	28.1	30.04	34.4	31.8	38.7	31.14
5	4.0	85.8	5.8	87.8	5.0	81.06	4.6	77.78
6	2.7	48.0	4.8	55.1	5.1	47.71	5.9	44.74
7	19.4		16.9		16.4		13.7	
Total 1,4,5,6	55.2	41.5	59.2	44.1	100.0	42.55	100.0	41.3

Note: Employment statuses include (1) self-employed worker, (2) employer assisted by temporary worker/unpaid worker, (3) employer assisted by permanent worker/paid worker, (4) regular wage employee, (5) casual employee in agriculture, (6) casual employee not in agriculture and (7) unpaid family workers

Source: Calculated from Sakernas

2.3.7 *Youth NEET*

On the discussion of the quality of employment, a certain category of those who are unemployed or out of the labour force that needs special attention is the youth group. They are called youth NEET, defined as youth (aged 15–24) who are not engaged in employment or education as the percentage of youth population of the age range. In short, it is the percentage of idle youth. It indicates underutilisation and unused potential with long-term adverse socio-economic effects as it may also create social instability. Such unused potential is particularly important for Indonesia to reap demographic dividend, which is projected to last only till 2030. The prospect for demographic dividend arises when the proportion of people in the productive age group (15–64 years) reaches a maximum and the dependency ratio is at its lowest level. Having a significant proportion of idle youths while the country is experiencing a youth bulge is not only economically wasteful but also politically risky as this group, especially male youth NEET, is most likely to engage in violent and destabilising activities. In other words, unless sufficient productive jobs are created to absorb a growing labour force, demographic dividend may turn into a curse.

Thus, youth NEET broadens the perspective on youth unemployment beyond its conventional definition. "This measure is particularly relevant for youth because it captures those who are not investing in their future either by acquiring human capital through education or training or by gaining experience on the job" (Assaad and Levison 2013: 15). While the prevalence of youth NEET is economically and politically important to look at, this is relatively an unexplored variable and not generally available for most developing countries. What follows is probably the first detailed estimate of the magnitude of youth NEET in Indonesia.

The magnitude of youth NEET is quite high. Overall, it is nearly one-third of the youth aged between 15 and 24, with a huge gender gap. The youth NEET peaked at around 33 per cent in 2003–2005, increased from 28 per cent in 1996. This is the period when the economy struggled to recover from the AFC. Youth NEET declined from 2005 until 2012, then remained stagnant at around 25 per cent, despite stable economic growth at around 6 per cent.

The incidence of youth NEET among female population was 73 per cent higher in 2016 than that of the male counterpart; this gender gap is

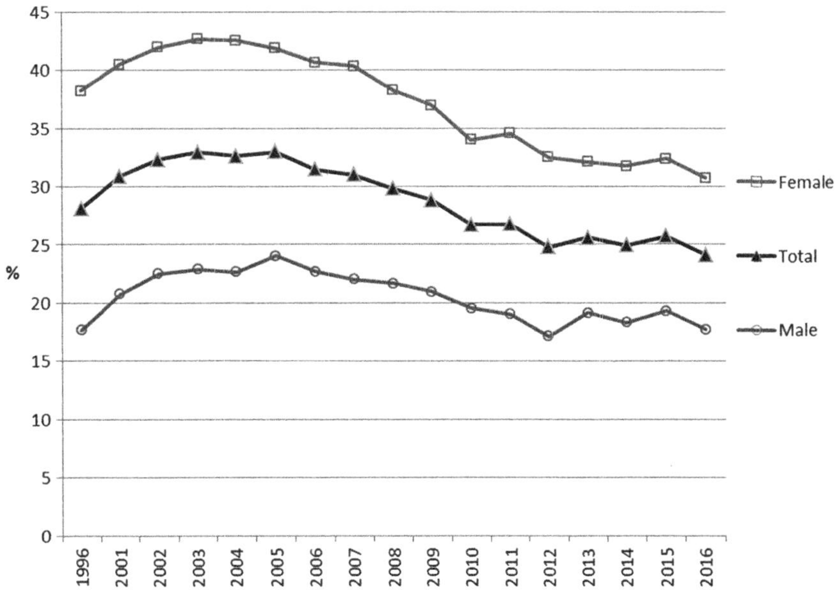

Fig. 2.13 Youth NEET (neither in employment nor in education or training) 1996–2016 by gender (%). (Source: Calculated from Sakernas)

huge, but there is an improvement over 1996 (Fig. 2.13). The significantly higher percentage of youth NEET among female population may be due to the fact that females are mostly responsible for parenting and doing other unpaid household tasks.

2.4 Concluding Remarks: Employment Quality Matters

This chapter has presented the most updated data on employment-related indicators in Indonesia. It has been shown that the unemployment rate is not a good indicator of development progress in poor or developing countries like Indonesia in the absence of decent social security provisions. While a steady reduction in the unemployment rate has been recorded since 2005, this trend has not been followed by an equivalent progress in terms on employment quality. The proportion of good quality employment in the form of regular employment has increased only slowly, while the casualisation rate, especially in the industrial sector, has been on the rise. Furthermore, the level of wage inequality, too, has been on the rise as with the incidence of low pay. Therefore, attention should be focused more towards improving the quality of employment rather than mere unemployment reduction.

For the first time, Indonesia's medium-term planning document (RPJMN 2004–2009) defined decent work as employment in the formal sector or regular employment, and continuous expansion of formal employment was treated as a key development objective. The next RPJMN 2010–2014, too, has the objective to continuously improve quality of employment by expanding the relative size of regular employment; but like the previous RPJMN, the document does not include any target for regular employment. For the first time, the latest RPJMN 2015–2019 includes the target of expanding the coverage of formal employment from 40.5 per cent to 50 per cent during 2014–2019. As mentioned in Chap. 1, the expansion of regular or "quality" employment features prominently in the long-term plan 2005–2025 RPJPN on strengthening the national industrial base. This highlights the importance the GOI attaches to reinvigorating the industrial sector.

However, expansion of regular (formal sector) employment or the industrial base would not be sufficient to address socio-economic development deficits, such as rising inequality, vulnerability and working poverty. Industrial revitalisation strategies must include policies to deal with the increasing trends in casualisation and incidence of low pay, especially in the industrial sector.

References

ACOSS 2015. *Poverty in Australia 2014.* Sydney: Australian Council of Social Services.

Aspinall, E. and M. Sukmajati, eds. 2016. *Electoral dynamics in Indonesia: Money politics, patronage and clientelism at the grassroots.* Singapore: NUS Press.

BPS and ILO 2010. *Working children in Indonesia 2009.* Jakarta: BPS and ILO.

Dhanani, S., I. Islam and A. Chowdhury 2009. *The Indonesia labour market: Challenge and changes.* London: Routledge.

Harris, J.R. and M.P. Todaro 1970. "Migration, unemployment and development: A two-sector analysis." *American Economic Review* 60(1): 126–142.

ILO 2004. *Working out of poverty: An ILO submission for the Indonesia PRSP.* Jakarta: ILO.

ILO 2008. *Social security in Indonesia: Advancing the development agenda*. Jakarta: ILO.

ILO 2011. *Indonesia: Decent work country profile*. Jakarta: International Labour Organization.

Majid, N. 2012. "How not to count the employed in developing countries." *Employment Working Paper* no. 136. Geneva: ILO.

Purnagunawan, R. and V. Pirmana 2013. "Labor market development in Indonesia: Has it been for all?" *Working Papers in Economics and Development Studies (WoPEDS)* no. 2013-17. Bandung: Padjadjaran University.

Tadjoeddin, M.Z. 2013. "Miracle that never was: Disaggregated level of inequality in Indonesia." *International Journal of Development Issues* 12(1): 22–35.

Tadjoeddin, M.Z. 2014. "Decent work: On the quality of employment in Indonesia." *Asian Journal of Social Science* 42(1–2), 9–44.

Tadjoeddin, M.Z. 2015. "Spatial dimensions of key employment outcomes in Indonesia." *Comparative Asian Development* 14(3): 466–509.

World Bank 1993. *The East Asian miracle: Economic growth and public policy*. Washington, DC: World Bank and Oxford University Press.

Yusuf, A.A. 2014. *Has prosperity been for all? Revisiting the trend of various dimension of inequality in Indonesia*. Jakarta: INFID.

CHAPTER 3

Earnings, Productivity and Inequality

3.1 Introduction

As seen in Chap. 2, economic growth in Indonesia post-AFC has not been accompanied by parallel improvements in employment quality. In particular, there has been growing incidence of low pay and increasing casualisation in the industrial sector, resulting in growing earnings inequality. However, Indonesia is not unique in this respect. Increasing casualisation and growing inequality during the recent decades are observed globally. Thus, in this chapter, we examine real wage-earnings, productivity and earnings inequality in Indonesia, disaggregated into provinces and economic sectors, to see, in particular, whether the post-Asian financial crisis (AFC) and democratic Indonesia mimics the global trend of disconnection between wage and productivity growth. This disconnection has three consequences. *First*, it affects income or earnings distribution. We argue that the declining income share of labour, or declining wage-productivity ratio, may help explain the continuous rise in economic inequality in Indonesia since the late 1990s' AFC. *Second*, it implies a vicious circle of low-wage economy, instead of a productivity-driven high-wage dynamic trajectory of an economy. *Third*, it opens the discussion on the broader issue of quality of growth.

M. Z. Tadjoeddin, A. Chowdhury, *Employment and Re-Industrialisation in Post Soeharto Indonesia*, Critical Studies of the Asia-Pacific, https://doi.org/10.1057/978-1-137-50566-8_3

3.2 Trends in Real Wage Earnings

Wage earning is taken in this study to refer to net wage/income earned by the following employment categories: (1) self-employed, (4) regular waged employees, and (5 and 6) casual workers in agriculture and non-agriculture.[1] The four employment categories accounted for 66 per cent of total employment in 2016 (Table 3.1). As mentioned in Chap. 2, the National Labour Force Survey (Sakernas) does not collect earning data for the remaining three employment statuses: (2) self-employed assisted by temporary/unpaid workers, (3) employers and (7) unpaid family workers.[2] It is interesting to note an increase in the share of regular waged employees, while the shares of other employment categories either declined or remained constant.

As can be seen in Fig. 3.1, real wage earnings in post-AFC, democratic and decentralised Indonesia are relatively stagnant.[3] Average real earnings increased in the early and later part of this period, namely 2001–2004, and again in 2008–2016. They declined during 2004–2008. However, until 2015 they remained below the peak reached during the early part of the

Table 3.1 Employment status (%), 2001, 2010 and 2016

Employment status		*2001*	*2010*	*2016*
1	Self-employed worker	19.2	19.4	16.9
2	Self-employed assisted by temporary/unpaid workers	22.4	20.0	16.4
3	Employer assisted by permanent worker/paid worker	3.1	3.0	3.7
4	Regular wage employee	29.3	30.1	38.7
5	Casual employee in agriculture	4.0	5.4	4.6
6	Casual employee not in agriculture	2.7	4.7	5.9
7	Unpaid family worker	19.4	17.3	13.7
	Total	100	100	100

Source: Calculated from the Sakernas

[1] This coverage is more comprehensive than, for example, a recent study on earnings in Indonesia by Comola and de Mello (2013), which only covers earnings of salaried workers in the 2004 Sakernas.

[2] The numbering of the employment statuses follows the Sakernas' order. This would allow for generating the overall figure for earnings as well as disaggregated figures across the four employment categories.

[3] The year 2001 is used as the starting point since new definitions of unemployment have been adopted only since the 2001 survey.

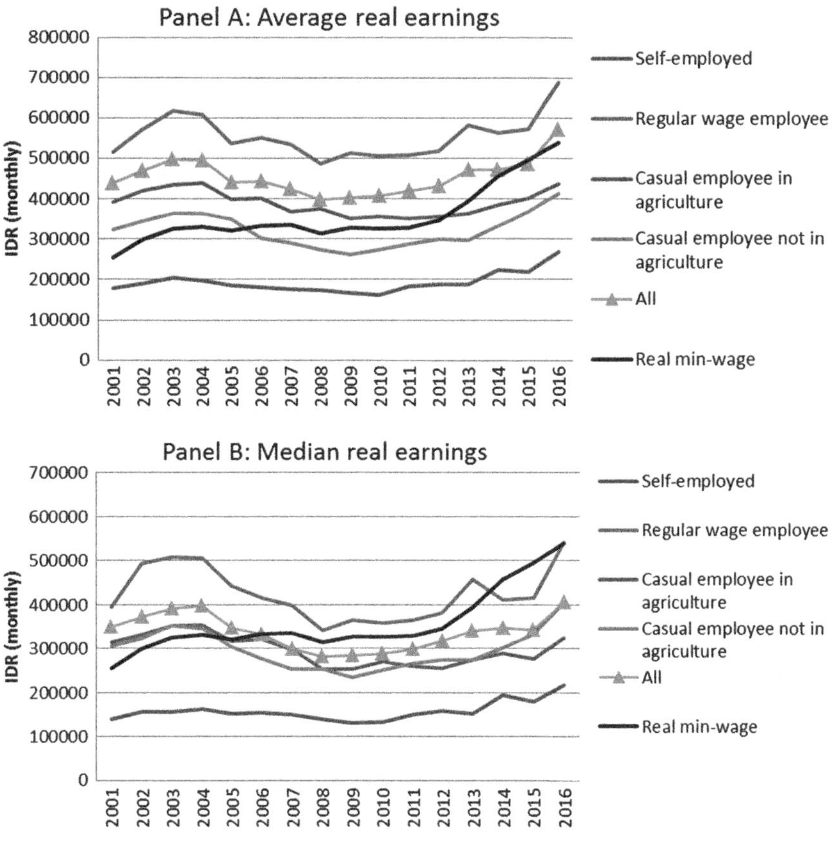

Fig. 3.1 Real average and median earnings and real minimum wage by employment status, 2001–2016 (IDR, monthly, 2000 constant prices). (Source: Calculated from the Sakernas)

previous decade; in 2015 monthly real average earning was IDR 486,000 (in 2000 prices, based on the gross domestic product [GDP] deflator), lower than the average monthly earnings in 2003 (IDR 499,000).[4] A roughly consistent trend was found across employment categories. The most impressive increase in real earnings occurred in 2016.

[4] IDR stands for Indonesian Rupiah, the local currency of Indonesia.

Average monthly real minimum wage displayed a clear increasing trend between 2001 and 2004,[5] but showed a declining trend during 2004–2008, slowly increasing again since then (Fig. 3.1). The increasing trend in the early 2000s coincided with a series of reforms to labour legislations, culminating in the adoption of the 2003 Manpower Act. Figure 3.1 also reveals that the median earnings of regular waged employees (status 4) began declining from 2004 after rising during 2001–2004 and converged towards the real minimum wage, following its trends since 2008. This indicates that the minimum wage in effect has become the default wage for the category of regular waged employees. That is, a high proportion of wages were paid close to the minimum wage level. Moreover, the level of the minimum wage was higher than the overall median earnings and median earnings of self-employed and casual workers, pointing to significantly a low level of earnings for the other employment categories.

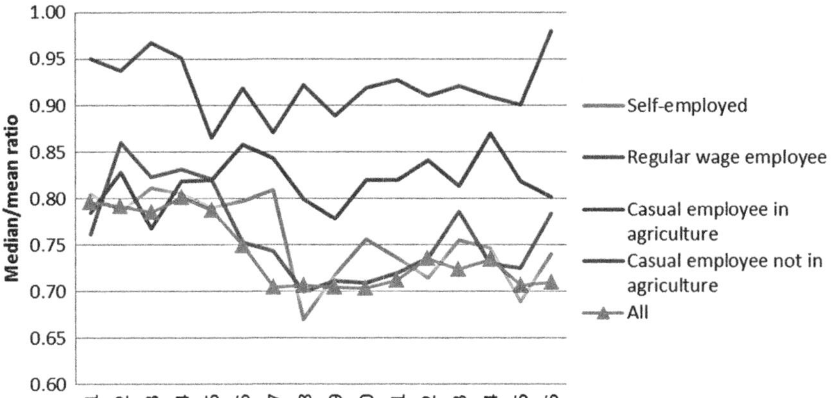

Fig. 3.2 Median to mean ratio of real earnings across employment status, 2001–2016. (Source: Calculated from the Sakernas)

[5] GDP deflator is also used to convert nominal minimum wage into the real wage. The national figure of minimum wage is the simple average of provincial minimum wages.

Although median earnings mimicked the trend of average real earnings, Fig. 3.2 shows a clearer decreasing trend of median to mean ratio across employment categories for which we have data. This is an early indication of increasing earnings inequality. The declining trend of the ratio of median to mean real earnings (Fig. 3.2) confirms the rising earnings inequality trend as highlighted in the previous chapter. The declining ratio is clearly discernible for overall earnings and the earnings of all employment categories, except for casual labourers in agriculture.

3.2.1 *Trends Across Sectors*

The declining or stagnant trends in real earnings are found in most economic sectors (Fig. 3.3). Among the dominant economic sectors as in Panel A (Fig. 3.3), while real earnings were largely stagnant in agriculture, trade and services, real earnings in the manufacturing sector declined during 2001 and 2008 but showed an increasing trend since then. The period of declining manufacturing real earnings coincides with the period of rising inequality and declining share of regular employment in industry. While the opposite trend is found in the period after 2008, employment quality in the industry sector started to improve in terms of increased share of regular employment and increased real earnings.

A sharp increase in real earnings is noticeable only in the non-tradable transport-communication sector. But this sector's contribution to overall employment was not significant, absorbing only 4.7 per cent of total employment in 2016, declining from 4.9 per cent in 2001. This sector also recorded the highest growth in labour productivity among the non-dominant sectors (Fig. 3.5b). It seems that the transport and communication sector have been the main beneficiaries of the country's economic growth during the past one and a half decades, but workers in this sector did not share the benefits.

3.2.2 *The Gender Dimension*

Figure 3.4 depicts the gender gap in real earnings. In general, female workers received slightly over three-quarters of their male counterparts. The gap has narrowed during the last one and a half decades. The female

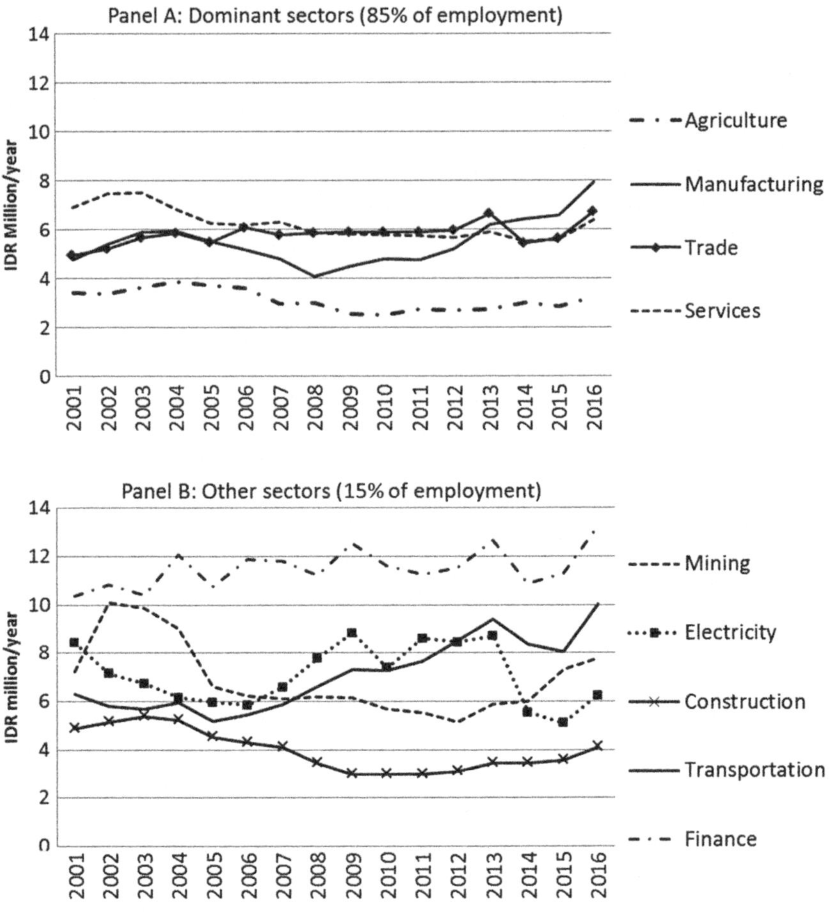

Fig. 3.3 Declining real earnings in most sectors, 2001–2016 (Average yearly earning, IDR million per year, 2000 constant prices). (Source: Calculated from the Sakernas)

to male real earnings ratio in overall employment increased from 0.67 to 0.77. However, the closing of the gender gap in real earnings was slow in the formal sector of regular wage employment.

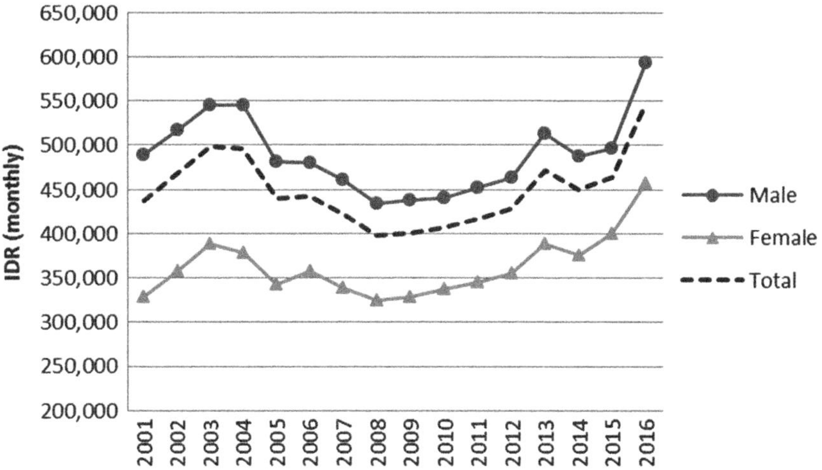

Fig. 3.4 Gender gap of real average earnings, 2001–2016 (IDR, monthly, 2000 constant prices). (Source: Calculated from the Sakernas)

3.3 Labour Productivity Trends

In developed economies with more sophisticated available data, productivity is measured as value added per worker per hour of work (Sharpe et al. 2008). In the Indonesian context, however, differences in hours of work among workers are difficult to factor in. Therefore, we measured labour productivity as value added or output per worker. It is also not possible to differentiate the wages of individual workers within a firm, because the data at firm level are obtained by dividing total labour cost with total workers of the firm.

Trends in labour productivity across economic sectors are presented in Fig. 3.5. All four dominant economic sectors accounting for 85 per cent of total employment experienced continuous productivity increase during 2001–2016. Among them, the manufacturing sector was most productive, and in 2016, manufacturing labour productivity was more than double the next highest trade sector. The manufacturing sector also recorded the highest labour productivity growth during the post-AFC period, increasing from around IDR 32 million in 2001 to over IDR 50 million in 2016. This, again, points to the importance of the manufacturing sector in the Indonesian economy.

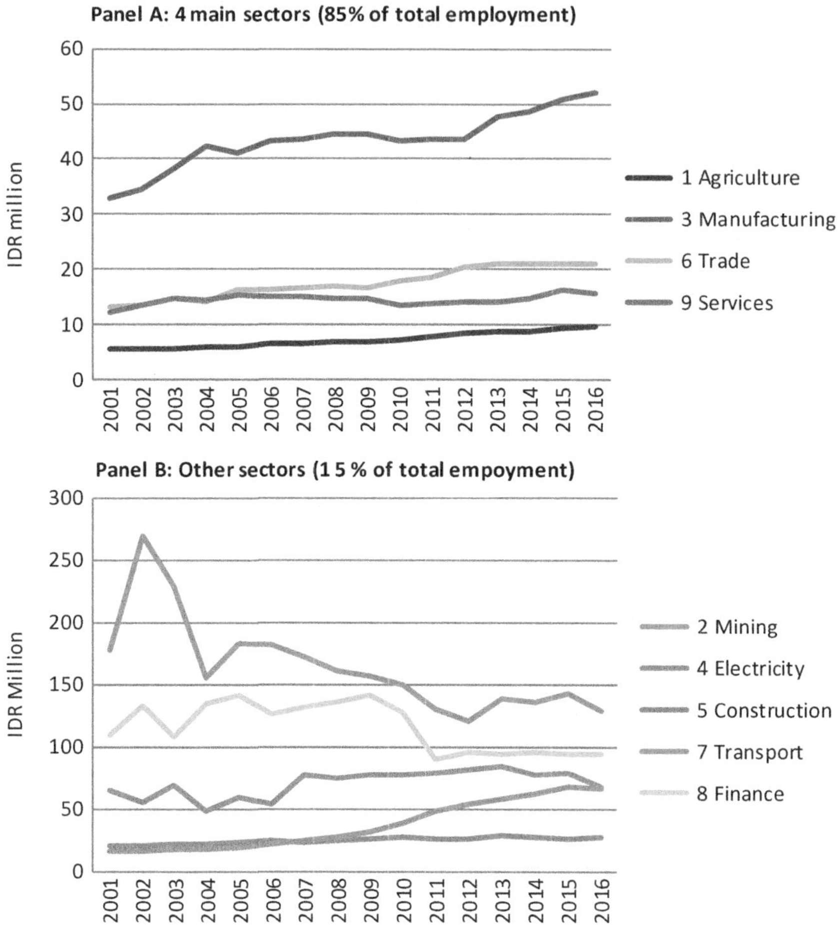

Fig. 3.5 Productivity trend by economic sector, 2001–2016. (Source: Calculated from BPS data)

Agriculture has the lowest productivity, less than one-fifth of the manufacturing sector, due to the dominance of informal employment of less educated and unskilled workers and traditional farming. As expected, it also experienced the least increase in productivity. The service sector's productivity has been just above the agriculture sector and stagnant, confirming low-level service sector activities commonly found in developing countries.

The productivity growth of the other sectors, accounting for only around 15 per cent employment in total, was more volatile. The mining sector which enjoyed a boom during the post-AFC period experienced a steep fall in labour productivity from around IDR 274 million in 2004 to around IDR 126 million in 2016. The finance sector also experienced a fall in labour productivity since 2009. Transport is the only sector that recorded improvements in labour productivity since 2009, from around IDR 25 million to around IDR 74 million in 2016.

3.4 Productivity, Real Wages and Employment: Theoretical Perspectives

The International Labour Organization (ILO) in its 2012/2013 Global Wage Report drew attention to a more than decade-long growing disjoint between wages and labour productivity in many countries. It revealed that since the early 1980s a majority of countries have experienced a downward trend in the "labour income share". That is, increasingly a lower share of national income has gone into labour compensation and a higher share into capital incomes. This has happened most frequently where wages have stagnated but also in some countries where real wages have grown strongly. The ILO linked this phenomenon to rising inequality worldwide. This section attempts to explain this phenomenon within extant theories before examining the situation in Indonesia.

3.4.1 Productivity and Real Wages

Labour productivity is generally understood as total value added (output) per employee. Labour productivity and real wages could be regarded as two sides of the same coin. The former is what a worker produces, while the latter is what a worker receives from his/her employer for what he/she produces. In other words, the real wage is the price of a worker for his/her productivity. Thus, according to the mainstream or neoclassical economic theory, real wage is equal to marginal product of labour.

Therefore, real earnings and labour productivity should move in a similar direction, assuming that the labour supply is not infinitely elastic as assumed by Keynes in the context of the great depression (Fabricant 1959). Higher labour productivity should lead to higher real earnings and vice versa as predicted by the marginal productivity theory and efficiency wage theory (Goh 2009).

The marginal productivity theory suggests that productivity should positively affect real wage. The theory maintains that highly productive workers are highly paid and vice versa. A rise in real wage results in increased labour cost in the short run. But higher labour cost, in turn, should induce substitution oflabour with capital, thus, raising capital-labour ratio or capital intensity. This should raise both marginal and average productivity of labour, which, in turn, should stimulate labour demand, thus unleashing dynamic interactions between high wage and high productivity (Goh 2009).

The positive effect of wages on productivity is also hypothesised by the efficiency wage theory. Firms may find it profitable to pay wages higher than market-clearing level. Higher than market-clearing wage can stimulate worker effort and strengthen long-term employment relationships as in Shapiro and Stiglitz (1984). When firms increase pay, workers should work harder out of a sense of loyalty or for fear of being caught shirking and not being able to find a similarly paid job as in Akerlof (1982).[6]

3.4.2 Employment, Wages and Productivity

Higher wages, thus, not only induce higher productivity but also lead to more employment in an expanding economy. This occurs when higher wages raise share of wages in GDP, which, in turn, increases consumption demand. If the rise in consumption demand is more than the adverse impact of higher wage cost on net exports, there will be higher profit expectations leading to increase in investment. This is likely to be the case as the workers' marginal propensity to consume is generally very high,

[6]The dynamic relationship among working conditions (especially pay), productivity and effective demand was understood long ago during the early 1990s by the fathers of modern industrialisation. For example, Robert Bosch, the German industrialist, engineer and inventor, founder of Robert Bosch GmbH (electrical company), said: "I don't pay good wages because I have a lot of money; I have a lot of money because I pay good wages" when he introduced eight-hour working days in 1906, free Saturdays in 1910 and other benefits for his workers, Similarly, Henry Ford, the American industrialist, founder of the Ford Motor Company, and sponsor of the development of the assembly line technique of mass production, said: "Of course the higher wage drew a more productive worker. But that wasn't the real reason. The fact was, it was no good mass-producing a cheap automobile if there weren't masses of workers and farmers who could afford to buy it" when he doubled the pay of his workers to $5 a day in 1914. While Bosch was referring to the boost in productivity due to better working and pay conditions, Ford's rationale for higher pay was effective demand. The quotes are from Schmid (1995, p. 433).

almost close to one, and wage-induced increased productivity can offset the impact of higher wages on international competitiveness. "When wages rise in line with productivity increases they are both sustainable and create a stimulus for further economic growth by increasing households' purchasing power" (ILO 2013, p. v).

This is the wage-led growth within the post-Keynesian paradigm, where employment and unemployment are determined in the product market (King 2015). However, once wage-induced productivity growth is considered, a high wage-high employment scenario can also be consistent with the neoclassical paradigm where the downward-sloping labour demand curve is the marginal product curve of labour. While in a static neoclassical world, higher wages result in lower labour demand, in a dynamic world with wage-induced productivity growth, the labour demand curve continuously shifts to the right to produce a positive relationship between wages and employment, provided the labour supply curve does not shift commensurately (see Figs. 3.6b and 3.6c).

Another important aspect of the wage and productivity relationship is the wage-productivity ratio. This equals the share of income that belongs to worker (Sharpe et al. 2008) as can be seen from the following expressions:

$$W/AP = W/\ (Y/L) = W.L/Y = \text{wage share}$$

where W = real wage, L = No. of employment, Y = output.

The ratio must be less than unity in the standard neoclassical microeconomic framework, as the downward-sloping portion of the marginal product curve (representing the labour demand curve and real wage) is below the average product curve (see Fig. 3.6a). It is clear that, at any point of employment (number of labour) along the labour demand curve (marginal product of labour), average productivity is always higher than wage. As employment increases with declines in real wage, the gap between real wage and average labour productivity grows larger, resulting in progressively lower wage-productivity ratios and declining wage share in a static framework.

Figures 3.6b and 3.6c depict the relationship between employment, wages and productivity in a more dynamic framework, where labour's marginal and average productivity curves shift upward due to productivity growth, implying that the same workers can produce more. This can happen due to a number of factors, such as technological progress, improvements in labour skills, higher capital intensity, better management or corporate restructuring. When marginal product curve shifts upward (Fig. 3.6b), the demand curve for labour shifts to the right (Fig. 3.6c). In

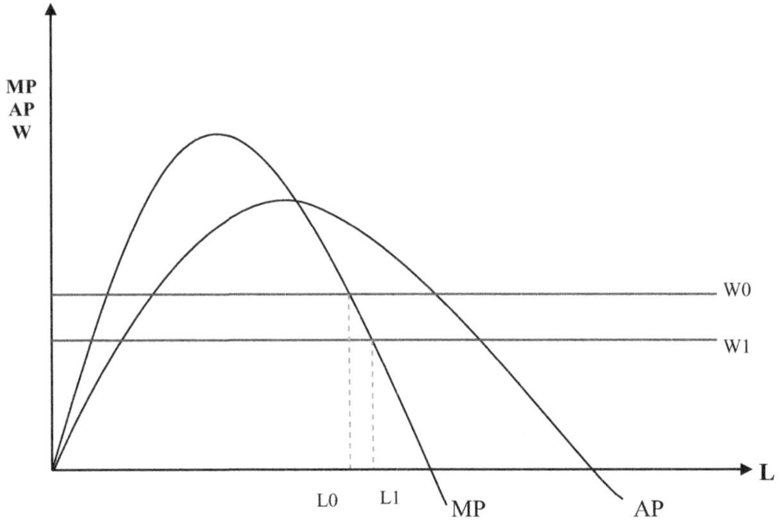

Fig. 3.6a Marginal product and average product curves

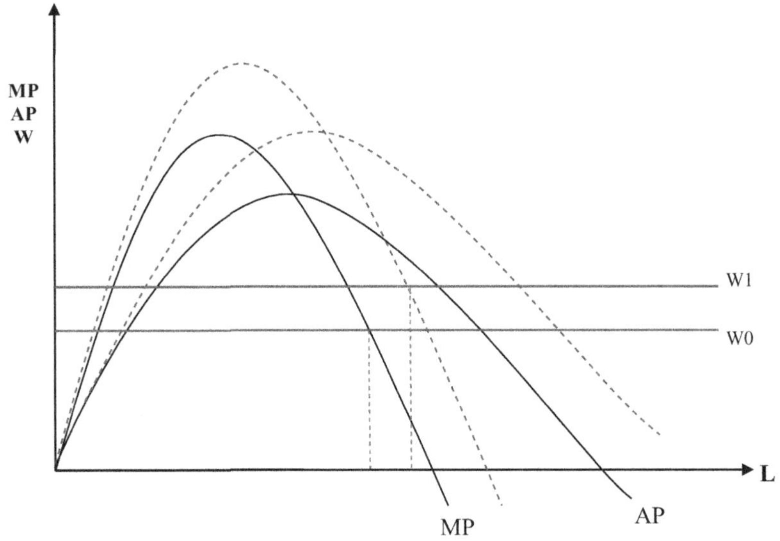

Fig. 3.6b Outright shift of marginal product and average product curves

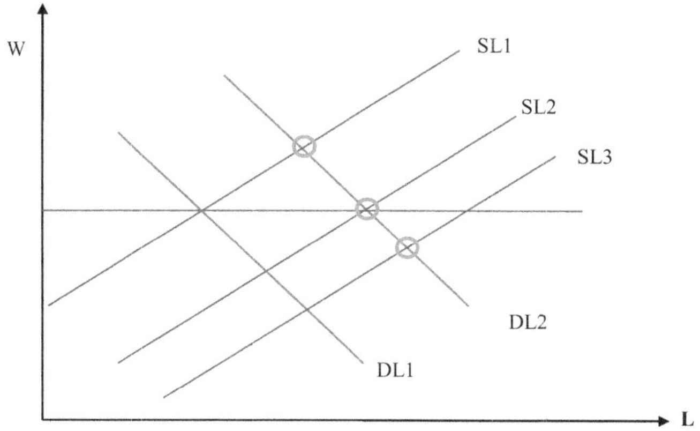

Fig. 3.6c Different supply responses to demand shift

this scenario, the expansion of employment could be achieved with higher real wages, higher productivity and higher wage share within a growing economy, provided the shift in the labour demand curve caused by productivity growth is larger than the shift in labour supply curve to absorb the growing labour force. If, however, productivity growth is not sufficient to absorb the growing labour force, resulting in a larger shift in the labour supply curve than the shift in labour demand curve, real wages will fall, creating a disjoint between real wage growth and productivity growth at the individual firm or micro levels. However, labour market institutions such as lack of union and weaker bargaining power of labour as well as non-compliance with minimum wage legislations can also create a disjoint between real wage and productivity growth.

At the macro or national level, this disjoint between real wage growth and productivity growth can happen when a falling wage share leads to declines in consumption demand not offset by increases in net exports and investment demand, especially when net positive migration and increased labour force participation rate can shift the labour supply curve more than the shift in the labour demand curve, pushing wages down. This situation can be exacerbated by a procyclical restrictive macroeconomic policy framework which emphasises fiscal consolidation and targets a low single-digit inflation rate regardless of causes of inflation with depressing impacts on aggregate demand.

Weaker labour unions (or lack of them) and the dominance of procyclical macroeconomic policies could explain the global trend of dealignment of real wage and productivity or observed declining share of labour income, especially since the early 1980s in developing countries, and since the 1970s in developed countries, as documented in ILO (2013, 2015). The trend of excessive executive pays and bonuses, widely exposed during the 2008–2009 global financial crisis (GFC), has only made the matter worse. The company executives belong to a different class of labour since they are very much on the side of the employers mainly representing the interest of capital especially in short-time gains as highlighted by Chang (2010).

3.5 Disjoint Between Labour Earnings and Productivity in Indonesia

The disjoint between labour earnings and productivity was evident in post-AFC Indonesia, both at the economy-wide and province levels as well as across sectors. While growth in wage earnings kept pace with productivity growth before the 1997–1998 economic crisis (Dhanani et al. 2009), the story was very different after the crisis. During 2001–2016, real earnings only grew at 1.7 per cent annually, while productivity grew at an annual rate of 3.7 per cent.

The data of functional distribution of income are usually derived from input-output (I-O) tables as presented in Table 3.2. There are discrepancies in data between labour's share of income from the I-O table and wage-productivity ratio derived from the labour force survey (Sakernas) and National Accounts data. In 2008, the labour's share of income from

Table 3.2 Functional distribution of income (%), 1975–2008

I-O code		*1975*	*1980*	*1985*	*1990*	*1995*	*2005*	*2008*
201	Wages	24.9	24.1	27.7	27.4	30.5	30.7	30.9
	Gross operating surplus	*75.1*	*75.9*	*72.3*	*72.6*	*69.5*	*69.3*	*69.1*
202	Operating surplus	68.1	71.2	63.8	60.7	56.8	57.6	58.7
203	Depreciation	5	5.4	6.4	7.4	8.1	10.1	10.4
204	Indirect tax	2	2.3	2.9	5	4.6	3.9	3.8
205	Subsidy	0	−3.1	−0.8	−0.6	0	−2.3	−3.8
209	*Gross value added*	*100*	*100*	*100*	*100*	*100*	*100*	100

Source: Input-output tables (BPS), various years

the I-O table was 30.9 per cent, while wage-productivity ratio from Sakernas for the overall economy was 24 per cent. Moreover, we cannot construct a continuous long series from I-O tables to observe trends. Therefore, we shall use Sakernas data.

3.5.1 Delinking at the National and Sectoral Levels

Sectoral disaggregation is particularly important since the overall economy-wide picture hides variations across economic sectors, which is not helpful for analysing causes and possible remedies. The disjoint between wage and productivity growth can be seen more clearly from the declining wage-productivity ratio than from the declining share of labour income derived from the I-O tables. Figure 3.7 depicts the evidence of delinked wages and productivity growth. The earnings to productivity ratio consistently declined, both for the overall economy and across six out of the nine economic sectors, covering 96 per cent of the total employed workforce. In the remaining three sectors (electricity, mining and finance), the ratio has been either stagnant or slightly increased (finance). The agricultural sector, which has the largest share of informal employment, experienced the greatest decline in the earnings-productivity ratio. A possible cause is the decreasing earnings of the largely less educated and unskilled agricultural sector workforce, relative to other dominant sectors such as manufacturing, trade and services. The agriculture sector experienced only modest productivity gains, even after the exodus of workers from the sector. During 2004–2015, the employment share of agriculture sector declined sharply from 44.5 per cent to 33 per cent. The two sectors that did not show the delinking trend were mining and finance, comprising only 4.2 per cent of total employment.

Figure 3.8 demonstrates the delinking trend in a slightly different way by showing the divergent trend of the earning index vis-à-vis the productivity index for the overall economy and the four main economic sectors absorbing 85 per cent of total employment. It has to be noted that the delinking between labour productivity and real earnings growth was more pronounced during four years between 2004 and 2008, when the two indicators moved in opposite directions, labour productivity rising while real earnings declining. Following this short period, real earnings rose again, however, at a slower pace than labour productivity, as a result unable to break the delinking process. The manufacturing sector, however, showed a converging trend between real wage and productivity growth since 2008.

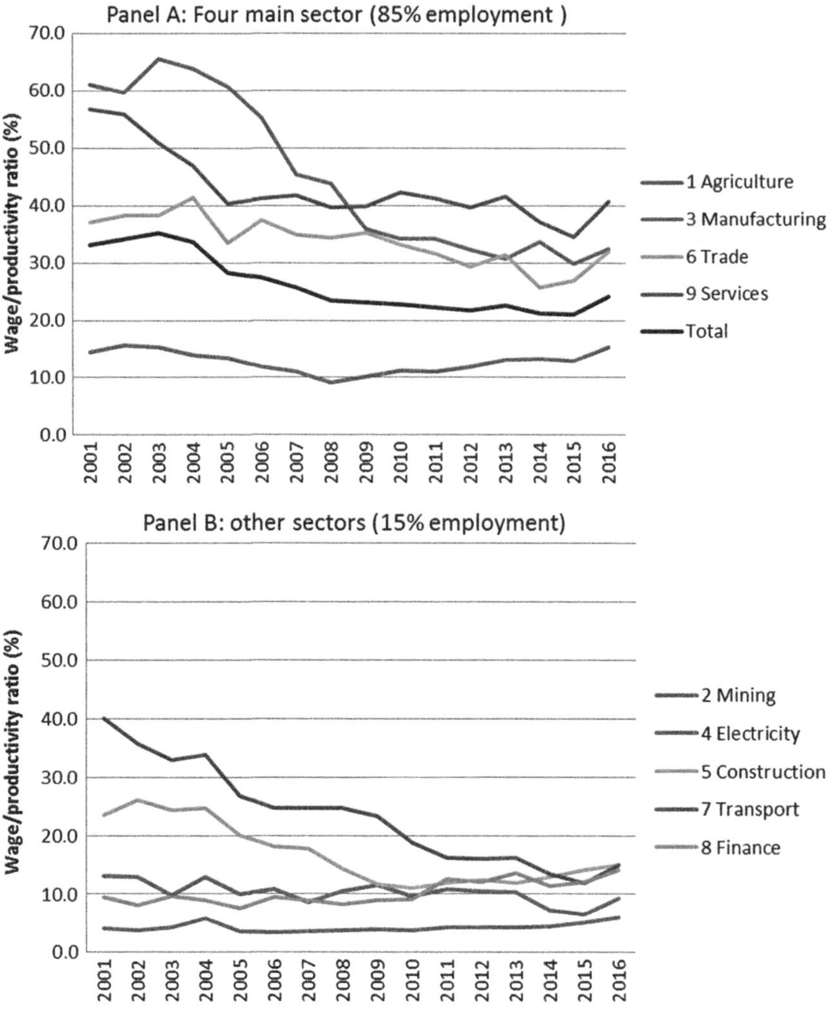

Fig. 3.7 Wage earnings-productivity ratio (%) across sectors, 2001–2016. (Source: Calculated from the Sakernas)

3.5.2 Delinking at the Province Level

The delinking between earnings and productivity is noticeable in the majority of Indonesian provinces. In order to see the differences in the delinking trend across the 33 provinces, the earnings-productivity ratio

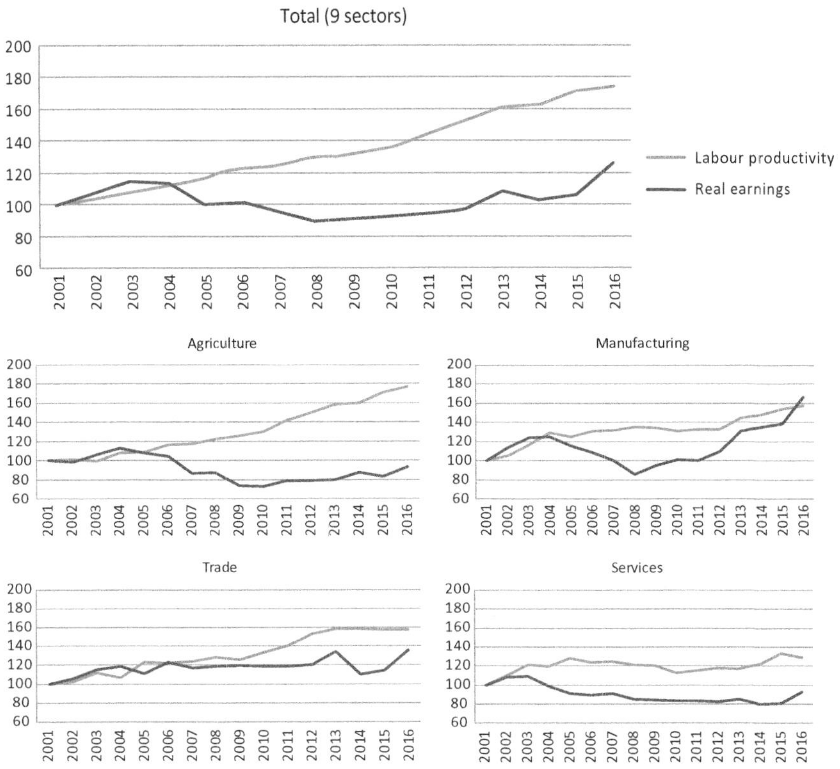

Fig. 3.8 Labour productivity and real earnings, 2001–2016 (2001 = 100). (Source: Calculated from the Sakernas (annual: 2001–16) and the National Account (annual: 2001–16))

trends of each province from 2001 to 2011 are plotted. Based on the slopes of the trend in each province, the provinces are classified into the following three groups:

Group 1: 17 provinces with decreasing earning-productivity ratio (slope ≤ −0.20)

Group 2: 8 provinces with constant earning-productivity ratio (−0.20 < slope < 0.20)

Group 3: 8 provinces with increasing earning-productivity ratio (slope ≥ 0.20)

Table 3.3 Provinces grouping based on earnings-productivity slope

Group 1		*Group 2*		*Group 3*	
Decreasing (slope ≤ −0.20)		*Constant (−0.20 < slope < 0.20)*		*Increasing (slope ≥ 0.20)*	
Province	*Slope*	*Province*	*Slope*	*Province*	*Slope*
West Sulawesi	−2.78	West Sumatera	−0.17	South Kalimantan	0.24
West Papua	−1.41	East Kalimantan	−0.09	Maluku	0.35
Central Java	−0.96	West Kalimantan	−0.05	Bangka-Belitung	0.49
Lampung	−0.68	DKI Jakarta	−0.04	East Nusa Tenggara	0.58
South Sulawesi	−0.65	South Sumatera	−0.02	Banten	0.67
West Java	−0.64	DI Yogyakarta	0.00	Aceh	0.87
North Sulawesi	−0.63	Papua	0.12	Bengkulu	1.07
East Java	−0.60	West Nusa Tenggara	0.16	Riau Islands	1.16
Central Sulawesi	−0.60				
Gorontalo	−0.59				
Riau	−0.56				
Jambi	−0.55				
Bali	−0.53				
North Sumatera	−0.35				
Central Kalimantan	−0.29				
North Maluku	−0.25				
South East Sulawesi	−0.20				

Source: Calculated from the Sakernas and National Account

The details of the provinces grouping are presented in Table 3.3.

The above groupings are used to calculate the average earnings-productivity ratio, the average growth of real regional GDP (RGDP) and the average growth of their shares in the national GDP. The results indicate distinctive characteristics of each provincial group. By graphing the average trend in each group, as shown in Fig. 3.9, provinces in Group 1 turn out to be the best performing economies experiencing increasing trends in economic growth and in the growth of their RGDP share in the national GDP over the past decade. However, the earnings-productivity ratio in the Group 1 provinces was decreasing, indicating the delinking between earnings and productivity growth. This is an unfortunate correspondence, as good economic performance seemed to have been achieved at the cost of labour since their real earnings did not keep pace with labour productivity growth. Thus, the quality of growth in these provinces is questionable.

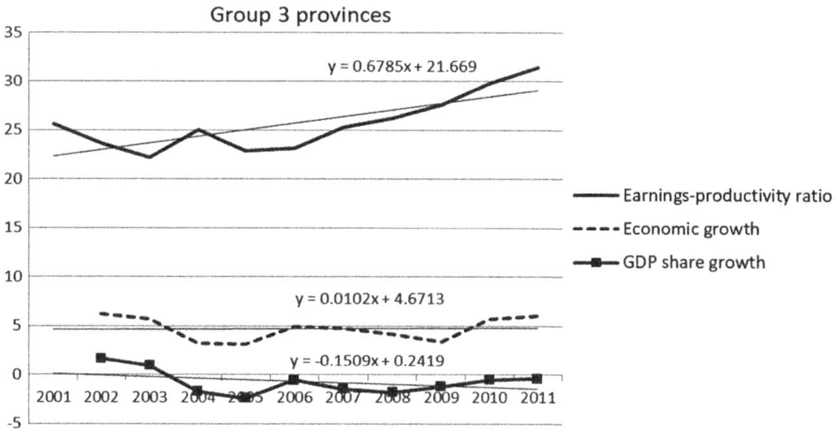

Fig. 3.9 Average earning-productivity ratio, average economic growth and average growth of GDP share for each provincial group (%). (Note: Ordinary least squares (OLS) regressions are used to estimate the trend lines; Source: Calculated from the BPS data (Sakernas and National Account))

Provinces in Group 2, where the earnings-productivity ratio was relatively constant during the last ten years, exhibit a slightly increasing trend in their RGDP growth but a decreasing trend in their average share in the national GDP. In Group 3 provinces, the earnings-productivity ratio shows an increasing trend but more volatile average GDP growth compared to Group 2 provinces. Moreover, the growth of their shares in the national GDP shows a decreasing trend.

In short, the 17 provinces in Group 1 were the best performing economically, with the highest positive slope for their economic growth and increasing share in the national GDP. In 2011, this group comprised more than 70 per cent of total employment and contributed nearly 60 per cent to total GDP. These 17 provinces were the backbone of the country's economic growth, but ironically wage share in these provinces declined, raising doubts about the quality of growth. The worst economic performance was found in the eight provinces of Group 3, yet they experienced the increasing earnings-productivity ratio. The employment and GDP shares of Group 3 provinces were only 12 per cent and 10 per cent respectively and most were located in remote outer islands.

The above finding on the delinking between earnings and productivity growth indicates that, despite the relatively good performance of the Indonesian economy, the post-AFC growth pattern has been increasingly unfavourable for most Indonesians. The delinking phenomenon highlights at least three implications: first, it leads to an increase in overall inequality; second, the quality of economic growth should be questioned, especially from the employment perspective; third, the phenomenon should be factored into any discussion/estimation on employment elasticities, or the employment effect of economic growth. While the next section discusses the linkage between delinking and inequality, the issue of sectoral employment function at various levels will be taken up in Chap. 5. We reflect on the issue of quality of growth in the concluding section.

3.6 Wage-Earnings Inequality

As highlighted in Chap. 2, the democratic and decentralised Indonesia has witnessed rising economic inequality (Tadjoeddin 2015; World Bank 2015). In general, during the past decade, wage-earnings inequality has also been on the rise, which is consistent with the more well-known measure of Gini measures of household expenditure. In fact, the overall wage-earnings Gini is higher than that of expenditure, on average by 18 per cent. The lower level of expenditure Gini is partly due to the smoothing effect of consumption, where saving and dis-saving play a role. The wage-earning Gini peaked earlier in 2009 and 2015 at staggering levels of 0.46 and 0.47 respectively as depicted in Fig. 2.10. Earnings inequality increased in the period 2004–2008, was relatively stable since till 2015 and declined in 2016. The trend was more or less echoed across the nine economic sectors depicted in Fig. 3.10.[7] Among the economic sectors, mining has the highest earnings inequality followed by the manufacturing sector. Earnings inequality in the mining sector increased sharply during the mining boom reaching its peak in 2008 and significantly dropped since then.

The rise in economic inequality (either consumption or earnings/income) has paralleled the decline in wage-productivity ratio during the

[7] In addition to the Gini index, two other measures to show the increasing trend of wage-earning inequality are employed: (1) D9/D1 ratio that measures earning dispersions between the highest and lowest deciles, and (2) median/mean ratio that measures the gap between the median and the mean. Both measures consistently show increasing trend of wage-earning inequality. Detailed results are available from the authors.

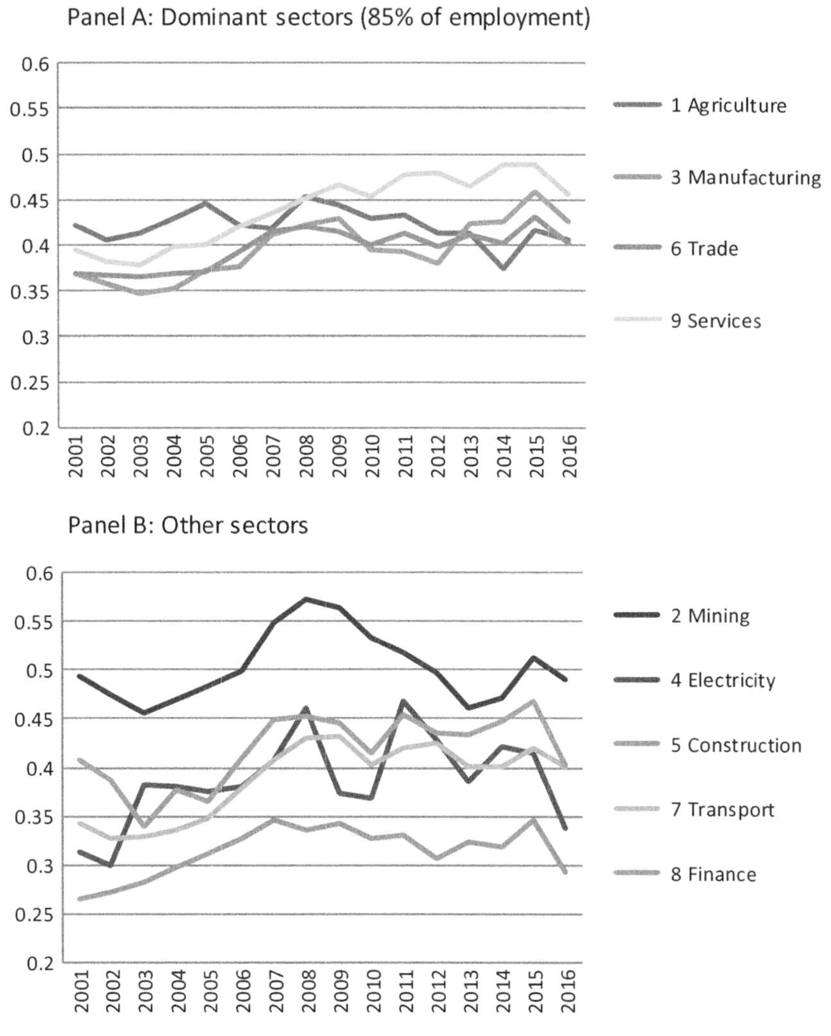

Fig. 3.10 Gini coefficients of wage earnings across economic sectors, 2001–2016. (Source: Calculated the Sakernas)

post-AFC period. The decline, however, is not unique to Indonesia as this has been a global phenomenon since the past three decades (ILO 2015; IMF 2017). The declining wage-productivity ratio (akin to declining labour shares of income), in fact, could be seen as one possible reason, among others, for the rise in economic inequality. On this, at the cross-country level, IMF (2017) finds that lower labour shares of income are strongly associated with higher income inequality (measured by Gini coefficients) both across countries and over time within countries. We find a similar negative association between wage-productivity ratio and the consumption Gini index across Indonesian provinces as depicted in Fig. 3.11.

Furthermore, in emerging markets, such as Indonesia, the IMF study points to the forces of global integration, particularly the expansion of global value chains contributing to the rising overall capital intensity in production, as the main driver of the declining labour shares. Guschanski and Onaran (2017) identify three channels via which global value chains can negatively affect the wage share: first, integration into global value chains increasing capital intensity of production, as offshored tasks are likely to be more capital intensive in emerging economies than domestic tasks in capital-scarce countries; second, offshoring leading to a change in the elasticity of substitution between capital and labour; and third, global value chains altering the bargaining power in favour of capital. By using data from seven emerging economies, including Indonesia, Guschanski and Onaran (2017) cast doubt on the first two channels but find evidence for a negative impact of globalisation on the bargaining power of labour in emerging economies.

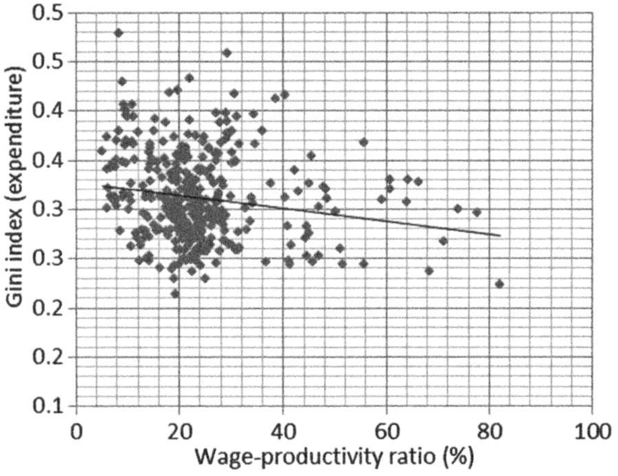

Fig. 3.11 Wage-productivity ratio and Gini index, 33 provinces, 2001–2011. (Source: Calculated from BPS data)

Within the political economy framework, Stiglitz (2012) has identified another source for declining labour's share. According to him, the increase in personal inequality affects the command over resources and power relations. Increasing economic and political power in the hands of a small elite allows them "regulatory capture" to limit redistribution as well as to shape the rules in areas ranging from corporate governance to product and labour market regulation in their interest. Consequently, there would be a negative effect of personal distribution on the wage share.

The above implies that the decline in the wage share is not an inevitable outcome of trade integration or growth but can be altered by institutions for a level playing field. That is, in democratic Indonesia, an increase in workers' bargaining power has the potential to increase the wage share for a given capital-output ratio. Among several variables representing labour bargaining power, minimum wage could be the most important one. Higher minimum wage compliance indicates improved bargaining power of labour; therefore, it should improve the labour share of income and in turn reduce inequality. This is confirmed by our findings on how minimum wage compliance would significantly reduce inequality in Indonesia as explained in Box 3.1.

Box 3.1 Minimum Wage Compliance and Inequality

One of the key progresses on reforms related to the labour market institutions since the democratic transition of the late 1990s is the minimum wage setting across Indonesian provinces. This has always been a contentious issue pointing out pros and cons by the proponents and opponents of labour market flexibility. The opponents hold the view that the minimum wage legislation introduces labour market inflexibility, deters hiring and hence adversely affects the very people, the low-skilled workers, the legislation intends to help.

In this subsection, we examine possible impacts on minimum wage compliance on inequality. Two following scenarios are used to gauge the possible impact of minimum wage compliance on wage-earnings inequality: (1) concentrating only on earnings of regular wage employment (status no. 4 in the Sakernas) and (2) concentrating on earnings of all employment for which earnings data are available, covering self-employed workers (status no. 1), regular wage employment

(*continued*)

Box 3.1 (continued)

(status no. 4) and casual employment (status nos. 5 and 6). The wage-earnings data are from the August series of Sakernas covering the period 2001–2014.

Two Gini indices are calculated for each group. The first one is the primary wage Gini. The second one is a new Gini index, calculated by assuming that the level of minimum wage compliance reaches 100 per cent. For this, the wage-earnings level of workers receiving less than the provincial minimum wages is upgraded to the level of provincial minimum wages. The Indonesian provincial minimum wages data are taken from the ILO database.

Minimum wage compliance in Indonesia has been continuously declining since 2001 as shown in Fig. 3.12. In 2014, more than half of total employment earned less than provincial minimum wages; among regular wage employment representing the formal sector, the rate of non-compliance was 46 per cent. The year 2014 recorded the steepest rise in the rate of non-compliance.

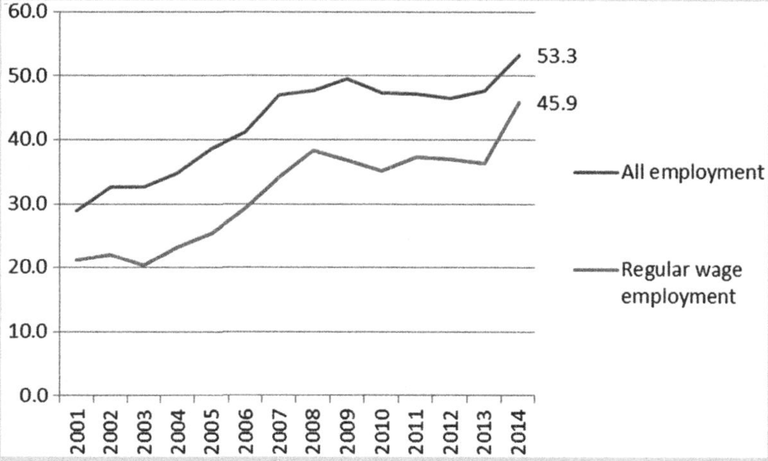

Fig. 3.12 Percentage of workers earning less than provincial minimum wages, 2001–2014. (Source: Calculated from Sakernas and ILO database)

(*continued*)

Box 3.1 (continued)

The primary wage Gini index for all employment and regular wage employment is presented in Fig. 3.13 for 2001–2014. In general, the level of inequality has been on the rise, and the wage inequality of all employment is higher than that of regular wage employment. However, in 2014, the primary wage Gini of regular wage employment reached the record level of 0.46, surpassing that for all employment. On average during 2001–2014, the primary wage Gini for all employment was 5.5 per cent higher than that for regular wage employment. It has to be noted that "all employment" means that all employment for which earnings data are available (own account worker, regular wage employment and casual employment). In 2014, the three categories of employment accounted for 65 per cent of total employment.

Next, we calculate a scenario based on what would have happened to the level of wage inequality if the level of minimum wage compliance reached 100 per cent. In other words, we want to know the effect of 100 per cent minimum wage compliance on the reduction of wage inequality.

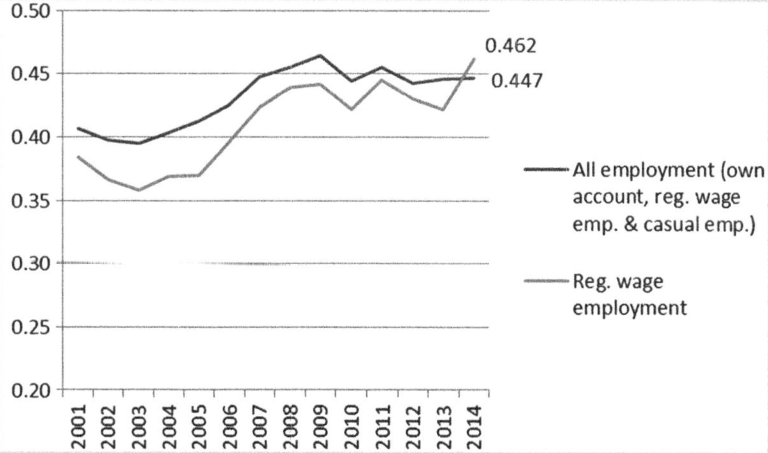

Fig. 3.13 Primary wage Gini, 2001–2014. (Source: Calculated from Sakernas)

(continued)

Box 3.1 (continued)

Figure 3.14 presents the scenario for regular wage employment only. In 2014, the Gini index of wage inequality would have fallen from 0.46 to 0.35 representing a reduction by 25 per cent if all regular waged employees received earnings level no less than their respective provincial minimum wages. Overall, on average during 2001–2014, the full compliance with minimum wage would have reduced wage Gini by 16 per cent. If we look at the trend during 2007 and 2014, the full minimum wage compliance would flatten wage inequality at the Gini index of around 0.35, while the primary wage Gini was on the rise without full minimum wage compliance.

Figure 3.15 depicts the impact of full compliance of provincial minimum wages on the reduction of wage inequality for all employment. The effect of full minimum wage compliance is larger in the case of all employment than in the case of regular wage employment only. This is understandable since the proportion of workers receiving earnings less than the minimum wages is way larger. On average

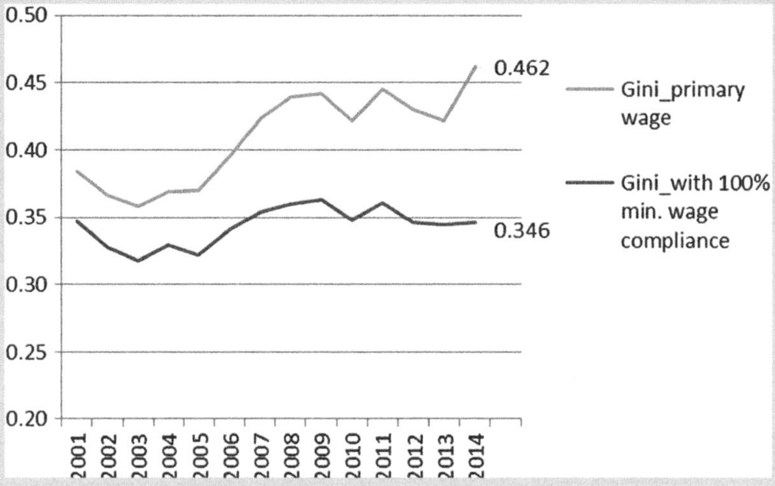

Fig. 3.14 Gini index of wage earnings: *Regular wage employment*, 2001–2014. (Source: Calculated from Sakernas and ILO database)

(continued)

Box 3.1 (continued)

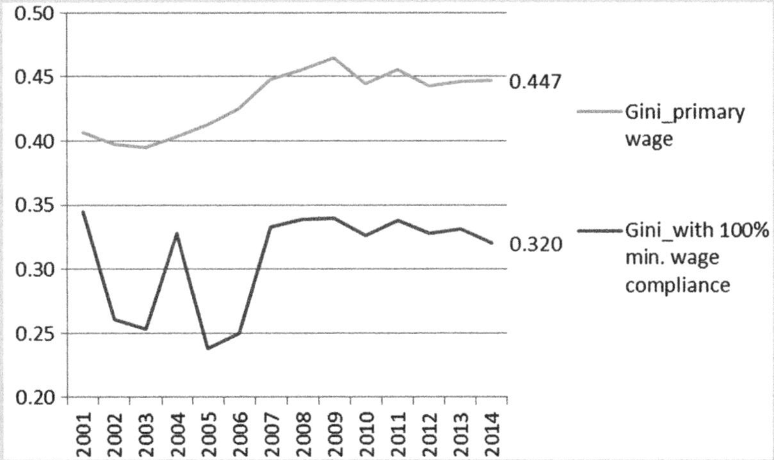

Fig. 3.15 Gini index of wage earnings: *All employment*, 2001–2014. (Source: Calculated from Sakernas and ILO database)

during 2001–2014, the 100 per cent minimum wage compliance would have reduced wage inequality by 28 per cent.

Thus, minimum wage compliance has a great potential to reduce earnings inequality, but this potential has been largely overlooked. Full minimum wage compliance could reduce wage-earnings inequality between 16 per cent and 28 per cent. While the level of minimum wage non-compliance has been on the rise mimicking the rising trend of wage-earnings inequality, reducing the level of non-compliance becomes important especially among regular wage employment.

3.7 Concluding Remarks: Attacking Inequality

This chapter has demonstrated that post-Soeharto and democratic Indonesia displays the global trend of disconnection between earnings and productivity growth: labour productivity continues to rise while real wage-earnings stagnate. This has contributed to stagnant wage share in GDP and rising overall wage-earnings inequality. The findings, thus, raise doubts about the sufficiency of Indonesia's so-called triple-track strategy, which combines the traditional pro-growth focus of development policy with pro-poor and pro-jobs creation orientation in attacking inequality.

We find that full compliance with minimum wage has a great potential in reducing wage-earnings inequality. Minimum wage compliance should also reduce consumption inequality due to a close association among wage, income and consumption. Since the full compliance would improve earnings of those at the lower end of income distribution, it should have a larger effect on economic activities as their marginal propensity to consume is very high—almost close to 1, and they mostly spend on locally produced products.

The net effect should also consider the effect of minimum wage compliance on employment, especially in the formal sector. One may argue that minimum wage reduces employment opportunity and hence contributes to poverty and inequality—it harms the very people (poor) that it intends to help. However, it has to be noted that the compliance rate is currently less than 50 per cent—it is just like having no minimum wage in practice; yet employment did not rise, and inequality did not fall. Instead, inequality rose. Furthermore, studies did not find any convincing overall empirical evidence of a negative relationship between the level of minimum wage and the level of employment.[8] Therefore, ensuring minimum wage compliance is an option that should be utilised to reduce economic inequality. However, targeting minimum wage compliance among regular wage employment is a more straightforward strategy than increasing the level of compliance for all employment.

References

Akerlof, G.A. 1982. "Labour contracts as partial gift exchange." *Quarterly Journal of Economics* 97(4): 543–69.

Chang, H.J. 2010. *23 things they don't tell you about capitalism*. New York: Bloomsbury.

Comola, M. and L. de Mello 2013. "Salaried employment and earnings in Indonesia: New evidence on the selection bias." *Applied Economics* 45(19): 2808–16.

Dhanani, S., I. Islam and A. Chowdhury 2009. *The Indonesia labour market: Challenge and changes*. London: Routledge.

[8] See, for example, Islam and Nazara (2000).

Fabricant, S. 1959. "Basic facts on productivity change." *Occasional Paper 63.* New York: NBER.

Goh, S.K. 2009. "Is productivity linked to wages? An empirical investigation in Malaysia." *MPRA Paper* No. 18095. (https://mpra.ub.uni-muenchen.de/18095/)

Guschanski, A. and Ö. Onaran 2017. "Why is the wage share falling in emerging economies? Industry level evidence." *Greenwich Papers in Political Economy* No. 52. University of Greenwich.

ILO 2013. *Global wage report 2012/13: Wages and equitable growth.* Geneva: International Labour Organization.

ILO 2015. *Global wage report 2014/15: Wages and income inequality.* Geneva: International Labour Organization.

IMF 2017. *World economic outlook 2017.* Washington, DC: International Monetary Fund.

Islam, I. and S. Nazara 2000. *Estimating employment elasticity for the Indonesian economy.* Jakarta: International Labor Organization.

King, John 2015. *Advanced introduction to post Keynesian economics.* Cheltenham, UK: Edward Elgar.

Schmid, G. 1995. "A new approach to labour market policy: A contribution to the current debate on efficient employment policies." *Economic and Industrial Democracy* 16(3): 425–56.

Shapiro, C. and J.E. Stiglitz 1984. "Equilibrium unemployment as a worker discipline device." *American Economic Review* 74(3): 433–44.

Sharpe, A., J.F. Arsenault and P. Harrison 2008. "The relationship between labour productivity and real wage growth in Canada and OECD countries." *CSLS Research Report* No. 2008-8. Ottawa: Centre for the Study of Living Standards (CSLS).

Stiglitz, J.E. 2012. *The price of inequality.* New York: W.W. Norton.

Tadjoeddin, M.Z. 2015. "Spatial dimensions of key employment outcomes in Indonesia." *Comparative Asian Development* 14(3): 466–509.

World Bank 2015. *Indonesia's rising divide: Why inequality is rising, why it matters and what can be done.* Washington, DC: World Bank.

CHAPTER 4

Wages, Employment, Productivity in the Manufacturing Sector

4.1 Introduction

In light of the findings in the previous chapter that real wage-earnings growth fell behind productivity growth across the economy, this chapter examines the dynamics of wage inequality and productivity in the manufacturing sector, arguably the most dynamic sector in the economy. The manufacturing sector maintains its role as the largest contributor to the overall gross domestic product (GDP) and is the main engine of growth. However, in addition to experiencing a disjoint between productivity and earnings growth in the manufacturing sector, the Indonesian economy seems to have experienced negative de-industrialisation since the Asian financial crisis (AFC) in the sense that its share in GDP has fallen prematurely. This has been a result of slower growth of manufacturing value added (MVA) compared to GDP. Furthermore, growth has been "jobless" as employment growth lagged behind albeit slower growth of both MVA and GDP. Despite these trends, the manufacturing sector is still viewed as the mainstay for creating quality employment, and many have advocated for its revitalisation.

Arguably, the dynamics of de-industrialisation and delinking trends as well as employment elasticity are unlikely to be homogeneous within the manufacturing sector. For example, there could be significant differences

M. Z. Tadjoeddin, A. Chowdhury, *Employment and Re-Industrialisation in Post Soeharto Indonesia*, Critical Studies of the Asia-Pacific, https://doi.org/10.1057/978-1-137-50566-8_4

between large-medium (LM) and micro-small (MS)[1] manufacturing firms' wage-productivity gaps, and all types of manufacturing firms may not exhibit the signs of de-industrialisation. The employment-creating potential may also vary between LM and MS firms. This chapter, thus, examines wage-productivity trends within the manufacturing sector by firm size.

4.2 Employment, Productivity and Real Wage

Tables 4.1 and 4.2 present a snapshot of sectoral productivity and real wage growth, and output and employment shares during the post-AFC period. As can be seen in Table 4.1, the manufacturing sector's productivity growth was only 3.7 per cent, below that of agriculture and trade (4.6 per cent and 4.5 per cent respectively), and less than the overall productivity growth of the economy (4.6 per cent), indicating that the sector is losing steam. The bulk of the 9.8 percentage point decline of agriculture's employment share was absorbed by the service sector (4.0 percentage points) and the construction sector (2.1 percentage points), with productivity growth of only 1.7 per cent and 2.1 per cent respectively, much lower than the overall productivity growth of the economy. The manufacturing sector did not

Table 4.1 Sectoral GDP, employment and productivity, 2001 and 2016

	2001		*2016*		*Productivity growth*	*Change in employment share (% point)*
	% Employment	*% GDP*	*% Employment*	*% GDP*	*(% annual average)*	
Agriculture	43.8	15.5	31.9	11.7	3.9	−11.9
Mining	1	11.7	1.2	6.0	−0.6	0.2
Manufacturing	13.3	27.7	13.1	25.2	3.2	−0.2
Electricity	0.2	0.6	0.3	0.7	1.7	0.1
Construction	4.2	5.6	6.7	6.8	2.0	2.5
Trade	19.2	16.2	22.5	17.5	3.2	3.3
Transportation	4.9	4.9	4.7	11.7	10.3	−0.2
Finance	1.2	8.6	3.0	10.3	−0.1	1.8
Services	12.1	9.3	16.4	9.5	1.8	4.3
Total	100	100	100	100	3.6	0.0

Source: Calculated from BPS data

[1] Micro firms and cottage firms are used interchangeably.

Table 4.2 Regular waged employment: sectoral share and wage index, 2001–2016

	Total employment share (%)		*Regular waged employment share (%)*		*Wage index of regular waged emp. (Indonesia = 100)*	
	2001	*2016*	*2001*	*2016*	*2001*	*2016*
Agriculture	43.8	31.9	10.6	7.0	60	65
Mining	1.0	1.2	1.5	1.6	146	164
Manufacturing	*13.3*	*13.1*	*28.6*	21.0	*88*	*92*
Electricity	0.2	0.3	0 .4	0.7	147	132
Construction	4.2	6.7	7.3	6.3	87	94
Trade	19.2	22.5	11.4	16.2	83	83
Transportation	4.9	4.7	5.6	5.1	115	125
Finance	1.2	3.0	3.8	6.4	183	144
Services	12.1	16.4	30.8	35.7	123	105
Total	100	100.0	100	100	100	100
Inter-sector wage inequality (CV)					0.39	0.32

Source: Calculated from the Sakernas

contribute in absorbing the drop in agriculture's employment share. That is, the surplus labour from agriculture was primarily absorbed by those sectors which were not the most dynamic and well performing. More strikingly, the transport-communication sector that has experienced significantly higher (22.6 per cent) productivity growth has reduced its employment absorption by 0.4 percentage point, although this sector has been the main beneficiaries of the robust economic growth during the past decade.

Furthermore, the following three observations reveal the manufacturing sector's weak employment performance during the post-crisis period. *First,* manufacturing sector's contribution to regular waged employment has significantly declined far more than the decline in the sector's contribution to the overall employment (Table 4.2). Note that regular waged employment accounts for more than 90 per cent of formal employment.

Second, consistent with the above trend, there has been an increase in the level of casualisation of employment in the manufacturing sector as highlighted in chapter. Between 2001 and 2016, the share of casual employment in the total manufacturing employment (regular *plus* non-regular) increased from 3.1 per cent to 4.3 per cent, while casualisation in the overall economy increased from 6.7 per cent to 10.5 per cent.[2] The category of casual employment was introduced for the first time in the 2001 National Labour Force Survey (Sakernas), so the situation cannot be compared with the pre-crisis period.

Third, real wage of regular employees in the manufacturing sector was relatively depressed vis-à-vis other sectors. The last two columns in Table 4.2 present wage index across sectors by assigning the value of 100 for the average wage. The wage index of the manufacturing remained less than 100, and the manufacturing wage remained the third lowest among the nine economic sectors.

More disturbingly, slow catch up of the manufacturing wages was observed when wages were converging across sectors as indicated by the declining trend of the coefficient of variation of sectoral wages. This finding casts doubts on the argument of those who believe that the labour market has become more rigid causing poor employment outcomes of the manufacturing sector. For example, Yusuf et al. (2013:4) define labour market rigidity as "constant or increasing real wage", implying that flexible labour market is represented by declining real wages. They claim that increased capital utilisation as a result of labour market "rigidity" caused jobless growth in the manufacturing sector and argue for a "flexible" labour market.

4.3 Wages and Productivity Trends in Manufacturing

As highlighted in chapter, real wage earnings of the manufacturing sector are at par with the overall earnings of the economy in terms of level and trend (Fig. 3.3). However, the magnitude was lower than most other sectors, except for agriculture and construction. Moreover, the gap between earnings and productivity in the manufacturing sector is quite striking. In 2015, real wage earnings in manufacturing were still at 13 per cent of its labour productivity, slightly lower than 14.4 per cent in 2001. However, the ratio improved to 15.3 in 2016. The sector's wage-productivity ratio was among the lowest and showed a declining trend between 2002 and 2008 (Fig. 3.7), indicating the delinking trend between wages and productivity in the manufacturing sector.

[2] Matsumoto and Verick (2011) also argued for the increased casualisation of employment in the Indonesian economy, but they did not provide disaggregated analysis into the sectoral level.

This section looks at the gap between real wages and productivity at three levels: across manufacturing sub-sectors, by firm size—LM and that of MS establishments within manufacturing industry—and by factor intensity.

4.3.1 *Wage-Productivity Gaps Across Manufacturing Sub-sectors*

The trends of real earning across manufacturing sub-sectors at the ISIC 2 digit level are similar to the general trend of real earnings in the overall manufacturing sector. Average real wage earnings of food and textile sub-sectors are among the lowest, less than the overall real wages of the manufacturing sector (Fig. 4.1). The trend of delinking until 2008 between wages and productivity was also apparent across manufacturing sub-sectors, as the wage-productivity ratios declined in most of sub-sectors (Fig. 4.2).

4.3.2 *Wage-Productivity Gaps in Large-Medium and Micro-Small Establishments*

Following the Statistics Indonesia definitions, large firms have 100 workers or more, medium firms have 20–99 workers, small firms have 5–19 workers and micro firms have less than 5 workers (including firms with

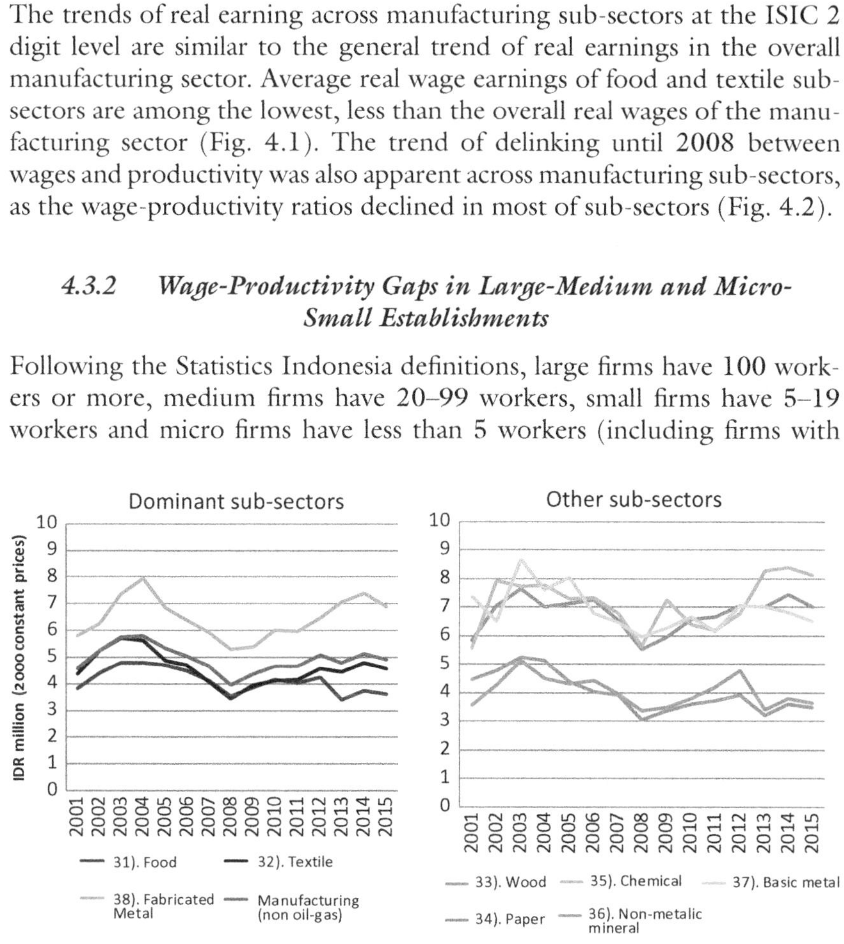

Fig. 4.1 Real wage earnings, manufacturing ISIC 2, 2001–2015 (IDR million/year, 2000 constant prices). (Source: Calculated from the Sakernas)

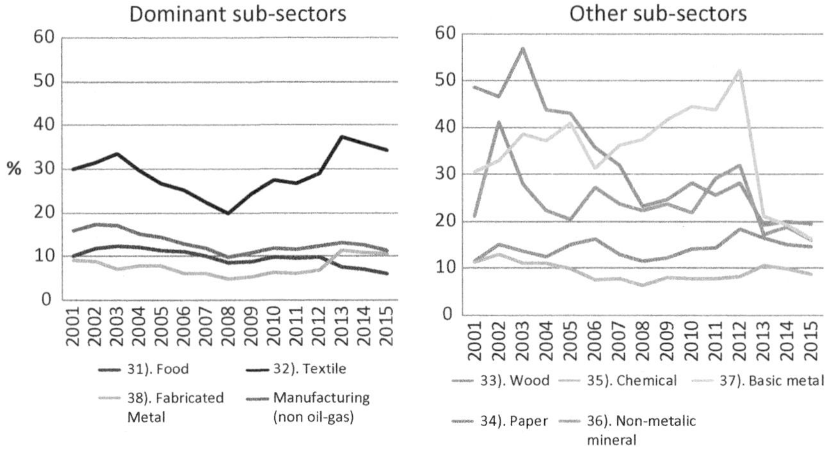

Fig. 4.2 Wage-productivity ratio (%), manufacturing ISIC 2, 2001–2015. (Source: Calculated from BPS data)

unpaid workers). Several steps are needed to construct the required data from the existing sources, such as the *National Income Account* and the *National Labour Force Survey* (Sakernas), which contain data on sectoral GDP or value added, employment and wages for the overall manufacturing sector disaggregated into nine manufacturing sub-sectors (ISIC 2). Similar data are also available for LM firms from the *Large and Medium Manufacturing Statistics.* Combining the two datasets (overall manufacturing and LM manufacturing), data for MS manufacturing can be calculated. The data construction steps are explained briefly as follows.

First, wages and employment data for total manufacturing and nine manufacturing sub-sectors from the national statistics are used to generate labour cost, as the product of wages and employment, at the national level. *Second*, by multiplying labour cost per worker data from the large and medium manufacturing statistics with the number of workers, we get the total labour cost for medium and large manufacturing firms. *Third*, after deducting the total labour cost of large and medium firms from the labour cost of the overall manufacturing sector, we obtain the labour cost for micro and small firms. *Finally*, after dividing the labour cost by the number of workers in micro and small manufacturing, we can get the wages for micro and small firms. The number of workers in the MS firms is obtained by deducting LM manufacturing employment from national manufacturing employment.

Thus, we generate employment, wages, total value added and productivity data for the manufacturing sector disaggregated into LM and MS firms. With regard to the nine manufacturing sub-sectors, we focus only on the three with the highest employment shares, namely sub-sector 31 (food), 32 (textile) and 38 (fabricated metal). As mentioned earlier, these sub-sectors represent resource-based and labour-intensive industry (food), footloose labour-intensive industry (textile) and capital-intensive industry (fabricated metal).

As expected, the difference between wages-productivity gaps in LM and MS firms is quite striking. During 2001–2014, the trend of diverging productivity in LM and MS firms was much clearer than that of real wages (Fig. 4.3). Both LM and MS firms showed declining trends of wage-productivity ratio, indicating the delinking of wages and productivity. Although productivity of LM firms increased at a much faster rate than productivity of MS firms, in the past decade, the value-added share of LM firms in overall manufacturing industry stagnated at 54 per cent and their employment share, in fact, declined from 36 per cent to 32 per cent (Fig. 4.4). This observation is consistent with the overall finding on the process of de-industrialisation in the Indonesian economy.

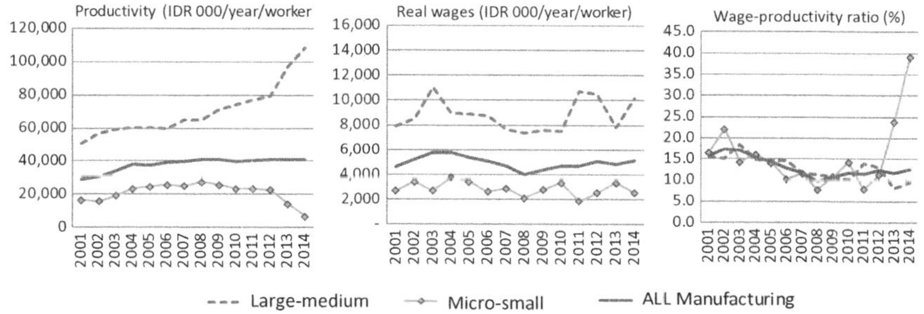

Fig. 4.3 Manufacturing: ALL, large-medium (LM) and micro-small (MS), 2001–2014. (Source: Calculated from BPS data)

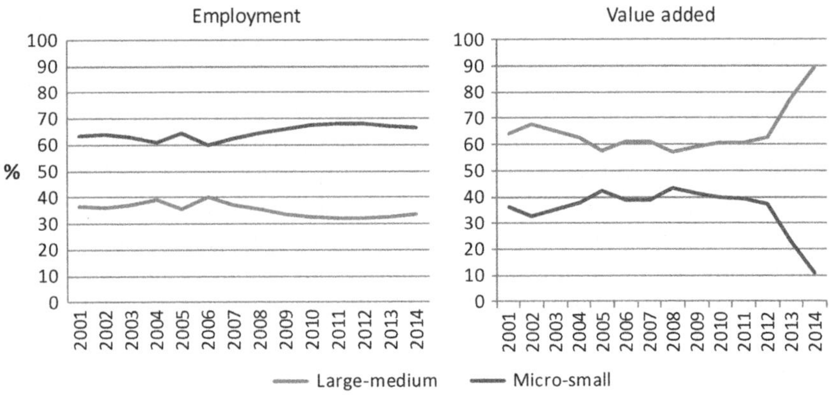

Fig. 4.4 Employment and value-added shares of LM and MS firms, 2001–2014. (Source: Calculated from BPS data)

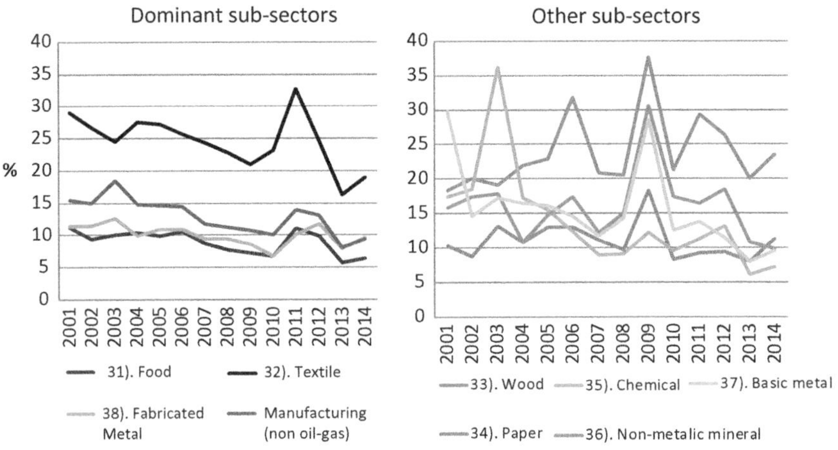

Fig. 4.5 Wage-productivity ratio (%) across sub-sectors of LM industry, 2001–2014. (Source: Calculated from BPS data)

It is interesting to find that the trend of declining wage-productivity ratio was also experienced by the more modern and organised LM firms. However, the picture is not homogeneous across sub-sectors of the LM industry as depicted in Fig. 4.5. For example, the dominant sub-sectors (textiles, food and fabricated metal) experienced a secular decline in the wage-productivity ratio, although it improved between 2009 and 2011.[3] On the other hand, the non-dominant sub-sectors experienced more fluctuations.

4.3.3 Wage-Productivity Gaps Within Manufacturing by Factor Intensity

There are two sources of firm-level data for the manufacturing sector: the long-standing Large and Medium Manufacturing Survey (*Survei Industri Besar dan Sedang*) and the Micro and Small Manufacturing Survey (*Survei Industri Mikro dan Kecil*) since 2008. BPS (*Badan Pusat Statistik* or Statistics Indonesia) publishes aggregate data on employment, value added and labour cost disaggregated at the ISIC 2 level. Furthermore, the ISIC 2 manufacturing sub-sector could be aggregated into three categories of factor intensity: labour intensive, resource intensive and capital intensive. Table 4.3 details the grouping of ISIC 2 sub-sectors into three categories of resource intensity, following the approach of Aswicahyono et al. (2010).

Wage-Productivity Gaps in Large and Medium (LM) Firms by Factor Intensity

Wages and productivity in LM firms are disaggregated by factor intensity as showed in Fig. 4.6a. As expected, levels of wage and productivity are the highest among capital-intensive firms, followed by resource-intensive and labour-intensive categories. Productivity gaps are larger than wage gaps across factor intensity. However, during 2008–2013, a generally increasing trend of wages and productivity is observable across three categories of factor intensity; capital-intensive firms recorded the steepest increase.

During the period, a general trend of increasing wage-productivity ratio is observable across factor intensity categories (Fig. 4.6b), meaning that labour share of income in LM firms was on the rise. This trend is consistent with the increasing wage-productivity ratio in the overall manufacturing sector during the same period (2008–2013) depicted earlier in Fig. 3.7. As expected, the labour share of income in labour-intensive firms is far higher (more than twice) than labour share of income in resource- and capital-intensive LM firms.

[3] The three dominant manufacturing sub-sectors account for around two-thirds of manufacturing employment.

Table 4.3 The grouping of ISIC 2 manufacturing sub-sector based on factor intensity

ISIC2	***Labour Intensive***
13	Manufacture of textiles
14	Manufacture of wearing apparel
15	Manufacture of leather and related products
16	Manufacture of wood and of products of wood and cork, except furniture
31	Manufacture of furniture
32	Other manufacturing
33	Maintenance and repair of machinery and equipment
	Resource Intensive
10	Manufacture of food products
11	Manufacture of beverages
12	Manufacture of tobacco products
17	Manufacture of paper and paper products
18	Printing and reproduction of recorded media
19	Manufacture of coke and refined petroleum products
20	Manufacture of chemicals and chemical products
21	Manufacture of basic pharmaceutical products and pharmaceutical medicine
22	Manufacture of rubber and plastics products
	Capital Intensive
23	Manufacture of other non-metallic mineral products
24	Manufacture of basic metals
25	Manufacture of fabricated metal products, except machine
26	Manufacture of computer, electronic and optical products
27	Manufacture of electrical equipment
28	Manufacture of machinery and equipment n.e.c.
29	Manufacture of motor vehicles, trailers and semi-trailers
30	Manufacture of other transport equipment

Source: Aswicahyono et al. (2010)

Wage-Productivity Gaps in Micro and Small (MS) Firms by Factor Intensity

Tables 4.4a and 4.4b present wage and productivity data for micro and small firms disaggregated by the three factor intensity categories (labour, resource and capital). The wage and productivity data are presented in IDR million per year in 2000 constant prices, where the nominal value is adjusted with GDP deflator of non-oil-gas manufacturing sector.

One characteristic of MS firms is their informality, where significant portions of their employment are unpaid workers. The share of paid employment is the lowest among micro firms at around one-fifth to a half. Therefore we consider only the number of paid employment in calculating

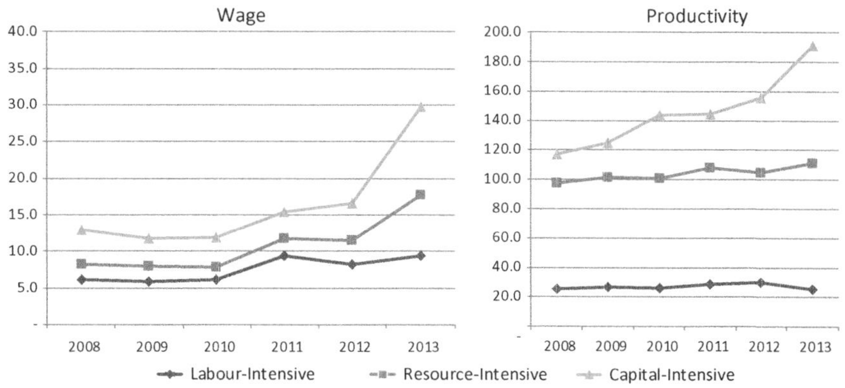

Fig. 4.6a Wage and productivity in large-medium firms manufacturing (IDR million/year, 2000 constant prices). (Source: Calculated from BPS data [micro-data of Large and Medium Manufacturing Survey])

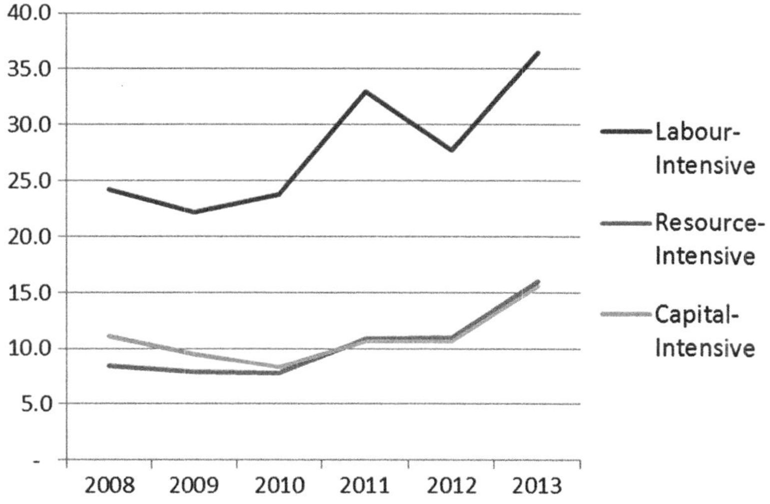

Fig. 4.6b Wage-productivity ratio in large-medium firms (per cent). (Source: Calculated from BPS data [microdata of Large and Medium Manufacturing Survey])

Table 4.4a Wage and productivity: Micro firms (IDR million/year, 2000 constant prices)

	Micro firms				
	2010	*2011*	*2012*	*2013*	*2014*
Wage					
Labour intensive	3.6	0.7	7.0	7.1	4.8
Resource intensive	1.9	0.4	5.1	4.9	2.9
Capital intensive	3.7	0.8	7.6	6.8	4.7
Productivity					
Labour intensive	4.2	1.0	3.5	4.0	5.9
Resource intensive	6.1	0.8	3.5	3.9	4.9
Capital intensive	5.8	1.5	5.6	5.6	8.3
Wage-productivity ratio (%)					
Labour intensive	85.3	74.1	199.4	176.3	80.2
Resource intensive	30.9	52.8	145.1	123.9	58.9
Capital intensive	63.1	48.9	135.2	119.7	56.8

Source: Calculated from BPS data

Table 4.4b Wage and productivity: Small firms (IDR million/year, 2000 constant prices)

	Small firms				
	2010	*2011*	*2012*	*2013*	*2014*
Wage					
Labour intensive	3.9	0.9	5.0	7.4	6.6
Resource intensive	2.0	0.8	5.0	6.1	4.9
Capital intensive	3.7	0.8	6.8	6.8	5.3
Productivity					
Labour intensive	13.4	2.2	6.9	10.0	15.5
Resource intensive	9.2	1.8	9.1	10.2	11.6
Capital intensive	12.0	1.8	7.2	11.1	14.6
Wage-productivity ratio (%)					
Labour intensive	29.3	42.1	71.8	73.6	42.3
Resource intensive	21.3	41.4	54.5	59.9	42.1
Capital intensive	31.1	45.1	94.3	61.5	36.1

Source: Calculated from BPS data

Table 4.4c Paid employment at firm level (per cent)

Micro firms	**2010**	**2011**	**2012**	**2013**
Labour Intensive	32.6	32.5	31.4	29.3
Resource Intensive	26.0	22.6	21.5	22.3
Capital Intensive	52.5	57.3	52.6	47.1
Small firms	**2010**	**2011**	**2012**	**2013**
Labour Intensive	80.8	79.9	82.7	82.3
Resource Intensive	78.4	72.3	81.6	74.0
Capital Intensive	84.9	85.0	81.8	85.2
Medium firm		**2011**	**2012**	
Labor Intensive		99.3	98.2	
Resource Intensive		99.5	98.0	
Capital Intensive		99.6	98.9	
Large firm		**2011**	**2012**	
Labor Intensive		100.0	99.9	
Resource Intensive		100.0	99.9	
Capital Intensive		100.0	100.0	

Source: Calculated from microdata of *Large and Medium Manufacturing Survey* and *Micro and Small Manufacturing Survey*

average wage. However, total employment (paid and unpaid) is used to calculate labour productivity. Detailed data on the percentage of paid workers across firm sizes and factor intensity are presented in Table 4.4c.

The following two anomalies are noticeable from the wage and productivity data for MS firms presented in Tables 4.4a and 4.4b. *First*, wage and productivity levels of MS firms in 2011 were far lower than in other years (2010, 2012 and 2014). *Second*, wage-productivity ratios of MS firms in 2012 and 2013 were much higher than in other years (2010, 2011 and 2014). In the case of micro firms, wage-productivity ratios were more than 1, while it should be less than 1 to account for the share of profit. Such anomalies could only be explained by survey irregularities in the relevant years. Because of these anomalies in the surveys, the yearly trends of wage and productivity data in the case of MS firms seem to be meaningless.

Nevertheless, a quick comparison between 2010 and 2014 data reveals a broad picture of wage and productivity in MS firms during the period. There is a general trend of increasing levels of wages and productivity in MS firms across the three categories of factor intensity. A general trend of increasing wage-productivity ratio is noticeable in small firms across factor intensity, which is consistent with the overall trend in the manufacturing sector and among LM firms. A different trend is noticeable in the case of micro firms, where the wage-productivity ratio seems to show a declining trend. As noted earlier, most of the micro firms operate in the informal sector, and the majority of their workers are unpaid. Jobs in micro firms are largely categorised as self-employed involving family members.

The comparison of wage and productivity data across firm size and factor intensity in a single year of 2010 also reveals a few general patterns (Fig. 4.7a and Fig. 4.7b). *First*, levels of wage and productivity increased with the firm size. However, wage increases were far lower than productivity increases. This meant a declining share of labour income when firm sizes got larger, which is likely due to increased capital intensities. *Second*, the decline in the labour share of income when the firm sizes got larger

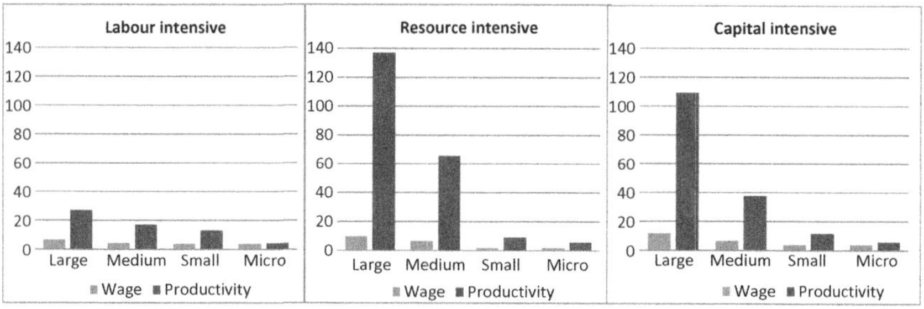

Fig. 4.7a Wage and productivity, manufacturing, 2010 (IDR million/year, 2000 constant prices). (Source: Calculated from BPS data)

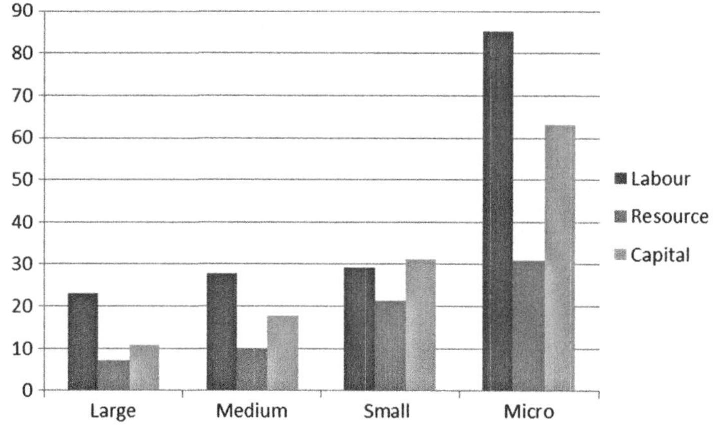

Fig. 4.7b Wage-productivity ratio (per cent), 2010: firm sizes and factor intensity. (Source: Calculated from BPS data)

was the steepest in capital-intensive industries. *Third*, there were relatively small wage differentials across firm size in labour-intensive industries, while the differences were much larger in resource- and capital-intensive firms. *Fourth*, wages were the lowest among micro and small firms in the resource-intensive category.

There is one key implication of the observation that levels of wage and productivity increased with the firm size—smaller firms need to graduate into larger firms. In this case, transition from micro-small firms into medium-large firms is crucial, as can be gleaned from Table 4.5. The phenomenon of "missing middle", discussed previously, is evident with regard to employment shares. Medium-sized firms contribute only approximately 6 per cent to total employment in the manufacturing sector, one-third is contributed by large firms and the largest part is contributed by MS firms.

A key policy challenge is, therefore, to encourage MS firms to upgrade themselves into medium firms to tackle the problem of the "missing middle".[4] A review of challenges faced by MS firms would be useful. A short discussion of the challenges based on the *micro and small enterprise survey* data is provided in the box.

Table 4.5 Shares of employment and value added (%), 2010

Employment	*Factor intensity*			
Firm size	Labour	Resource	Capital	All
Large	34.3	33.1	44.2	35.3
Medium	5.0	6.2	6.6	5.8
Small	14.8	15.5	13.5	14.9
Micro	45.9	45.1	35.7	44.0
All	*100*	*100*	*100*	*100*
Value Added				
Firm size	Labour	Resource	Capital	All
Large	63.8	77.7	89.7	79.0
Medium	6.4	11.9	4.4	8.6
Small	15.1	3.5	2.6	5.3
Micro	14.7	6.8	3.3	7.1
All	*100*	*100*	*100*	*100*

Source: Calculated from BPS data

[4] The "missing middle" situation could possibly be linked to the wide spread use of "home-workers" in Indonesia. The term "homeworker" is used to refer to industrial outworkers who carry out paid work from their home, for firms/business or their intermediaries, typically on a piece-rate basis. These hide the true number of workers employed by firms.

Box 4.1 Problems Faced by Micro and Small Firms

Problems experienced by micro and small manufacturing firms are summarised in Fig. 4.8. Out of the list of problems perceived by micro and small firms, three main problems stand out: access to finance, raw materials and market. Financing is consistently the highest reported problem during the survey period from 2009 to 2013. The highest percentage was in 2010 when 34.6 per cent of micro and small firms reported that they have difficulties in financing their activities. This figure remained around the 30 per cent band until the 2013 survey. Access to raw materials is the second highest perceived problem with the trend increasing from 14.1 per cent in 2009 and peaking in 2011 when 20.2 per cent of micro and small firms reported this problem. The figure slightly decreased to 17.1 per cent in 2013. Marketing their products is the third highest problem reported by an average of 17 per cent of the sample over the period.

Other problems, including energy, transportations, workers' skills and labour costs, appear to be less important throughout the period covered. It is necessary to note that labour cost is one of the lowest reported problems, contrary to the claims by many that the legislations on minimum wage and severance pay are obstacles, particularly for small and micro firms.

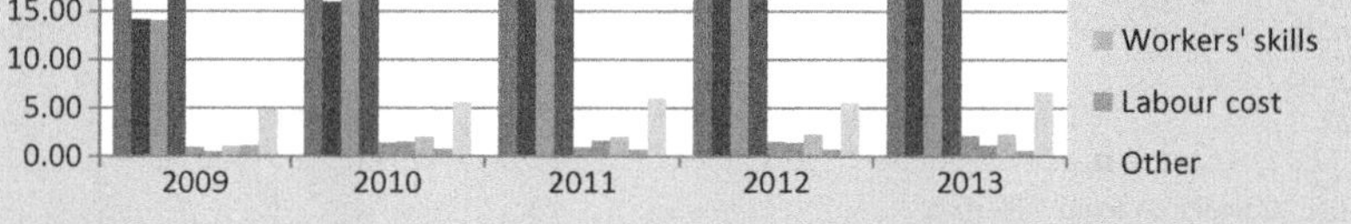

Fig. 4.8 Problems faced by micro and small manufacturing firms (per cent), 2009–2013. (Source: Calculated from BPS data [Micro and Small Manufacturing Survey])

(*continued*)

Box 4.1 (continued)

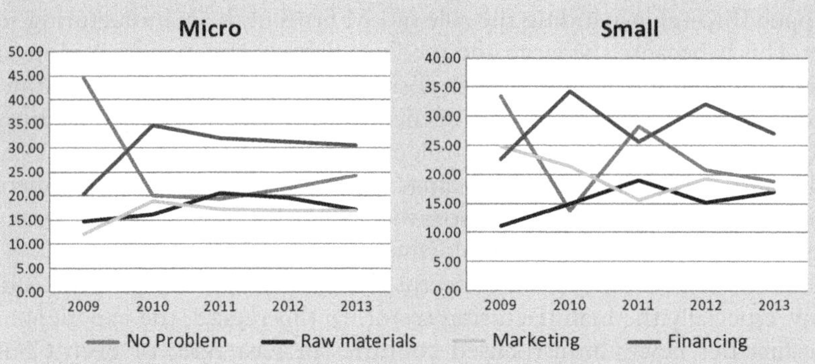

Fig. 4.9 Three main problems of micro and small manufacturing firms (per cent), 2009–2013. (Source: Calculated from BPS data [Micro and Small Manufacturing Survey])

Disaggregating the data into micro and small firms and focusing on the three most common problems show the different characteristics between the two. As shown in Fig. 4.9, it appears that problems experienced by small firms tend to fluctuate more than the micro firms. This may reflect a more uncertain business environment faced by the small firms relative to the micro firms.

4.4 Concluding Remarks: Implications for Re-industrialisation

It is clear that the Indonesian manufacturing industries have failed to move to a higher level and diversify into more sophisticated activities beyond the traditional resource-based and labour-intensive industries. The recent policy attention for re-industrialisation by emphasising value addition, especially in the resource sector and establishing economic corridors, including special economic zones, as articulated in the Master Plan of National Industry Development (*Rencana Induk Pembangunan Industri Nasional—RIPIN 2015–2035*) seems a step in the right direction.[5]

[5] Singapore and South Korea are excellent examples of successful industrial restructuring and catching up industrial developments of Japan, North America and Western Europe.

A preliminary implication of the observed wage and productivity trends is that revitalisation of Indonesian industries or re-industrialisation has to happen through expanding the role of LM firms in the manufacturing sector. This is because the large and medium firms in the manufacturing sector are expected to be in a better position to make significant investment and technological advancement needed for revitalising the manufacturing sector. Therefore, a key policy challenge is how to push numerous establishments categorised as micro-small firms into medium firms. Such a transition would significantly boost the levels of productivity and wage as well as create better quality employment.

A second key implication concerns the overall upgrading of the economy, especially the manufacturing sector. In this regard, the experience of the first-tier newly industrialised countries in East Asia, or even China, underscores the importance of government's role in industrial development and subsequent restructuring. As argued by Chang (2010, 2011), governments in these countries used "selective" policy interventions in the form of a policy package to create and support, not to pick "winners". Therefore, re-industrialisation would require sophisticated industry policy which can avoid the pitfalls of "picking the winners" strategy and do not encourage "rent-seeking" activities. As elaborated by Chowdhury (2008), Singapore used wages policy to restructure their industries in the 1980s. Wages policy is neutral and can avoid the pitfalls of picking winners. Indonesia is a diverse country, and its different regions may need different kinds of policies in accordance with their resource endowments and level of industrial development. In this regard, regional minimum wages can be an effective policy tool.

References

Aswicahyono, H., H. Hill and D. Narjoko. 2010. "Industrialisation after a deep economic crisis: Indonesia." *Journal of Development Studies* 46(6): 1084–1108.

Chang, H.J. 2010. *23 things they don't tell you about capitalism*. New York: Bloomsbury.

Chang, H.J. 2011. "Industrial policy: Can we go beyond an unproductive confrontation?" In J. Lin and B. Pleskovic (eds.). Annual World Bank Conference on development economics 2010, global: Lessons from East Asia and the global financial crisis. Washington, DC: World Bank.

Chowdhury, A. 2008. "Labour market policies as instruments of industry policy: What can Europe learn from Southeast Asia?" *American Journal of Economics and Sociology* 67(4): 661–81.

Matsumoto, M. and S. Verick. 2011. "Employment trends in Indonesia over 1996–2009: Casualization of the labour market during an era of crises, reforms and recovery." *Employment Working Paper* No. 99. Geneva: International Labour Organization.

Yusuf, A.A., A. Komarulzaman, M. Purnagunawan and B. Resosudarmo. 2013. "Growth, poverty, and labour market rigidity in Indonesia: A general equilibrium investigation." *Working Paper in Economics and Development Studies* (WoPEDS) 201304. Bandung: Padjadjaran University.

CHAPTER 5

Determinants of Employment, Wage and Productivity

5.1 Introduction

Having discussed the trends in employment, wages and productivity at various levels (e.g., national, provincial, sectoral and enterprise) in previous two chapters, this chapter investigates their determinants by using relevant econometric techniques. This exercise is important to identify policy instruments in order to influence their trends at various levels to achieve the desired objective of guiding the economy towards a high-wage and high-productivity trajectory and to address socio-economic deprivation such as working poverty and earnings inequality. The chapter begins with an examination of wage and productivity functions, followed by employment functions.

5.2 Wage and Productivity Functions

As discussed in Chap. 3, real wage and productivity are linked according to both neoclassical and non-neoclassical theories. They influence each other, especially in a dynamic context. Higher productivity translates into higher wages, while higher wages induce higher productivity.

From a micro-level perspective at the firm level, the determinants of wage and productivity are also linked to the characteristics of firms and individual workers. Individual workers' characteristics may include workers' experience (or age as a proxy), workers' level of education and training

M. Z. Tadjoeddin, A. Chowdhury, *Employment and Re-Industrialisation in Post Soeharto Indonesia*, Critical Studies of the Asia-Pacific, https://doi.org/10.1057/978-1-137-50566-8_5

(indicating skills) and gender.[1] Firms' characteristics may comprise size, capital intensity, technology penetration, export orientation and foreign investment.[2]

We estimate productivity and wage functions separately at the firm level in the manufacturing sector. We model productivity as a function of wage and, then, wage as a function of productivity along with firm characteristics. Due to lack of data, we could not include workers' characteristics. The analysis is divided into large-medium (LM) firms and micro-small (MS) firms because they use different survey data and different set of firm characteristics.

5.2.1 Large-Medium Firms

For LM firms, we postulate that wages and productivity are causally and positively related, while both are also influenced by individual firm characteristics. Three characteristics of firm are considered: (1) capital intensity (CAP), measured by the end year real value of capital/machinery per worker; (2) export intensity (EXPORT), measured as the percentage of exported output to total value of output and (3) intensity of foreign ownership/investment (FOREIGN), measured as the percentage of foreign ownership in the firm. More specifically, we want to know whether capital intensity positively affects wages and productivity, as for example in Arai (2003); whether workers become productive and enjoy higher wages if they are employed by more export-oriented firms, as for example in Amiti and Konings (2007) and Amiti and Davis (2011); whether firms with larger share of foreign investment are more productive and pay their workers higher wages, as for example in Martins (2011) and Hijzen et al. (2013). The analyses are disaggregated by firm size and factor intensity. The following two separate functions are specified for both wage and productivity.

$$\begin{aligned}\text{Ln RW}_{it} = \alpha_0 + \alpha_1 \text{ Ln RW}_{it-1} + \alpha_2 \text{ Ln PROD}_{it} + \alpha_3 \text{ Ln CAP}_{it} \\ + \alpha_4 \text{ EXPORT}_{it} + \alpha_5 \text{ FOREIGN}_{it} + \upsilon_i + \varepsilon_{it}\end{aligned} \tag{5.1}$$

[1] For relevant empirical exercises, among others, see Lebedinski and Vandenberghe (2014), van Ours and Stoeldraijer (2010), Galindo-Rueda and Haskel (2005) and Hellerstein et al. (1999).

[2] Some relevant empirical exercises are Hijzen et al. (2013), Amiti and Davis (2011), Amiti and Konings (2007) and Arai (2003), just to name a few.

$$\begin{aligned}\text{Ln PROD}_{it} = {}& \beta_0 + \beta_1 \text{ Ln PROD}_{it-1} + \beta_2 \text{ Ln RW}_{it} + \beta_3 \text{ Ln CAP}_{it} \\ & + \beta_4 \text{ EXPORT}_{it} + \beta_5 \text{ FOREIGN}_{it} + \upsilon_i + \varepsilon_{it}\end{aligned} \tag{5.2}$$

RW stands for real wage, PROD represents labour productivity, lag-dependent variable is included to capture path dependence or the dynamic nature of overtime progress of wage and productivity, meaning that current realisations of the dependent variable are influenced by its past values.

The wage and productivity functions are estimated by using dynamic panel data (DPD) regression of difference method, known as GMM, which is more suitable for situations with "small T, large N" panels, meaning few time periods and many individual firms (Roodman 2009). The choice of difference GMM implies that the firm-fixed effects have been controlled for. In addition to this, we also include year-fixed effects in the estimations in order to net out from the estimates the effect of common time shocks on firms' productivity and wages. Furthermore, the GMM technique helps in dealing with the issue of endogeneity between wage and productivity.

Having foreign ownership and export orientation as independent variables might be problematic because the two could be positively related, as found by Ramstetter and Takii (2006) in pre-crisis Indonesia and Fu, Wu and Tang (2010) in China. We have checked for this possibility and confirmed that foreign ownership is not a significant determinant of firm exports during the period of our analysis (2008–2012) across firm size and factor intensity using dynamic panel estimation.[3]

The estimation results of Eq. 5.1 on the determinants of real wages are presented in Table 5.1. Several findings stand out. *First*, productivity appears to be the most important determinant of real wages, with an overall elasticity of 0.24.[4] This means that 1 per cent increase in productivity would be translated into a 0.24 per cent increase in real wage. The elasticity of wages with respect to productivity (in short, wage-productivity elasticity) in medium firms is a little bit higher than that in large firms, 0.25 and 0.22, respectively. The wage-productivity elasticity is the highest among firms in capital-intensive industry. It has to be noted that the strong, positive relationship between wage and productivity at the firm level is a very

[3] Detailed results are available from authors.

[4] This magnitude is roughly similar to the elasticity of wage with respect to productivity in the case of China's state-owned manufacturing firms (Zhang and Liu 2013).

Table 5.1 Determinants of real wage (difference GMM regression)

	Productivity (Elasticity)	*Capital intensity (Elasticity)*	*Export orientation*	*Foreign investment*	*Year-fixed effects*	*Obs.*
All firms	0.236***	0.044**	0.001	0.001	Yes	6818
Firm size						
Medium	0.253***	0.041**	0.001	0.002	Yes	2825
Large	0.222***	0.042	0.001	0.001	Yes	3993
Factor intensity						
Labour	0.254***	0.059**	0.002	0.0004	Yes	3312
Resource	0.188***	0.009	0.001	0.001	Yes	2286
Capital	0.330***	0.062*	−0.0005	0.004	Yes	1220

Notes: ***, ** and * indicate 1 per cent, 5 per cent and 10 per cent levels of significance respectively, regressions with robust standard error

common finding as, among others, in Bagger, Christensen and Mortensen (2014) and Zhang and Liu (2013).

Second, as expected, capital intensity per worker shows a positive and significant effect on wage levels, but the elasticity coefficients are very small. In resource-intensive industries, capital intensity shows no significant effect on wages. This finding is largely consistent with other studies as in Arai (2003).

Third, surprisingly, export orientation and foreign ownership have no significant effect on wage level across firm size and factor intensity. Higher export orientation does not lead to higher pay for the workers; higher foreign ownership also does not lead to higher wages. This echoes ILO's World Employment and Social Outlook (2015), which reports insignificant impact of global supply chain participation on sectoral wages. It has to be noted that, this analysis is based on 2008–2013 data, and the year 2008 was the beginning of the global financial crisis (GFC). It seems that domestic market and domestic sources of investment have become more important for the Indonesian manufacturing sector than foreign investment. This is in contrast to the situation prior to the Asian financial crisis (AFC). For example, in all ASEAN countries, including Indonesia, Ariff and Hill (1985) found that foreign ownership was a significant determinant of inter-industry wage differential and foreign-owned firms paid higher wages than domestic firms. Based on a survey conducted in Indonesia prior to the Asian crisis, Pangestu and Hendytio (1997) reported that exporting firms paid higher wages than firms that produced solely for the domestic market.[5]

The end of the oil boom in the early 1980s forced Indonesia to develop a more sustainable source of non-oil exports, particularly in the labour-intensive manufacturing sector. This led to the reorientation of industrial policy in Indonesia from import substitution to export promotion. It was during the period of the export promotion strategy of the mid-1980s till the mid-1990s (just before the Asian crisis) that Indonesia experienced rapid industrial growth in which export-oriented labour-intensive manufacturing industries played a major role, especially garment and footwear, as well as foreign direct investment (FDI) in those industries. At that time, cheap labour was Indonesia's main comparative advantage. The introduction of more liberal investment policies, the development of industrial estates close to the supply sources of cheap labour and the strict control over labour by Soeharto's authoritarian regime ensured a favourable industrial climate for FDI. Thus, the effects of export orientation and foreign ownerships on the wage level during the pre-AFC export promotion era are likely to be different from during the post-AFC period. In fact, the crisis was a turning point for awareness on the importance of Indonesia's large domestic market and domestic sources of investment financing.

Table 5.2 presents the determinants of productivity as formulated in Eq. (5.2). The elasticity of productivity with respect to wages (in short, productivity-wage elasticity) is much lower than the wage-productivity elasticity. This means that real wage is more responsive to changes in productivity than productivity to the changes in real wage. Capital intensity maintains its positive and significant effect on productivity as in the case of real wage. However, the effect of capital intensity on labour productivity in large firms is nearly twice as that of medium firms. Similar to the previous findings, export orientation and foreign ownership have no significant effect on labour productivity.

The consistency of GMM estimator depends on the validity of the assumption that the error terms do not display serial correlation and on the validity of the instruments. Two specification tests are used to deal with the problems (Arellano and Bond 1991; Arellano and Bover 1995; Blundell and Bond 1998). The first is the Arellano-Bond test, which examines the hypothesis that the error terms are not serially correlated. The second is a Sargan test of overidentifying restrictions, which tests the

[5] This confirms Marxian labour aristocracy hypothesis.

Table 5.2 Determinants of labour productivity (difference GMM regression)

	Real wage (Elasticity)	*Capital intensity (Elasticity)*	*Export orientation*	*Foreign investment*	*Year-fixed effects*	*Obs.*
All firms	0.134***	0.078***	−0.00007	0.0003	Yes	6819
Firm size						
Medium	0.121***	0.053**	0.001	−0.001	Yes	2825
Large	0.142***	0.094***	−0.0005	0.001	Yes	3994
Factor intensity						
Labour	0.101***	0.051***	−0.0004	0.001	Yes	3312
Resource	0.139***	0.115***	0.0001	−0.001	Yes	2287
Capital	0.236***	0.066*	−0.0002	0.0021	Yes	1220

Notes: ***, ** and * indicate 1 per cent, 5 per cent and 10 per cent levels of significance respectively, regressions with robust standard error

overall validity of the instruments. Failure to reject the null hypotheses of both tests provides support to our model specifications. Non-stationarity is not a big concern for panel data with small T (time periods).

With regard to regression in Table 5.1 (wage equation), only one regression does not survive the Arellano-Bond test, but none of the regressions pass the Sargan test at 5 per cent level of significance. Therefore, all regressions were rerun with fixed-effect estimation with the inclusion of time fixed effects without a lag-dependent variable, and consistent results are obtained. In most cases, the coefficients of productivity and capital intensity tend to be smaller in the case of GMM regressions.

All regressions in Table 5.2 (productivity equation) survive the Arellano-Bond test. For the Sargan test, however, only two (resource intensive and capital intensive) out of six regressions pass the test at 5 per cent level of significance. The other four regressions were rerun with fixed-effect estimation with the inclusion of time fixed effects without a lag-dependent variable, and we obtain consistent results. But the coefficients of real wage from the GMM regressions tend to be smaller than the coefficients from the fixed-effects regressions. These mean that regression results presented in Tables 5.1 and 5.2 are acceptable.

In order to check a possible selection bias due to the exclusion of newly listed firms and those which exited the market, and only include firms that form a balanced panel dataset during the observation years of 2008–2013, we performed the seemingly unrelated estimation (Suest) test. Ordinary least squares (OLS) regressions were run for the wage model in Eq. 5.1 for the whole survey sample and for only firms included in the balance panel for each observation year. Then, the coefficients of independent variables of the two sample groups (all and selected) were systematically compared. The Suest test is highly significant in five out of six observation years indicating general presence of selection bias; however, the bias is downward. Average productivity coefficient in the selected samples is 12 per cent lower than that in the overall samples.[6] This indicates that the estimated elasticity of productivity with respect to wage (productivity-wage elasticity in Eq. 5.1) in the panel setting is quite conservative and tends to be lower than the elasticity for the overall samples. In the case of the productivity model in Eq. 5.2, a similar result of downward bias (significant only in three out of six observation years) is found for real wage elasticity with respect to productivity. Average wage-productivity elasticity (Eq. 5.2) in the selected samples is 4 per cent lower than the elasticity for the overall samples.

5.2.2 *Micro and Small Firms*

We model wage and productivity functions for MS firm with a different set of firms characteristics, which include (1) capital ownership, measured as a percentage of business capital originated from own internal source; (2) firm age, measured by how many years the firm has been in operation; (3) cooperative membership, indicating whether a firm is a member of any cooperative association; and (4) business licence type, indicating whether a firm has any type of business licence.[7] These small and micro firm characteristics are different from those for large and medium firms, and are simply dictated by the differences in the design of manufacturing surveys for LM and MS firms.

The influence of ownership structure on firm performance has been investigated in various theoretical and empirical studies on firms' productivity and growth. In the case of small and medium enterprises (SMEs), the issue of ownership structure is also crucial as these firms are mostly family owned and run by a mix of family members and non-family members. Chu (2009) and Barbera and Moores (2011) show that ownership

[6] Detailed regression results and related Suest test are available from authors.

[7] While it would be interesting to identify the role of technology on wage and productivity, the survey design does not have specific and consistent information on this matter across the survey periods. However, it is necessary to note that micro and small manufacturing firm survey in 2009 and 2010 includes questions on the use of computer and internet, which can be used as a proxy for technology. Unfortunately, these questions are no longer available in the rest of the survey. We ran a separate regression for 2010 that included these questions, in addition to the robustness check regression using 2010 data since the year accounts for the bulk of the total observation.

structure, in terms of both managerial and capital, is an important determinant of SMEs' performance. In our model, the inclusion of capital represents a control on the role and contribution of SMEs' internal resources towards firms' productivity. Another key factor of a firm's performance is how long the firm has been in operation. Patel (2005), specifically focusing on the SMEs in the UK, finds that there are substantial differences between embryonic, emerging and established firms in terms of firms' financial performance. A study by Nunes et al. (2013), comparing young and old SMEs in Italy, also finds that firm age is a fundamental characteristic which determines firms' growth. In both studies by Patel (2005) and Nunes et al. (2013), hypothesis that ageing increases tangible performance of firms is supported. However, an opposite pattern is found in terms of firm innovation. Similar findings are also reported in a recent study by Smith and Hendrickson (2016) for the case of SMEs in Australia. In order to account for the impact of ageing, we include how long the firm has been in operation in our model.

Business network and collaboration has also been identified as an important factor in determining micro and small enterprises' performance. Both in developed and developing countries, cooperative is a common institution representing business network and collaboration within the SME world. Cooperatives represent an alternative model in organising and running business activities. London Economics (2008), in a report studying the performance of cooperative member versus non-member across Europe, finds that firms with cooperative memberships generally have higher turnover and labour productivity growth as opposed to the non-member firms. Villa and Bruno (2013) also emphasises the importance of SME collaboration via cooperative model as one of SMEs' business strategies. In the model, the cooperative membership represents a control on the possible importance of cooperative on firms' productivity measure. The last variable included in the model is business licensing. Any type of business licensing represents formalisation of micro and small firms. While it is a common practice in developed countries, it is still often considered less necessary by micro and small businesses in developing countries. Mourougane (2012), in the case of micro, small and medium enterprises in Indonesia, argues that one of the obstacles for enterprises' productivity growth is the formalisation of firms. Rand and Torm (2012), analysing manufacturing SMEs in Vietnam, find that becoming a formal business leads to higher profits and investments and also an increase in the number of permanent workers. Accounting for the importance of business formalisation, we include the ownership of business licence in our estimation model.

Estimating the regression model using only the observations that have wage data would be fine if the missing wage data occurred randomly. However, the decision to pay wage or not was made by individual firms. Thus, firms that do not pay wages may constitute a self-selected sample and not a random sample. It is likely some of the firms that have relatively small business activities and also have enough supply of workers from the owners' family members would choose not to pay formal wages; and this would account for much of the missing wage data, for micro firms in particular. Thus, it is likely that we will overestimate the wages paid by the firms in the population. In this case, we need to account for information that we have on the non-wage paying firms.

Two approaches were employed to estimate the wage and productivity models in the case of MS firms: pooled cross-section and pseudo panel. In the pooled cross-section setting, the wage and productivity functions can be estimated with OLS regression. However, as mentioned earlier, the firms without wage information might constitute of a self-selected sample, not a random sample. If this case is true, the OLS will be biased. Therefore, we estimated the wage and productivity functions using the Heckman method, in addition to the OLS. The Heckman selection model allows us to use information from non-wage paying firms to improve the estimates of the parameters in the regression model. The Heckman selection model provides consistent, asymptotically efficient estimates for all parameters in the model. We use Heckman Maximum Likelihood (ML) estimation, which allows for robust estimation.[8]

Table 5.3 summarises the estimation results for the wage equation. The Heckman ML approach confirms the presence of sample selection bias in the three specifications; thus, OLS tends to overestimate the effect of the explanatory variables. Therefore, we use the Heckman estimations in order to analyse the determinants of real wage. The most important finding is the positive and significant effect of productivity on real wage. For overall data of micro and small firms, the magnitude of elasticity of wage with respect to productivity is 0.117. The elasticity is much higher in small firms compared with micro firms, 0.9 and 0.28, respectively. For a robustness check, as the 2010 survey accounted for the 39 per cent of the total observations from 2009 to 2013, we carried out separate estimations for the year 2010 and the main finding holds.

[8] For more details on the Heckman selection model, see Cameron and Trivedi (2010) and Wooldridge (2002).

Table 5.3 Determinants of wage in micro and small firms (Heckman)

	All (Micro + small)		*Micro firms only*		*Small firms only*	
	(1)	*(2)*	*(3)*	*(4)*	*(5)*	*(6)*
	OLS Robust	*Heckman Robust*	*OLS Robust*	*Heckman Robust*	*OLS Robust*	*Heckman Robust*
Ln productivity	0.300**	0.117***	0.312**	0.0887*	0.280**	0.277***
	(0.0493)	(0.0356)	(0.0513)	(0.0361)	(0.0452)	(0.0518)
Own capital	−0.0003	0.0041***	−0.0010	0.0016***	0.0007	0.0008
	(0.0009)	(0.0008)	(0.0004)	(0.0004)	(0.0015)	(0.0014)
Cooperative	−0.0678**	0.116**	−0.0521**	0.163***	−0.0842	−0.0361
	(0.0094)	(0.0415)	(0.0089)	(0.0325)	(0.0334)	(0.0536)
Firm age	−0.00461*	0.00559***	−0.00316*	0.00952***	−0.00724**	−0.00457**
	(0.0011)	(0.0014)	(0.0009)	(0.0018)	(0.0015)	(0.0017)
Firm age (squared)	−0.000005	−0.00002	−0.00005	−0.0001**	0.00007	0.00008*
	(0.00002)	(0.00003)	(0.00002)	(0.00003)	(0.00003)	(0.00004)
Business licence	0.153***	0.287	0.0798*	0.237	0.234***	0.487***
	(0.0084)	(0.163)	(0.0191)	(0.165)	(0.0159)	(0.112)
Rho		−0.857		−0.871		−0.816
Sigma		1.103		1.210		0.790
Lambda		−0.945		−1.054		−0.644
P-Value for LR test		1.81e-47		5.81e-140		2.04e-16
Test age & age-sq	0.000012	0.0000	0.0007	0.0000	0.0120	0.0000
Obs	40678	134923	24400	116589	16278	18334
R-sq	0.226		0.225		0.232	
Year dummies	YES	YES	YES	YES	YES	YES

Notes: ***, ** and * indicate 1 per cent, 5 per cent and 10 per cent levels of significance respectively. Standard errors are in parentheses. Each regression is with a constant

Having more discussion on the role of other firm characteristics is beyond the scope of this chapter. However, we checked the role of technology proxied by the use of computer for which data are available in the 2010 survey and found that technology has a positive and significant effect on real wage for the overall (micro and small), micro and small (firm) observations.

The main finding of positive and significant elasticity of real wage with respect to productivity is also confirmed by the pseudo panel approach as presented in Table 5.4. The pseudo panels are formed by grouping observations into cohorts on the basis of invariant shared characteristics and constructing the cohort variables as the mean values of the included observations. The cohorts are then traced over time in each of the annual surveys, forming a panel. In this study, the cohorts are formed based on the year the firms started their operations.[9]

For the productivity function, we followed the same procedure of having pooled cross section (Heckman) and pseudo panel regressions. Both approaches confirm previous finding of a significant and positive effect of wage on productivity as presented in Tables 5.5 and 5.6 respectively. The Heckman model indicates that there is no sample selection problem in the overall sample (combined micro and small firms), thus OLS robust is not biased.

Table 5.4 Determinants of wage in micro and small firms (pseudo panel, difference GMM)

	All	*Micro*	*Small*
Ln productivity	0.5870***	0.5796***	0.6411***
	(0.0561)	(0.0593)	(0.0486)
Firm age	−0.1574**	−0.1292	0.0016
	(0.0677)	(0.0867)	(0.0979)
Firm age (squared)	0.0008**	0.0010**	−0.0006
	(0.0004)	(0.0005)	(0.0014)
Own capital	−0.0010	0.0006	0.0048**
	(0.0016)	(0.0021)	(0.0022)
No of obs.	226	186	97
No of groups	84	69	39

Notes: ***, ** and * indicate 1 per cent, 5 per cent and 10 per cent levels of significance respectively. Standard errors are in parentheses. Each regression is with a lag-dependent variable, a constant and robust standard errors, productivity is endogenous

[9] See Appendix 5.2 on the detail on how the pseudo panel is constructed.

Table 5.5 Determinants of productivity in micro and small firms (Heckman)

	All (Micro + small)		*Micro firms only*		*Small firms only*	
	(1)	*(2)*	*(3)*	*(4)*	*(5)*	*(6)*
	OLS Robust	*Heckman Robust*	*OLS Robust*	*Heckman Robust*	*OLS Robust*	*Heckman Robust*
Ln real wage	0.663***	0.657***	0.645***	0.753***	0.687***	0.663***
	(0.0264)	(0.0319)	(0.0287)	(0.0541)	(0.0332)	(0.0422)
Own capital	−0.0003	−0.0003	−0.0024**	−0.0019*	0.0014*	0.0014***
	(0.0002)	(0.0002)	(0.0003)	(0.0008)	(0.0005)	(0.0004)
Cooperative	−0.110**	−0.111***	−0.0952	−0.0732	−0.104*	−0.109**
	(0.0142)	(0.0127)	(0.0371)	(0.0501)	(0.0365)	(0.0373)
Firm age	−0.00253	−0.00255	−0.00486	−0.00434*	0.00137	0.00126
	(0.0016)	(0.0016)	(0.0023)	(0.0019)	(0.0014)	(0.0014)
Firm age (squared)	0.00003	0.00003	0.00007	0.0001	−0.00004	−0.00004*
	(0.00003)	(0.00003)	(0.00005)	(0.00006)	(0.00002)	(0.00002)
Business licence	0.101	0.109	0.0674*	−0.0714	0.138	0.164
	(0.0572)	(0.0588)	(0.0198)	(0.117)	(0.0844)	(0.0959)
Rho		0.0358		−0.658		0.132
Sigma		1.141		1.239		1.136
Lambda		0.0409		−0.815		0.150
P-Value for LR test		0.468		0.00237		0.0113
Test age & age-sq	0.3486	0.0000	0.1724	0.0000	0.2786	0.0000
Obs	40678	48940	24400	29617	16278	19323
R-sq	0.210		0.219		0.206	
Year dummies	YES	YES	YES	YES	YES	YES

Notes: ***, ** and * indicate 1 per cent, 5 per cent and 10 per cent levels of significance respectively. Standard errors are in parentheses. Each regression is with a constant

5.3 Employment Functions: Models and Empirics

Estimates of employment functions in Indonesia had been preoccupied with concerns on the magnitude of "employment elasticity",[10] which is a concept primarily focused on the ability of economic growth to generate

[10] That is, elasticity of employment with respect to output. Technically, it should be called output elasticity, but it is commonly referred to as employment elasticity in the literature.

Table 5.6 Determinants of productivity in micro and small firms (pseudo panel, difference GMM)

	All	*Micro*	*Small*
Ln real wage	0.9096***	0.9279***	1.0689***
	(0.0615)	(0.1061)	(0.0833)
Firm age	0.1993*	−0.0053	−0.0931
	(0.1077)	(0.0823)	(0.1403)
Firm age (squared)	−0.0009	−0.0004	0.0022
	(0.0006)	(0.0005)	(0.0021)
Own capital	0.0010	−0.0026	−0.0047
	(0.0025)	(0.0028)	(0.0035)
No. of obs.	224	186	94
No. of groups	84	69	38

Notes: ***, ** and * indicate 1 per cent, 5 per cent and 10 per cent levels of significance respectively. Standard errors are in parentheses. Each regression is with a lag-dependent variable, a constant and robust standard errors, productivity is endogenous

new employment as found in Lim (1997), Islam and Nazara (2000), and Suryadarma et al. (2007). One fundamental shortcoming of these studies is that none of the estimated employment functions had real wages as a determinant of employment.

A recently adopted common approach is to model employment as a function of wages and total value added (gross domestic product—GDP) as in Tadjoeddin and Chowdhury (2012) and also in Narjoko and Putra (2015). In deriving the employment function, as in Tadjoeddin and Chowdhury (2012), it is assumed that firms minimise cost subject to a given level of output. Thus, it incorporates two important characteristics of labour demand, that is, it is a derived demand (for a given level of output) and the profit-maximising (or cost-minimising) behaviour of firms. Employers employ workers by weighing the wage they have to pay against the prices they receive for their products (i.e., real wages). Additionally, employment decision, especially in the modern sector, is a marginal decision, that is, it depends on incremental changes from the prevailing configuration of output, employment and real wages. Therefore, the model postulates that employment is a function of output, real wages and past employment. Lagged employment is included to capture the "hysteresis" or the path-dependent nature of the labour market and control for endogeneity. In this model, all three independent variables are treated as exogenous. The common empirical finding, and also belief, is that real wage would have a negative sign and GDP would have a positive sign.

It means that higher employment could only be achieved with either higher GDP or lower real wages. The trade-off between real wages and employment follows the conventionally conceived negative association between price and quantity from the demand perspective. This line of argument has been used by the proponent of labour market flexibility to argue that higher wages (especially minimum wage) are harmful for employment creation. This, however, only tells us half of the story as price and quantity could also be positively related, particularly in the long run when demand expands with growth.

The estimated sectoral employment functions conducted by Tadjoeddin and Chowdhury (2012), covering both the pre- and post-1997–1998 crisis periods, revealed that output growth is the major determinant of employment and real wages are not a significant determinant of employment except in the mining and manufacturing sectors. Furthermore, the real wage elasticity of employment in the manufacturing sector is very low. This implies that a large cut in real wages will have marginal gains in employment, causing a decline in labour income. Therefore, they suggested that the strategy of lowering real wages is not only likely to increase the incidence of working poor but also likely to subdue the growth of aggregate demand and hence slow down economic growth.

Using firm-level data of large and medium manufacturing industry, Narjoko and Putra (2015) estimate an employment function with value added and real wages as their independent variables. In addition, they include two dummy variables for whether a firm has a component of foreign ownership and engages in export market. They perform independent cross-section estimations for the years of 1990, 1996, 2006 and 2009, and then make a comparison. Their main concern was to estimate elasticity parameters of employment with respect to real wages and output at the firm level. They found a positive output elasticity and a negative wage elasticity, with consistent results in cross-industrial sub-sector at the ISIC 2 level.

Declining output elasticity of employment was seen as a discouraging trend since the same level of economic growth now produces less new employment. Such concern is, however, missing an important factor, labour productivity, as declining output elasticity of employment also implies increasing labour productivity, where workers could enjoy higher wages. From this perspective, declining output elasticity of employment may indicate a progress as the economy shifts from lower productivity sectors to the higher ones.

Our innovation lies in revisiting the basic employment function used in Tadjoeddin and Chowdhury (2012) and Narjoko and Putra (2015) by formulating employment, wages and productivity in a simultaneous relationship. While employment is formulated as a function of real wages, at the same time, real wages are formulated as a function of labour productivity as in Blanchard and Katz (1999). In other words, the real wage variable is treated as endogenous.

This new employment function can also be seen as an improvement to Bhattacharya et al.'s (2011) model, where the three variables—employment, real wages and productivity—were modelled separately to estimate the effect of employment on productivity and the effect of real wages on productivity in a panel data setting across Indian manufacturing subsectors. They found that both employment and real wages exert a positive effect on labour productivity.

In a long-run framework, employment and real wages should move in the same direction when labour productivity positively affects real wages. This is an ideal situation for achieving higher productivity and real wages while the overall economy grows with both employment and output expanding. We find evidence for such a scenario: first is in the case of modern and organised LM manufacturing establishments across Indonesia's manufacturing subsectors at the ISIC 3 level. Second is in the individual firm-level analysis of LM and MS manufacturing establishments, which also allows us to control for firms' characteristics. These will be explained in more details later.

The simultaneous model of employment, real wage and productivity is tested for the following two cases. First is at the overall economy and sectoral level using aggregate provincial data. Second is for the modern and dynamic LM establishments of the manufacturing sector.

5.3.1 Employment Function: Overall Economy and Nine Economic Sectors

The simultaneous relationship between employment, real wage and productivity is expressed in the following two-step equations:

$$\mathrm{Ln\,RW}_{i,t} = \alpha_0 + \alpha_1 \mathrm{Ln\,PROD}_{i,t} + \alpha_2 \mathrm{Ln\,RW}_{i,t-1} + \upsilon_i + \varepsilon_{i,t} \quad \text{1st step} \quad (5.3)$$

$$\mathrm{Ln\,EMP}_{i,t} = \beta_0 + \beta_1 \mathrm{Predicted\_Ln\,RW}_{i,t} + \beta_2 \mathrm{Ln\,EMP}_{i,t-1} + \upsilon_i + \varepsilon_{i,t} \quad \text{2nd step} \quad (5.4)$$

The first-step regression specifies real wages (Ln RW) as a function of labour productivity (Ln PROD) and real wages in the previous year.[11] It has to be noted that real wages refers to real earnings of self-employed workers, regular waged employment and casual workers. This regression is a more systematic test for the postulated delinking between real wages and productivity, which will be indicated by insignificant or negative value of α_1. In the second-step regression, the dependent variable Ln $EMP_{i,t}$ is the natural log of number of (sectoral) employment of province *i* at time *t* and Ln $EMP_{i,t-1}$ is one period lagged of this variable. RW stands for real wages as an endogenous independent variable. Here, we use the predicted value Ln RW taken from the first-step regression. The remaining components in the model are the error terms: v_i represents time-invariant heterogeneity across provinces and $\varepsilon_{i,t}$ is the time-variant error term. The relationship between real wages and productivity is denoted by α_1, and wage elasticity of employment (i.e., change in employment with respect to real wage) is shown by β_1. Assuming that β_1 is positive, therefore, employment (EMP) will increase by β_1 per cent if real wages (RW) increases by 1 per cent.

Using the DPD regression of system GMM, the model is estimated for all nine sectors in the economy. The sectors are (1) agriculture, fisheries and forestry; (2) mining and quarrying; (3) manufacturing; (4) electricity, gas and water; (5) construction; (6) trade, hotel and restaurant; (7) transportation and communication; (8) finance and (9) services. Employment and real earnings data are taken from the annual publications of Sakernas (August series), while provincial real GDP data are from the regional accounts publications of the BPS (*Badan Pusat Statistik*). Sectoral real wages are obtained by deflating sectoral nominal wages by sectoral output deflators.[12] We have a balance panel dataset across 33 Indonesian provinces during 2001–2011.

Estimation results for the overall economy as well as the nine economic sectors are summarised in Table 5.7.[13] Supports for the delinking hypotheses between real wage earnings and productivity, as documented

[11] This is similar to Blanchard and Katz's (1999) specification. Another alternative formulation is to treat wage as a function productivity and unemployment, such as Goh and Wong (2010) for the Malaysia case.

[12] The use of GDP deflator is more appropriate than the alternative of using consumer price index (CPI) to maintain consistency with (real) productivity data.

[13] All regressions pass both the Sargan test of overidentifying restrictions and the Arellano-Bond test of serial correlation, both of which are important in GMM estimation.

Table 5.7 Employment functions: endogenous versus exogenous wage earnings

	Endogenous wage (two-step system GMM)		*Exogenous wage (two-step system GMM)*
	First step	*Second step*	
	(LnWage = LnProductivity, lagLnWage)	*(LnEmp = predictedLnWage, lagLnEmp)*	*(LnEmp = LnWage, lagLnEmp)*
	Productivity coefficient	*Wage coefficient*	*Wage coefficient*
All	−0.002	−0.169***	−0.043***
1 Agriculture	−0.041**	−0.153***	−0.111***
2 Mining	0.034***	−1.455***	−0.023
3 Manufacturing	0.033	−3.887***	−0.012
4 Electricity	−0.054***	2.368***	0.362***
5 Construction	0.036**	−0.193*	−0.494***
6 Trade	0.066*	−1.089***	0.134***
7 Transportation	0.098***	−0.798***	−0.195***
8 Finance	−0.042***	3.835***	−0.195***
9 Services	0.035**	−0.220***	−0.034

Notes: ***, ** and * indicate 1 per cent, 5 per cent and 10 per cent levels of significance respectively; detailed regression results are in Appendixes 5.1 and 5.2

in Chap. 3, are further found for the overall economy and across sectors as can be seen from the first-step regression. While the productivity coefficient is insignificantly negative for the overall economy, the situation across sectors is not homogeneous. In five sectors, the productivity coefficients are significantly positive, but the magnitude is negligible. Therefore, in most cases, productivity has no meaningful relationship with real wage earnings pointing to a situation where the two are not moving in the same direction, or do very marginally.

In the regression, we compare the effect of real wage earnings on employment in two scenarios: endogenous wage earnings and exogenous wage earnings. In general, similar to the previous studies, a negative relationship between real wage and employment is found. However, the strength of the negative coefficient of real wage is stronger in the endogenous setting than in the exogenous one. The finding is consistent for the overall economy and most of sectors. Not all economic sectors display a similar trend, for example, real wage and employment in the electricity and finance sectors are positively and significantly related.

However, we argue that the decoupling between real wage earnings and productivity in the first-step regression was the reason for the negative coefficient of real wages in the second-step regression (the employment function). If the increase in productivity is strongly followed by increased real wages, or in other words, the decoupling between real wage and productivity was not the case, we could expect a positive association between real wages and employment.

5.3.2 *Employment Function: Large-Medium Firms of the Manufacturing Sector*

We applied the same model exclusively to the modern and dynamic LM firms section of the manufacturing sector. In this case, we conducted two separate analyses: (1) across 66 manufacturing sub-sectors (aggregate) at the ISIC 3 level and (2) across individual firm data of LM manufacturing.

Across the 66 Manufacturing Sub-sectors

The summary results of the aggregate analysis across the 66 manufacturing sub-sectors are presented in Table 5.8, which contains two rows. The first one for the overall manufacturing sector, with province-year as the unit of observation, is copied from Table 5.7. The second row presents results from the LM firms only. This is to directly compare the two results.

Based on the wage-productivity ratio of the manufacturing sector and its sub-sectors presented in Chap. 4, the disjoint between real wages and productivity is apparent in the *overall* manufacturing sector. This finding is consistent with the insignificant coefficient of the productivity variable in the first-step regression that models real wages as a function of productivity (Table 5.8; row 1, column 1). This means that in the overall manufacturing sector, productivity has no significant effect on real wages. As a consequence, the predicted real wages variable in the second-step regression is negatively and significantly correlated with employment (column 2), which is in support of the negative association between real wages and employment. The negative and significant coefficient of the real wages variable in the employment function, however, disappears when the real wages variable is treated as exogenous (column 3). We argue that the negative and significant relationship between employment and real wages in the second-step regression (column 2) is because of the

Table 5.8 Employment function—manufacturing (overall and LM firms only)

	Endogenous wage (system GMM)		*Exogenous wage*
	First step	*Second step*	*System GMM*
	WAGE = f {PROD}	*EMP = f {pred_WAGE}*	*EMP = f {Wage}*
	PROD coef.	*Predicted WAGE coef.*	*Wage coef.*
Manufacturing sector (overall)	0.033	−3.887***	−0.012
Large and medium firms in manufacturing	0.243***	0.552***	0.009***

Notes: ***, ** and * indicate 1 per cent, 5 per cent and 10 per cent levels of significance respectively; regression results of the overall manufacturing sector are taken from Table 5.4; detailed regression results can be found in Appendixes 5.3 and 5.4

delinking between wages and productivity as the real wages variable is treated as endogenous to productivity.[14]

A similar regression conducted exclusively for the LM firms is also supportive of the above assessment. As mentioned earlier, although the delinking trend is still found in the overall LM firms, the trend is far from homogeneous across sub-sectors of LM firms. To dig deeper, we exploit the variation across sub-sectors of LM firms at the ISIC 3 level, and surprisingly we find a different result namely the delinking story is no longer valid (Table 5.8, row 2). In the first-step regression, the coefficient of productivity variable is *significantly positive* (0.24) meaning that 1 per cent increase in productivity leads to 0.24 per cent increase in real wages. As a consequence, in the second-step regression, the predicted real wages variable is significantly and positively related to employment with a coefficient of 0.55. This means that 1 per cent increase in predicted real wages leads to 0.55 per cent increase in employment. In contrast to the previous finding, increase in real wages can lead to higher employment in more modern

[14] In South Africa, Klein (2012) finds that the negative effect of real wages on employment is due to "excess" real wages, which refers to a situation where real wage growth far exceeds productivity growth. Excess real wages could be seen as the opposite of delinking between wage and productivity; both are unfavourable conditions. The former is not good for the economy, while the latter is unfair for the workers.

and better organised large and medium manufacturing industry. The positive and significant effect of real wage on employment is subject to positive effect of productivity on real wages. This is an ideal situation mentioned earlier.

As a matter of fact, we did find a rising wage-productivity ratio in the sub-sectors of LM firms since 2008 as reported in Chap. 4, indicating that the manufacturing sector is turning the corner, led by the large and medium firms.

The relationship between employment, wages and productivity should be framed in a more dynamic framework based on outward shifts of labour demand due to factors other than wage and employment. These factors could be technological progress, having more skilled workers, higher capital intensity, reforming management, corporate restructuring and so on. In this scenario, the expansion of employment could be achieved by having higher wages, higher productivity and an overall growth of the economy.

Firm-Level Analysis

We examine the previous findings further on the simultaneous relationship between productivity, real wages and employment in large and medium firms using firm-level data and controlling for individual firm characteristics. In essence, it is a combination of our previous approach and that of Narjoko and Putra (2015). Our main innovation is that the estimates are disaggregated into firm size (large and medium) and factor intensity (labour, resource and capital intensives).

The simultaneous relationship between employment, wages and productivity at the firm level can be expressed as follows:

$$\text{Ln RW}_{it} = \alpha_0 + \alpha_1 \text{ Ln RW}_{it-1} + \alpha_2 \text{ Ln PROD}_{it} + \upsilon_i + \varepsilon_{it} \tag{5.5}$$

$$\begin{aligned} \text{Ln EMP}_{it} = \beta_0 + \beta_1 \text{ Ln EMP}_{it-1} + \beta_2 \text{ Ln RW}_{it} + \beta_3 \text{ Ln PROD}_{it} \\ + \beta_4 \text{ Ln CAP}_{it} + \beta_5 \text{ EXPORT}_{it} + \beta_6 \text{ FOREIGN}_{it} + \upsilon_i + \varepsilon_{it} \end{aligned} \tag{5.6}$$

As before (Eqs. 5.1 and 5.2), RW stands for real wage, PROD represents labour productivity, CAP denotes capital intensity per worker, EXPORT stands for percentage of exported output to total value of firm output and FOREIGN denotes percentage of foreign investment to total firm investment. Lag-dependent variable is included to capture path dependence or the dynamic nature of overtime progress of wage and productivity.

The two equations are estimated with two-stage least squares (2SLS) regression. In addition to lag-dependent variable, time (year)-fixed effects are added to both equations. In the second equation, in addition to the variable of our main interest, RW (real wage), we also include variables PROD, CAP, EXPORT and FOREIGN to gauge the effects of labour productivity, capital intensity, export orientation and foreign ownership on employment respectively.

The inclusion of productivity in the second-stage regression would be in line with the New Keynesian (NK) perspective on the short-run effects of productivity shocks on employment. Under the NK model, some firms do not update the price in a given period. Therefore, their demand is fixed, which will lead to increases in real wage having no effect on employment, up to a certain point; however, as demand is fixed, an increase in productivity can reduce employment.

Estimation results of the simultaneous equations are reported in Table 5.9. From the first equation, the results of positive effect of productivity on real wages are consistent with findings in the previous section. In the second equation, the results are reported for each variable disaggregated into firm size and factor intensity.

Our findings support a generally positive relationship between real wages and employment after taking into account the effect of productivity on real wages. This is consistent with the previous finding at the ISIC 3 level for large and medium manufacturing. The overall wage elasticity of employment (in short, employment-wage elasticity) is 0.18. However, the elasticity varies across firm size, where employment-wage elasticity in medium firms is far larger than that in large firms, 0.26 and 0.07, respectively. Employment-wage elasticity is the lowest among resource-intensive firms.

The direct effect of labour productivity on employment is generally negative albeit very small, which is in line with the NK perspective explained earlier, while the indirect effect of labour productivity on employment is positive via wages. It has to be noted that the labour productivity variable enters both steps in our 2SLS regressions.

The use of firm-level data allows us to exploit individual firm characteristics. The first characteristic is capital intensity at the firm level. As expected, the elasticity of employment with respect to capital intensity is

Table 5.9 Employment function (2SLS regression, large-medium firms)

		Firm size		*Resource intensity*		
	All firms	*Medium*	*Large*	*Labour*	*Resource*	*Capital*
First stage (Dev. var: Ln real wage)						
Ln productivity	0.3087 ***	0.3537 ***	0.2535 ***	0.3336 ***	0.2517 ***	0.3385 ***
	(0.0055)	(0.0075)	(0.0085)	(0.0110)	(0.0085)	(0.0119)
Ln real wage_lag	0.1914 ***	0.1834 ***	0.1882 ***	0.1284 ***	0.2382 ***	0.1939 ***
	(0.0073)	(0.0096)	(0.0111)	(0.0112)	(0.0119)	(0.0163)
R-sq	0.34	0.3989	0.2331	0.2447	0.3332	0.4486
Second stage (Dep. var: Ln employment)						
Ln real wage	0.1821 ***	0.2582 ***	0.0698 **	0.2251 ***	0.1414 ***	0.2466 ***
	(0.0239)	(0.0330)	(0.0304)	(0.0547)	(0.0296)	(0.0618)
Ln productivity	−0.0630 ***	−0.0848 ***	−0.0419 ***	−0.0906 ***	−0.0434 ***	−0.0939 ***
	(0.0079)	(0.0124)	(0.0085)	(0.0185)	(0.0087)	(0.0226)
Ln capital	−0.0076 ***	−0.0104 ***	−0.0014	−0.0140 ***	−0.0038	−0.0067
	(0.0020)	(0.0023)	(0.0028)	(0.0031)	(0.0032)	(0.0050)
Export (%)	−0.0001	−0.0002 *	−0.0001	−0.0001	−0.0001	0.0002
	(0.0001)	(0.0001)	(0.0001)	(0.0001)	(0.0002)	(0.0003)
Foreign inv. (%)	0.0004 ***	0.0004 **	0.0003 ***	0.0005 ***	0.0002	0.0005 **
	(0.0001)	(0.0002)	(0.0001)	(0.0002)	(0.0002)	(0.0002)
Ln employment_lag	0.9583 ***	0.6636 ***	0.8623 ***	0.9693 ***	0.9487 ***	0.9506 ***
	(0.0026)	(0.0066)	(0.0047)	(0.0041)	(0.0043)	(0.0070)
R-sq	0.9081	0.5299	0.8338	0.9133	0.9026	0.8924
Year-fixed effects	Yes	Yes	Yes	Yes	Yes	Yes
Obs.	15,493	8417	7076	6781	5888	2824

Notes: ***, ** and * indicate 1 per cent, 5 per cent and 10 per cent levels of significance respectively. Standard errors are in parentheses. Each regression has a constant significantly negative, albeit with very low magnitude. This, however, indicates a substitutive relationship between the use of machinery capital and labour, implying that higher capital intensity correlates with lower employment.

The effect of foreign ownership on employment is largely negligible. Although the coefficient for overall large and medium firms is positive and significant, the magnitude is negligible. Not surprisingly, the export orientation of firms has no effect on employment. This is consistent with the deteriorating trend of Indonesian manufacturing exports. In the past decade, while the share of commodity exports has doubled, the export share of manufacturing product has fallen by half (World Bank 2012).

5.4 Concluding Remarks: Potential for Large-Medium Manufacturing

In contrast to the overall delinking trends in the economic sectors including manufacturing, the positive link between wages and productivity in the LM manufacturing industry has led to a positive correlation between real wages and employment. This is an ideal outcome where wages and employment increase when the overall economy (GDP) expands.

This finding is consistent across firm size and factor intensity and hence should affirm the call for re-industrialisation to reverse the trend of premature de-industrialisation since the 1997–1998 AFC. LM firms have the best potential for igniting productivity-led revitalisation of the manufacturing sector to create decent and quality jobs. That is, Indonesia does not have to be trapped in a low-wage, low-productivity vicious circle. This is a hopeful sign. However, this also highlights the need for active industry policy, especially to support graduation of small and micro firms to medium-sized operations.

Ironically, decentralised setting can be a challenge for a well-coordinated uniform nationwide approach to industry policy, especially when the regions race to the bottom and try to beggar their neighbours to attract investment. The democratic setting can also pose a challenge if demand for higher wages and better living spiral to outstrip productivity growth. National dialogue can mitigate these challenges.

APPENDICES

Appendix 5.1 Employment functions with *endogenous* wage (two-step system GMM, two-step estimator)

	All	*Agriculture*	*Mining*	*Manufacturing*	*Electricity*	*Construction*	*Trade*	*Transportation*	*Finance*	*Services*
First step (Dep. Var: Ln Real Wage)										
Ln Productivity	−0.002	−0.041**	0.034***	0.033	−0.054***	0.036**	0.066*	0.098***	−0.042***	0.035**
Ln Real Wage (lag)	0.285***	0.438***	0.245***	0.108***	0.204***	0.341***	0.081**	0.296***	0.160***	0.595***
Wald χ^2 *(P-value)*	0.000	0.000	0.000	0.000	0.000	0.000	0.000	0.000	0.000	0.000
Sargan test, *P-value* (H_0: overidentifying restrictions are valid)	0.987	0.990	0.992	0.987	0.9885	0.991	0.991	0.992	0.9898	0.9872
Arellano-Bond test (H_0: no autocorrelation)										
AR(1), *P-value*	0.000	0.000	0.010	0.007	0.000	0.000	0.001	0.000	0.000	0.000
AR(2), *P-value*	0.9913	0.364	0.388	0.162	0.368	0.094	0.056	0.521	0.857	0.259
Second step (Dep. Var: Ln Employment)										
Ln Real Wage (predicted)	−0.169***	−0.153***	−1.455***	−3.887***	2.368***	−0.193*	−1.089***	−0.798***	3.835***	−0.220***
Ln Employment (lag)	1.006***	0.905***	0.53612***	0.817***	0.152***	0.843***	0.914***	0.807***	0.484***	1.033***
Wald χ^2 *(P-value)*	0.000	0.000	0.000	0.000	0.000	0.000	0.000	0.000	0.000	0.000

Sargan test, *P-value* (H_0: overidentifying restrictions are valid)	0.991	0.987	0.989	0.991	0.991	0.988	0.993	0.989	0.988	0.992
Arellano-Bond test (H_0: no autocorrelation)										
AR(1), *P-value*	0.000	0.145	0.002	0.000	0.000	0.000	0.000	0.000	0.002	0.000
AR(2), *P-value*	0.560	0.950	0.104	0.455	0.156	0.512	0.201	0.018	0.714	0.281
No. of observations	330	330	330	330	330	330	330	330	330	330
No. of group (provinces/ sub-sectors)	33	33	33	33	33	33	33	33	33	33
No. of instruments used	56	56	56	56	56	56	56	56	56	56

Notes: ***, ** and * indicate 1 per cent, 5 per cent and 10 per cent levels of significance respectively; each regression has a constant term

Appendix 5.2 Employment functions with *exogenous* wage (two-step system GMM, two-step estimator)

	All	*Agriculture*	*Mining*	*Manufacturing*	*Electricity*	*Construction*	*Trade*	*Transportation*	*Finance*	*Services*
Ln Real Wage	−0.043***	−0.111***	−0.023	−0.012	0.362***	−0.494***	0.134***	−0195***	−0195***	−0.034
Ln Employment (lag)	0.999***	0.896***	0.499***	0.879***	0.202***	0.787***	0919***	0.812***	0.569***	1.052***
Wald χ^2 *(P-value)*	0.000	0.000	0.000	0.000	0.000	0.000	0.000	0.000	0.000	0.000
Sargan test, *P-value* (H_0: overidentifying restrictions are valid)	0.989	0.987	0.989	0.990	0.992	0.995	0.988	0.995	0.988	0.989
Arellano-Bond test (H_0: no autocorrelation)										
AR(1), *P-value*	0.000	0.156	0.005	0.000	0.000	0.000	0.000	0.001	0.001	0.000
AR(2), *P-value*	0.485	0.964	0.139	0.385	0.177	0.565	0.193	0.061	0.572	0.322
No. of observations	330	330	330	330	330	330	330	330	330	330
No. of group (provinces)	33	33	33	33	33	33	33	33	33	33
No. of instruments used	56	56	56	56	56	56	56	56	56	56

Notes: *** indicates 1 per cent level of significance; each regression has a constant term

Appendix 5.3 Employment functions of manufacturing sector with *endogenous* wage (two-step system GMM, two-step estimator)

	All manufacturing	*Large-medium (LM) firms*
First step (Dep. Var: Ln Real Wage)		
Ln Productivity	0.033	0.243***
Ln Real Wage (lag)	0.108***	0.084***
Wald χ^2 *(P-value)*	0.000	0.000
Sargan *test, P-value*	0.987	0.159
(H_0: overidentifying restrictions are valid)		
Arellano-Bond test		
(H_0: no autocorrelation)		
AR(1), *P-value*	0.007	0.000
AR(2), *P-value*	0.162	0.444
Second step (Dep. Var: Ln Employment)		
Ln Real Wage (predicted)	−3.887***	0.552***
Ln Employment (lag)	0.817***	0.721***
Wald χ^2 *(P-value)*	0.000	0.000
Sargan *test, P-value*	0.9913	0.191
(H_0: overidentifying restrictions are valid)		
Arellano-Bond test		
(H_0: no autocorrelation)		
AR(1), *P-value*	0.0001	0.0003
AR(2), *P-value*	0.455	0.700
No. of observations	330	648
No. of group (provinces/sub-sectors)	33	66
No. of instruments used	56	56

Notes: *** indicates 1 per cent level of significance; each regression has a constant term

Appendix 5.4 Employment functions of manufacturing sector with *exogenous* wage (two-step system GMM, two-step estimator)

	All manufacturing	*Large-medium (LM) firms*
Ln Real Wage	−0.012	0.009***
Ln Employment (lag)	0.879***	0.716***
Wald χ^2 *(P-value)*	0.000	0.000
Sargan test, *P-value*	0.9898	0.210
(H_0: overidentifying restrictions are valid)		
Arellano-Bond test		
(H_0: no autocorrelation)		
AR(1), *P-value*	0.0002	0.035
AR(2), *P-value*	0.385	0.551
No. of observations	330	648
No. of group (provinces/sub-sectors)	33	66
No. of instruments used	56	56

Notes: *** indicates 1 per cent level of significance; each regression has a constant term

References

Amiti, M. and D. Davis 2011. "Trade, firms, and wages: Theory and evidence." *Review of Economic Studies* 79(1): 1–36.

Amiti, M. and J. Konings 2007. "Trade liberalization, intermediate inputs, and productivity: Evidence from Indonesia." *American Economic Review* 97(5): 1611–38.

Arai, M. 2003. "Wages, profits, and capital intensity: Evidence from matched worker-firm data." *Journal of Labor Economics* 21(3): 593–618.

Arellano, T. and O. Bover 1995. "Another look at the instrumental variables estimation of error components models." *Journal of Econometrics* 68: 29–51.

Arellano, T. and S. Bond 1991. "Some tests of specification for panel data: Monte Carlo evidence and an application to employment equations." *Review of Economic Studies* 58(2): 277–97.

Ariff, M. and H. Hill 1985. *Export-oriented industrialisation: The ASEAN experience.* Sydney: Allen and Unwin.

Bagger, J., B.J. Christensen and D.T. Mortensen 2014. *Wage and labor productivity dispersion: The roles of total factor productivity, labor quality, capital intensity and rent sharing.* Mimeo, Royal Holloway.

Barbera, F. and K. Moores 2011. "The impact of family involvement on the productivity of the firm." *Working Paper.* Grand Valley State University. Available at: http://www.fambiz.org.au/wp-content/uploads/Impact-of-Family-Involvement-on-Productivity-Francesco-Barbera.pdf. Accessed on 22 February 2017.

Bhattacharya, M., P.K. Narayan, S. Popp and B.N. Rath 2011. "The productivity-wage and productivity-employment nexus: A panel data analysis of Indian manufacturing." *Empirical Economics* 40(2): 285–303.

Blanchard, O. and L.F. Katz 1999. "Wage dynamics: Reconciling theory and evidence." *American Economic Review* 89(2): 69–74.

Blundell, R. and S. Bond 1998. "Initial conditions and moment restrictions in dynamic panel data models." *Journal of Econometrics* 87: 115–43.

Cameron, A.C. and P.K. Trivedi 2010. *Microeconometrics using Stata.* Stata Press.

Chu, W. 2009. "The influence of family ownership on SME performance: Evidence from public firms in Taiwan." *Small Business Economics* 33(3): 353–73.

Fu, D., Y. Wu and Y. Tang 2010. "The effects of ownership structure and industry characteristics on export performance: Evidence from Chinese manufacturing firms." *Discussion Paper* 10/09. University of Western Australia – Business School.

Galindo-Rueda, F. and J. Haskel 2005. "Skills, workforce characteristics and firm-level productivity: Evidence from the matched ABI/employer skills survey." *IZA Discussion Paper* No. 1542. Bonn: IZA.

Goh, S.K and K.N. Wong 2010. "Analyzing the productivity-wage-unemployment nexus in Malaysia: Evidence from the macroeconomic perspective." *Discussion Paper* 12/10. Monash University.

Hellerstein, J.K., D. Neumar and K. Troske 1999. "Wages, productivity and worker characteristics: Evidence from plant-level production functions and wage equations." *Journal of Labour Economics* 17(3): 409–46.

Hijzen, A. P. Martins, T. Schank and R. Upward 2013. "Foreign-owned firms around the world: A comparative analysis of wages and employment at the micro-level." *European Economic Review* 60(C): 170–88.

ILO 2015. *World Employment and Social Outlook 2015: 'The changing nature of jobs'*. Geneva: International Labour Organization.

Islam, I. and S. Nazara 2000. *Estimating employment elasticity for the Indonesian economy.* Jakarta: *International Labor Organization.*

Klein, N. 2012. "Real wage, labour productivity, and employment trends in South Africa: A closer look." *IMF Working Paper* 12/92. Washington, DC: International Monetary Fund.

Lebedinski, L. and V. Vandenberghe 2014. "Assessing education's contribution to productivity using firm-level evidence." *International Journal of Manpower* 35(8): 1116–39.

Lim, D. 1997. "Forecasting employment growth in Indonesia." *Bulletin of Indonesian Economic Studies* 33(3): 111–19.

London Economics 2008. "Study on the impact of co-operative groups on the competitiveness of their craft and small enterprise members." *Final Report to European Commission DG Enterprise and Industry.* Available at: http://www.pedz.uni-mannheim.de/daten/edz-h/gdb/08/study_impact_cooperative_groups_final_report_jan_2008_3406.pdf. Accessed on 22 February 2017.

Martins, P. 2011. "Paying more to hire the best? Foreign firms, wages and worker mobility." *Economic Inquiry* 49(2): 349–63.

Mourougane, A. 2012. "Promoting SME development in Indonesia." *OECD Economic Department Working Papers* (995): 0_1.

Narjoko, D. and C.T. Putra 2015. "Industrialization, globalization and labour market regime in Indonesia." *Journal of the Asia Pacific Economy* 20(1): 57–76.

Nunes, P. M., M. Goncalves and Z. Serrasqueiro 2013. "The influence of age on SMEs' growth determinants: Empirical evidence." *Small Business Economics* 40(2): 249–272.

Pangestu, M. and M. Hendytio 1997. "Survey responses from women workers in Indonesia's textile, garment, and footwear industries." *World Bank Policy Research Working Paper* No. 1755.

Patel, S.H. 2005. *Business age and characteristics of SME performance.* Kingston Business School, Kingston University.

Ramstetter, E.D., and S. Takii 2006. "Exporting and foreign ownership in Indonesian manufacturing 1990–2000." *Economics and Finance in Indonesia* 54(3): 317–45.

Rand, J. and N. Torm 2012. "The benefits of formalization: Evidence from Vietnamese manufacturing SMEs." *World Development* 40(5): 983–98.

Roodman, D. 2009. "How to do xtabond2: An introduction to difference and system GMM in Stata." *The Stata Journal* 9(1): 86–136.

Smith, R. and L. Hendrickson 2016. *The effect of age on Australian small-to-medium enterprises. Research Paper* 1/2016. Available at: https://industry.gov.au/Office-of-the-Chief-Economist/Research-Papers/Documents/The-effect-of-age-on-Australian-Small-to-Medium-Enterprises.pdf. Accessed on 22 February 2017.

Suryadarma, D., A. Suryahadi and S. Sumarto 2007. "Reducing unemployment in Indonesia: Results from a growth-employment elasticity model." *SMERU Working Paper*, January.

Tadjoeddin, M.Z. and A. Chowdhury 2012. "Employment function for Indonesia: An econometric analysis at the sectoral level." *Journal of Developing Areas* 46(1): 265–85.

van Ours, J.C. and L. Stoeldraijer 2010. "Age, wage and productivity." *IZA Discussion Paper* No. 4765. Bonn: IZA.

Villa, A. and G. Bruno 2013. "Promoting SME cooperative aggregations: Main criteria and contractual models." *International Journal of Production Research* 51(23–24): 7439–7447.

Wooldridge, J.M. 2002. *Econometric analysis of cross section and panel data*. MIT Press.

World Bank 2012. *Picking up the pace: Reviving growth in Indonesia's manufacturing sector*. Jakarta: World Bank.

Zhang, J. and X. Liu 2013. "The evolving pattern of the wage–labor productivity nexus in China: Evidence from manufacturing firm-level data." *Economic Systems* 37(3): 354–68.

CHAPTER 6

Inequality, Employment and Manufacturing: Spatial Dimensions

6.1 Introduction

Having analysed broad trends in employment, wages and productivity at the national level, especially in the manufacturing sector, in the previous chapters, this chapter examines their variations at the provincial level.[1] It also contains results of an empirical exercise relating formal employment, real wage, productivity and human development at the regional level. Finally, the chapter provides a snapshot of regional diversity of Indonesia's manufacturing sector. It begins with a short discussion of the context and an overview of spatial inequalities in Indonesia. This chapter emphasises the importance of regional dimensions in such a large and diverse country in policymaking related to employment and re-industrialisation.

6.2 Indonesia's Spatial Inequality in Perspectives

As mentioned earlier, income inequality in Indonesia has been on the rise since the Asian financial crisis (AFC). During the first decade of the new millennium, the Gini index of household expenditure inequality increased by 32 per cent reaching a record high of 0.41, and the figure stays there

[1] The chapter uses provincial and regional interchangeably.

M. Z. Tadjoeddin, A. Chowdhury, *Employment and Re-Industrialisation in Post Soeharto Indonesia*, Critical Studies of the Asia-Pacific, https://doi.org/10.1057/978-1-137-50566-8_6

until recently. According to the Palma index, the expenditure inequality has increased by 66 per cent (Yusuf 2014).[2]

The rise in inequality is consistently found in all Indonesian provinces; however, the rates of increased inequality vary considerably. The province of Gorontalo in Sulawesi has the highest incremental increase in the Gini index. In 2000, among the 33 Indonesian provinces, Gorontalo had the lowest Gini index of 0.209; in 2015, it increased to 0.421 making it the sixth most "unequal" province in the country. East Kalimantan Province experienced the least incremental increase in the Gini index, from 0.307 in 2000 to 0.314 in 2015, representing a mere 2.2 per cent increase. However, there is no clear pattern, such as provinces with a lower Gini index value recording larger increases in inequality. For example, in 2015, North Maluku Province had the lowest Gini index of 0.280, increased from 0.236 in 2000, when the province's Gini index was the second lowest.

The overall expenditure inequality figure can be decomposed into two components of inequality: within provinces and between provinces. According to the decomposable Theil index measure of inequality, the overall inequality of household expenditure in Indonesia during 2000–2015 was largely contributed by within-province inequalities, and the share of within-province inequalities was on the rise (Figs. 6.1a and 6.1b). This means that the overall rise in inequality is due to the rise in within-province inequalities.

A further look at inter-provincial variation of the Gini index during the period reveals that several provinces seem to have driven the national inequality picture. In 2015, eight provinces recorded Gini index values higher than the overall expenditure Gini of Indonesia (Fig. 6.2). Four out of the eight provinces are located on the Java Island (Jakarta, West Java, Yogyakarta and East Java). Two of them (West Java and East Java), in fact, had Gini index values lower than national average back in 2000, which means that the rise in inequality in the two most populous provinces in the country has been remarkable during 2000–2015 (increased by more than 50 per cent). The other two Javanese provinces (Jakarta and Yogyakarta) have been consistently experiencing higher level of inequality than national average during the period.

[2] Palma (2011) index is the ratio of the income share of the richest 10 per cent of the population to the income share of the poorest 40 per cent of the population. The Palma index has been assessed to be more relevant for policymaking as it is concerned with the particular income segments where inequality is actually located (Cobham and Sumner 2013).

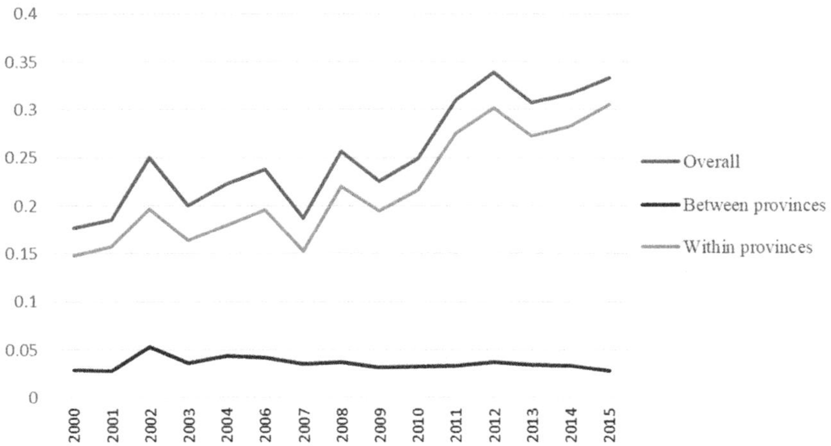

Fig. 6.1a Theil (T) index of expenditure inequality, 2000–2015. (Source: Calculated from BPS data)

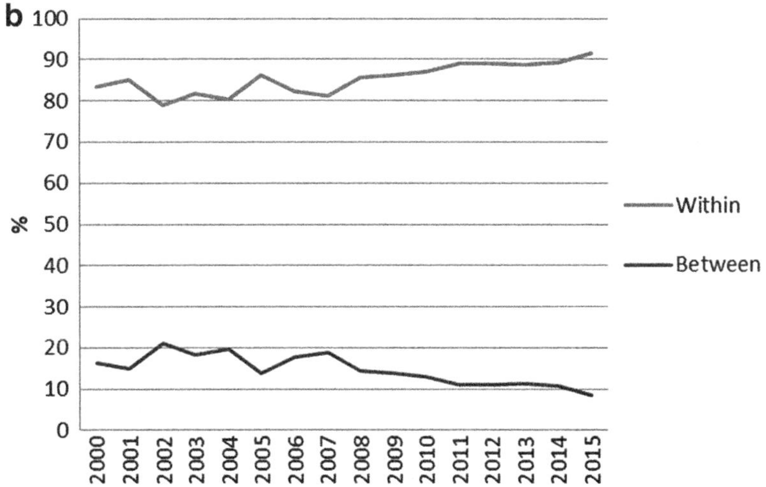

Fig. 6.1b Share of *within-* and *between*-provinces inequalities, 2000–2015. (Source: Calculated from BPS data)

Fig. 6.2 Gini index of eight provinces with Gini index higher than national average in 2015. (Source: Calculated from BPS data)

Furthermore, the magnitude of increase in the Gini index during 2000–2015 was larger in five of these eight provinces than at the national level (Table 6.1). Three of these five provinces are on the Java Island (West Java, East Java and Yogyakarta), while the other two are South Sulawesi and Gorontalo. Among these five provinces, West Java and East Java are the most important ones, being the most populous provinces in the country with 47 million and 39 million inhabitants respectively. These two provinces account for a little over one-third of the country's population. They are also among the most industrialised provinces in Indonesia. Labour productivities in these two provinces are about twice the national average with labour productivity growth slightly higher than national average. South Sulawesi is the most populous province and a growth centre in Eastern Indonesia. Gorontalo, a newly created province after the democratic transition in 1999, moved from a province with the lowest Gini index in 2000 to one of the highest in 2015 and recorded the highest incremental increase in the Gini index during the period (100.8 per cent).

The two provinces on the Island of Papua (Papua and West Papua) consistently appear on the list of provinces with higher level of income

Table 6.1 The eight provinces driving national inequality

Provinces	*Gini index*		*Change in Gini index*	*Labour productivity*	*Productivity growth*
	2000	*2015*	*2000–2015 (%)*	*2015 (IDR Mil, 2000 prices)*	*2000–2015 (% annual)*
91. West Papua	0.356	0.440	23.6	31.2	8.9
34. Yogyakarta	0.315	0.433	37.2	14.2	5.1
31. Jakarta	0.349	0.431	23.4	113.1	4.7
73. South Sulawesi	0.277	0.424	53.1	21.4	8.3
94. Papua	0.368	0.421	14.7	15.9	−2.1
75. Gorontalo	0.209	0.420	100.8	8.4	5.8
35. East Java	0.274	0.415	51.9	23.8	6.6
32. West Java	0.276	0.415	50.0	22.8	6.5
Indonesia	0.303	0.410	35.1	10.4	6.4

Source: Calculated from BPS data

inequality. This may be due to the mining enclave and socio-economic gaps between coastal and inland areas as well as between migrant and indigenous populations.

From a regional perspective, the above disaggregation indicates that the Island of Java is the area to focus on when identifying the source of the recent rise in inequality in Indonesia, especially the provinces of West Java and East Java. However, identifying the dynamics of various factors driving within-province inequality needs much more rigorous studies. For example, one needs to understand why two highly industrialised provinces, East Java and West Java, with higher than the national average labour productivity growth experienced larger increase in inequality, the factors behind the rapid rise in inequality in the growth centre, South Sulawesi, and consistently high inequality in Papua.

To see whether initial conditions of such factors as industrialisation, mining and human development have any influence on inequality, we present (Figs. 6.3a, 6.3b and 6.3c) correlations of their levels in 2000 with the incremental increase in the Gini index across provinces. The share of manufacturing in 2000 is negatively correlated with the increase in the Gini index (Fig. 6.3a). This indicates that the effort to re-industrialise should be inequality reducing. The share of mining in 2000 is also

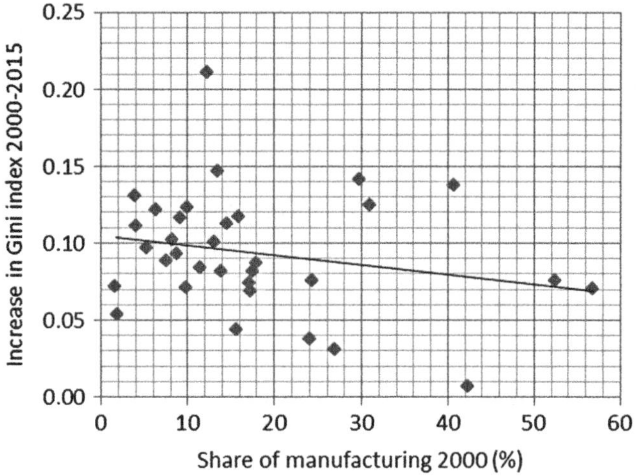

Fig. 6.3a Share of manufacturing (2000) and increase in Gini index (2000–2015). (Source: Calculated from BPS data)

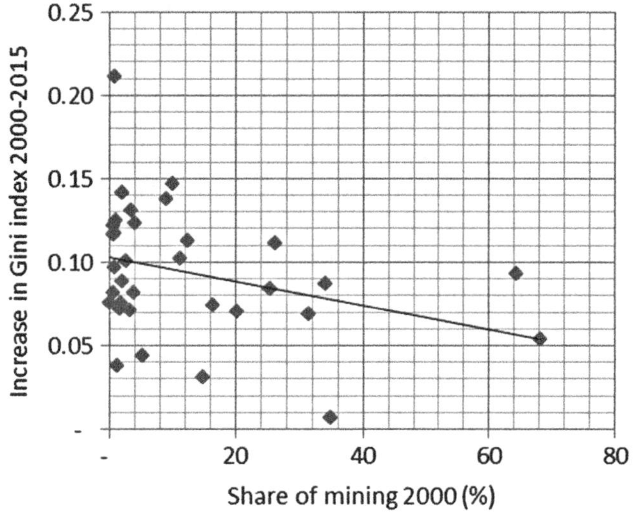

Fig. 6.3b Share of mining (2000) and increase in Gini index (2000–2015). (Source: Calculated from BPS data)

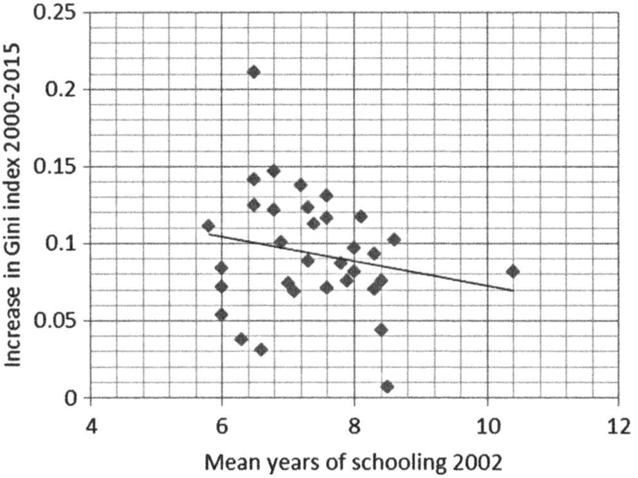

Fig. 6.3c Mean years of schooling (2002) and increase in Gini index (2000–2015). (Source: Calculated from BPS data)

negatively correlated with the increase in the Gini index (Fig. 6.3b). This, of course, does not negate the widely held view that the mining boom during 2004–2010 has contributed to the rise in inequality, which requires much more rigorous studies for validation. However, it does indicate that policies governing mining operations (licensing, ownership, industrial relations, etc.) must have played a greater role in causing inequality than the presence of a resource or mining sector per se. Finally, the negative correlation between the level of schooling in 2000 and the increase in the Gini index (Fig. 6.3c) implies that continuous improvement in human capital investment is good for tackling inequality.

Box 6.1 Studies on Indonesia's Spatial Inequality

Concern about spatial inequality or inequality across subnational entities in Indonesia was initially dominated by analyses of inter-regional variations of per capita regional gross domestic product (regional GDP [RGDP]). The variations were primarily generated by differences in the natural resource endowments across regions, particularly in the four resource-rich regions—Aceh, Riau, East

(*continued*)

Box 6.1 (continued)

Kalimantan and Papua. This kind of analysis was made possible due to the availability of national and regional income accounts since the mid-1970s. In this regard, Esmara's (1975) study is pioneering. The subsequent major studies of regional inequality in Indonesia have been undertaken by Uppal and Handoko (1986), Akita (1988), Akita and Lukman (1995) and Garcia and Soelistianingsih (1998). These studies have found considerably high degrees of spatial inequality with respect to per capita RGDP, primarily due to significant differences in resource endowments across provinces. Tadjoeddin et al. (2001) conducted across-district spatial inequality analysis (instead of across provinces) and found that the spatial inequality of per capita RGDP reduced by around 60 per cent if oil and gas incomes and the 13 richest districts were excluded.[3]

Inter-provincial inequality of per capita RGDP increased sharply in the early years of the New Order development (1968–1972), but it was relatively stable between the 1970s and mid-1980s (Esmara 1975; Akita 1988). Despite uneven resource endowments across provinces affecting regional productive capacity, regional convergence of per capita RGDP across provinces was evident in longer-term analyses covering the period between the 1970s and mid-1990s (Garcia and Soelistianingsih 1998; Hill 2000; Tadjoeddin 2011). Hill (2000: 235) notes "there is no case of a high-income province growing much faster than the national average, or conversely of a poor province falling sharply behind." The regional income convergence continues after the late 1990s' democratisation and decentralisation, but at a much slower speed, termed as weak convergence (Vidyattama 2013; Hill and Vidyattama 2014).

In addition to per capita RGDP, studies also looked at per capita household expenditure based on the Susenas. These studies, following Hughes and Islam (1981), Islam and Khan (1986), and Akita and Lukman (1999), indicate that the magnitude of regional expenditure inequality was much lower than per capita RGDP inequality.

(*continued*)

[3] The calculation is based on weighted coefficient of variation (CV). After oil and gas incomes were excluded, the study also excluded the 13 richest enclave districts, which are financial, manufacturing and trade centres.

Box 6.1 (continued)

Systematic comparisons of inter-district regional variations in per capita RGDP, as a measure of *regional prosperity*, and a series of indicators representing the degree of *community welfare* (e.g., health, education, purchasing power and the overall Human Development Index [HDI]), were conducted by Tadjoeddin et al. (2001), who found that regional disparities with respect to measures of community welfare were much lower than the relatively high degree of inequality with respect to per capita RGDP. This seems to be an outcome of the New Order regime's equalisation policy.

6.3 Spatial Inequalities of Employment Outcomes

This section presents the trends in selected indicators of employment quantity and quality disaggregated at the provincial level. It also presents the magnitudes and trends associated with the inter-provincial variations of key indicators, which include (i) unemployment rate, (2) formal employment and (3) vulnerable employment. Such exploration on spatial inequalities of employment outcome is probably among the early attempts.

6.3.1 Unemployment Rate

Unemployment rates across Indonesian provinces vary considerably as presented in Table 6.2. In the table, provinces with unemployment rates and per capita RGDP higher than the respective national figures are shown in grey shade. It reveals that provinces with per capita RGDP higher than the national figure tend to also have higher unemployment rates. This is confirmed by Fig. 6.4 showing a positive correlation between the unemployment rate and per capita RGDP.

There could be a number of plausible factors behind this association. First, this may be due to internal migration dynamics *a la* the Harris-Todaro model. That is, the high RGDP or more economic activities are acting as a pull factor to draw in people from depressed outer regions, thus swelling the ranks of unemployed. Second, this could also be due to higher labour force participation rate encouraged by more economic activities. Third, this could reflect "jobless" growth, that is, the failure of the growth process to generate sufficient number of jobs, which in turn may imply greater capital intensity of the growth process.

Table 6.2 Unemployment rates and RGDP per capita across provinces

Province	*Unemployment rate (%)*			*RGDP per capita (current prices, IDR million, 2016)*
	2001	*2010*	*2016*	
11. Aceh	7.7	8.4	7.6	26.9
12. North Sumatera	9.1	7.4	5.8	44.6
13. West Sumatera	8.7	7.0	5.1	37.2
14. Riau	6.1	8.7	*7.4*	*105.0*
15. Jambi	5.6	5.4	4.0	49.6
16. South Sumatera	6.3	6.7	4.3	43.6
17. Bengkulu	6.0	4.6	3.3	29.1
18. Lampung	6.4	5.6	4.6	34.3
19. Bangka Belitung	7.1	5.6	2.6	46.5
21. Riau Islands	7.4	6.9	*7.7*	*106.8*
31. Jakarta	15.1	11.1	*6.1*	*211.8*
32. West Java	11.8	10.3	89	34.9
33. Central Java	6.2	6.2	4.6	32.1
34. Yogyakarta	5.2	5.7	2.7	29.6
35. East Java	6.5	4.2	4.2	47.5
36. Banten	12.3	13.7	8.9	42.3
51. Bali	2.9	3.1	1.9	46.5
52. West Nusa Tenggara	5.8	5.3	3.9	23.7
53. East Nusa Tenggara	4.3	3.3	3.3	16.2
61. West Kalimantan	4.8	4.6	4.2	33.2
62. Central Kalimantan	6.1	4.1	4.8	44.1
63. South Kalimantan	5.9	5.3	5.5	36.1
64. East Kalimantan	6.8	10.1	*7.6*	*137.8*
71. North Sulawesi	10.2	9.6	6.2	41.3
72. Central Sulawesi	8.2	4.6	3.3	41.2
73. South Sulawesi	11.1	8.4	4.8	44.1
74. Southeast Sulawesi	7.5	4.6	2.7	38.0
75. Gorontalo	7.8	5.2	2.8	27.7
76. West Sulawesi	5.5	3.3	3.3	27.5
81. Maluku	11.3	10.0	7.0	21.6
82. North Maluku	9.3	6.0	4.0	24.6
91. West Papua	6.1	7.7	*7.5*	*74.6*
94. Papua	5.7	3.6	3.3	55.6
Indonesia	8.1	7.1	5.6	48.0

Source: Calculated from BPS data

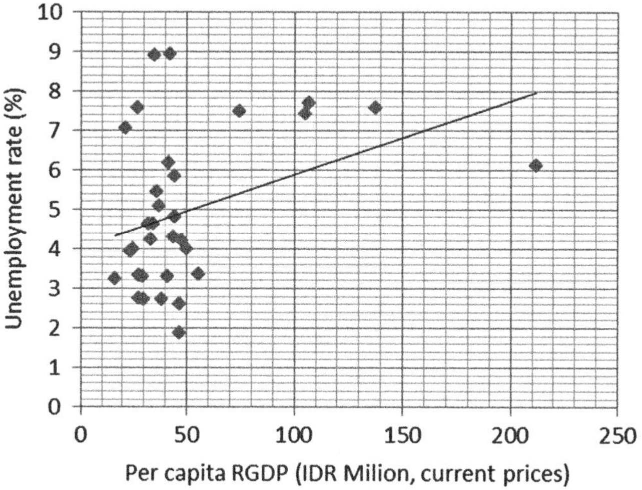

Fig. 6.4 Unemployment rates (2016) and per capita RGDP (2015) across provinces. (Source: Calculated from BPS data)

Out of the total 33 provinces in Indonesia, 12 provinces still recorded unemployment rates in 2016 higher than the pre-AFC level of national unemployment rate. On average, their unemployment rates were 1.8 percentage points higher than the pre-crisis level. The relatively high degree of inter-provincial variation of unemployment rates is detailed in Table 6.3. The inter-provincial variation, measured by simple coefficient of variation (CV), is used to gauge the degree of inter-provincial (regional/spatial) inequality or disparity. The CV is defined as the ratio of the standard deviation to the mean.[4] It measures how far the unemployment rates of individual provinces on average deviate in a relative term from the national unemployment rate. Regional disparity in terms of inter-provincial variation of unemployment rates remained more or less stable, except rising in 2011. This may reflect the lagged effect of the global financial crisis (GFC) which affected the provinces differently depending on their direct and indirect external exposer.

[4] Coefficient of variation (CV) has been widely used to measure spatial inequality, popularised by Williamson (1965).

Table 6.3 Open unemployment rate and regional variation, 1996–2016

	1996	*2001*	*2002*	*2003*	*2004*	*2005*	*2006*	*2007*	*2008*	*2009*	*2010*	*2011*	*2012*	*2013*	*2014*	*2015*	*2016*
Total																	
Unemployment (%)	5.4	8.1	9.1	9.7	9.9	11.2	10.3	9.1	8.4	7.9	7.1	6.6	6.1	6.2	5.9	6.2	5.6
CV (inter-provincial)	0.37	0.32	0.34	0.32	0.36	0.31	0.31	0.33	0.33	0.34	0.36	0.41	0.36	0.36	0.35	0.32	0.35
Male																	
Unemployment (%)	4.6	6.6	7.5	7.9	8.1	9.3	8.5	8.1	7.6	7.5	6.1	5.9	5.8	6.1	5.7	6.1	5.7
CV (inter-provincial)	0.32	0.36	0.35	0.32	0.31	0.31	0.31	0.34	0.34	0.34	0.34	0.44	0.38	0.35	0.33	0.29	0.35
Female																	
Unemployment (%)	6.9	10.5	11.8	12.7	12.9	14.7	13.4	10.8	9.7	8.5	8.7	7.6	6.8	6.5	6.3	6.4	5.5
CV (inter-provincial)	0.52	0.49	0.47	0.46	0.53	0.47	0.45	0.45	0.40	0.44	0.49	0.44	0.38	0.44	0.44	0.44	0.40
Female/male ratio of unemployment rate	1.50	1.60	1.57	1.61	1.59	1.58	1.57	1.33	1.28	1.13	1.42	1.29	1.18	1.07	1.09	1.05	0.96

Source: Calculated from Sakernas

Regional disparity in terms of inter-provincial variation of female unemployment rates is much higher than that of male. But the inter-provincial variation of unemployment rates for both male and total worsened, especially during 2005–2011 when the overall unemployment rate started to decline. On a positive note, the gender gap of unemployment rates has consistently improved since 2001, reaching parity in recent years from 60 per cent in 2001.

The worst unemployment situation is in Banten (Fig. 6.5), which is a highly industrialised province. Likewise, Jakarta, the most industrialised province, has a higher rate of unemployment. In both Jakarta and Banten, the unemployment rates are above the national average. On the other hand, poor provinces, such as North Maluku Utara and East Nusa Tenggara (NTT) with insignificant industrial activities, have unemployment rates below the national level. As in the case of association between RGDP and unemployment rates, this can also be explained by the internal migration dynamics. Comparative cases of Banten and NTT presented in Chap. 2 have illuminated this point. This may also reflect increased capital intensity of manufacturing causing "jobless" growth.

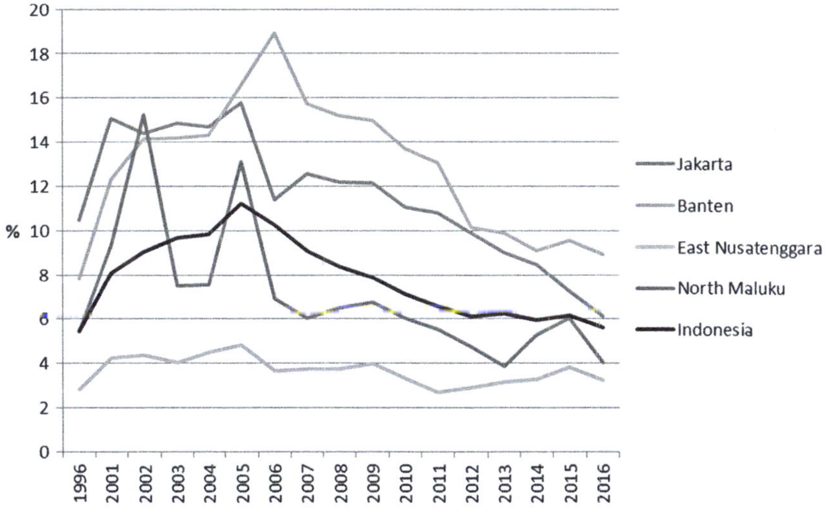

Fig. 6.5 Unemployment rate in selected provinces (%), 1996–2016. (Source: Calculated from Sakernas)

As emphasised in Chap. 2, reducing unemployment is different from improving the quality of employment. For example, it is meaningless to talk about unemployment reduction in Indonesia's poorest province of NTT, where the open unemployment rate was 2.7 per cent, but with only 20 per cent of labour force in formal employment. Lowering the unemployment rate in the province of NTT would not be a meaningful indicator of greater economic welfare; it is the improvement in the quality of employment that would eventually reduce poverty.

6.3.2 Formal (Regular) Employment[5]

For the quality of employment, the most important indicator is likely the size of formal employment, which is akin to regular employment, discussed in Chap. 2. At the same time, we can also look at the size of informal or vulnerable employment.

The definition of formal employment is based on the status of respondent's main job in the national labour force survey (Sakernas). As mentioned in Chap. 2, since 2001 Sakernas has recorded seven employment statuses.[6] Table 6.4 provides the breakdown of employment by status. The category of formal employment used in this chapter consists of the following two employment status: employers assisted by permanent employees and regular wage employment (statuses 3 and 4 respectively). It has to be noted that this definition follows the traditional definition of formal-informal employment in Indonesia, which is solely based on employment status. A wider definition of formal-informal employment is based on a combination of two indicators, status of employment and types

[5] In Chap. 2 we call it regular employment. However, the term "formal employment" resonates better in the Indonesian context.

[6] See Sect. 2.2.1. Prior to 2001, only five employment statuses were listed, excluding casual employee as in status numbers 5 and 6. BPS defines regular employee as a person who work permanently for other people or institution/office/company and gains money/cash or goods as wage/salary. A labourer without permanent employer is not categorised as a regular employee but casual worker. A labourer is considered to have a permanent employer if he/she is employed by the same employer during the past one month, with an exception of three months for a labourer in the construction sector. If the employer is an institution, more than one employer is allowed.

Table 6.4 Employment status (%), 2001–2016

No	*Employment Status*	*2001*	*2002*	*2003*	*2004*	*2005*	*2006*	*2007*	*2008*	*2009*	*2010*	*2011*	*2012*	*2013*	*2014*	*2016*
1	Own account worker	19.2	19.2	18.2	19.5	18.4	20.4	20.3	20.4	20.1	19.4	17.7	16.6	16.9	17.9	16.9
2	Employer assisted by temporary/unpaid workers	22.4	24.0	24.1	23.0	22.3	20.9	21.0	21.2	20.9	20.0	17.9	16.9	16.8	16.8	16.4
3	Employer assisted by permanent worker/ paid worker	3.1	3.0	2.9	3.2	3.0	3.0	2.9	2.9	2.9	3.0	3.4	3.5	3.4	3.6	3.7
4	Regular wage employee	29.3	27.3	26.0	27.2	27.7	28.1	28.1	27.5	27.8	30.1	34.4	36.4	37.0	37.0	38.7
5	Casual employee in agriculture	4.0	4.9	5.0	4.8	5.9	5.8	5.9	5.8	5.6	5.4	5.0	4.8	4.6	4.4	4.6
6	Casual employee not in agriculture	2.7	3.9	3.5	4.0	4.6	4.8	4.5	5.2	5.4	4.7	5.1	5.6	5.4	5.6	5.9
7	Unpaid family worker	19.4	17.6	20.3	18.5	18.0	16.9	17.3	16.9	17.4	17.3	16.4	16.2	15.9	14.7	13.7
	Total	100	100	100	100	100	100	100	100	100	100	100	100	100	100	100
	Formal employment (3 + 4)	32.3	30.4	28.9	30.3	30.7	31.1	31.0	30.4	30.7	33.1	37.8	39.9	40.4	40.6	42.4
	Informal employment (1 + 2 + 5 + 6 + 7)	67.7	69.6	71.1	69.7	69.3	68.9	69.1	69.6	69.4	66.9	62.2	60.1	59.6	59.4	57.6
	Vulnerable employment (1 + 7)	38.6	36.8	38.5	38.0	36.4	37.3	37.6	37.3	37.5	36.7	34.1	32.8	32.8	32.6	30.6

Source: Calculated from Sakernas

of employment.[7] Using the wider definition, we get a slightly higher share of formal employment than in the case of traditional definition; however, both definitions show similar trends over time.[8] The traditional definition is deliberately used in this study to enable us to compare with the situation prior to the 1997–1998 AFC.

Across provincial variation of formal employment (as a percentage of total employment) can be seen from Table 6.5. Few provinces have their rates of formal employment higher than the national level. They are provinces in the most industrialised and developed Island of Java and few outer Island provinces which are also highly industrialised such as Riau, Riau Islands and East Kalimantan. The seemingly positive association between the size of formal employment and the share of manufacturing in the provincial economy is confirmed by the scatter plot in Fig. 6.6. This finding has a clear implication; that is, Indonesia has to industrialise to improve quality of employment, proxied by formal employment.

In addition to the overall magnitude of formal employment at the national level, Table 6.6 also shows the trend of inter-provincial disparity of formal employment. During the first half of the 2000s, variation of formal employment across provinces, measured by CV, was much higher than the pre-crisis figure in 1996. In fact, the variation was on the rise. It declined during the second half of the decade reaching the pre-crisis level of the regional variation in 2011 and has continued to decline since then. The overall gender gap with respect to formal employment has also been continuously declining. The gender gap of formal employment in 2016 was much smaller than in 1996. However, the regional variation of the female formal employment rate remains nearly twice the figure for the male counterpart.

6.3.3 Vulnerable Employment

Notwithstanding the relatively high prevalence of vulnerable employment as reported in Chap. 2, inter-provincial disparity of vulnerable employment

[7] Types of employment includes (1) professional, technical and related worker; (2) administrative and managerial workers; (3) clerical and related workers; (4) sales workers; (5) services workers; (6) agriculture, animal husbandry, forestry workers, fishermen and hunters; and (7) production and related workers, transport equipment operators and labourers.

[8] See Nazara (2010) for details.

Table 6.5 Formal employment across provinces, 2001, 2010 and 2016

Province	*Formal employment (%)*		
	2001	*2010*	*2016*
11. Aceh	24.7	35.9	42.8
12. North Sumatera	33.8	31.5	40.0
13. West Sumatera	30.6	30.6	38.2
14. Riau	30.5	42.8	46.4
15. Jambi	28.0	35.2	37.9
16. South Sumatera	19.8	26.9	39.3
17. Bengkulu	18.4	24.9	34.1
18. Lampung	18.9	23.5	29.9
19. Bangka Belitung	29.6	41.0	44.4
21. Riau Islands	48.2	64.9	66.2
31. Jakarta	77.2	62.1	68.7
32. West Java	38.7	37.3	51.4
33. Central Java	30.0	28.5	37.9
34. Yogyakarta	35.3	34.5	45.1
35. East Java	31.1	29.1	37.9
36. Banten	45.7	46.5	61.5
51. Bali	38.9	35.8	45.7
52. West Nusa Tenggara	19.5	18.9	26.9
53. East Nusa Tenggara	12.1	17.2	25.2
61. West Kalimantan	23.8	27.5	38.2
62. Central Kalimantan	21.6	33.2	41.4
63. South Kalimantan	25.7	32.2	37.8
64. East Kalimantan	49.0	50.2	55.5
71. North Sulawesi	39.2	40.4	38.7
72. Central Sulawesi	20.8	25.4	33.5
73. South Sulawesi	25.1	29.2	35.1
74. Southeast Sulawesi	17.1	27.9	31.5
75. Gorontalo	27.6	28.7	39.7
76. West Sulawesi	15.1	19.9	29.9
81. Maluku	20.7	29.0	35.8
82. North Maluku	35.7	28.0	36.0
91. West Papua	26.7	32.6	40.6
94. Papua	13.2	14.9	21.6
Indonesia	32.3	33.1	42.4

Source: Calculated from BPS data

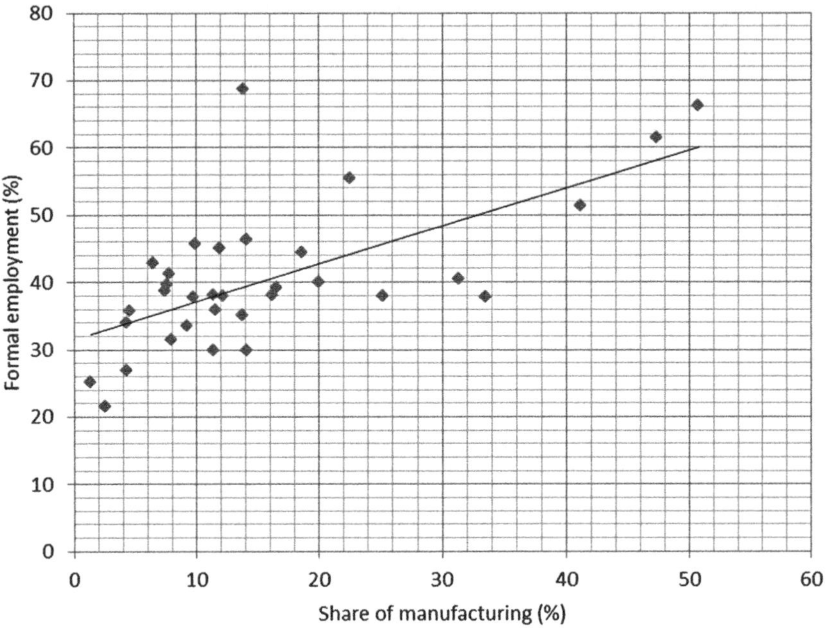

Fig. 6.6 Formal employment (2016) and share of manufacturing (2015). (Source: Calculated from BPS data)

was relatively low and showed a declining trend (Table 6.7). But the prevalence of vulnerable employment among female is nearly twice as that of male, and the gender gap shows an increasing trend.

Table 6.8 presents detailed variations of the prevalence of vulnerable employment across Indonesian provinces. It is clear that the rates of vulnerable employment are lowest among provinces in Java, the most developed Island in the country. On the other hand, the rates of vulnerable employment are generally higher than the national figure of vulnerable employment in outer Island provinces. As can be seen from Fig. 6.7, vulnerable unemployment is high in poorer provinces with low per capita RGDP. Without implying any causality, this observation can be interpreted in two ways. That is, poorer provinces are unable to generate sufficient number of decent jobs, and at the same time, vulnerable employment involves low-productivity activities resulting in low per capita RGDP. Thus, there is a vicious circle of vulnerable employment-low productivity-low per capita RGDP. On the other hand, high-productivity decent jobs create a virtuous circle resulting in high per capita RGDP.

Table 6.6 Formal employment: magnitude at the national level (per cent of total employment), regional variation and gender gap, 1996–2016

	1996	*2001*	*2002*	*2003*	*2004*	*2005*	*2006*	*2007*	*2008*	*2009*	*2010*	*2011*	*2012*	*2013*	*2014*	*2015*	*2016*
Total																	
Formal employment (%)	35.7	32.3	30.4	28.9	30.3	30.7	31.1	30.9	30.4	30.7	33.1	37.8	39.9	40.4	40.6	42.2	42.4
CV (inter-provincial)	0.32	0.40	0.41	0.46	0.42	0.46	0.41	0.37	0.36	0.35	0.34	0.32	00.31	00.31	00.30	00.30	00.25
Male																	
Formal employment (%)	40.3	36.1	33.5	31.9	33.4	32.8	32.9	33.7	32.8	32.5	35.2	40.3	42.8	43.4	43.5	44.9	45.1
CV (inter-provincial)	0.28	0.35	0.37	0.38	0.36	0.42	0.36	0.32	0.32	0.31	0.30	0.30	0.29	0.29	0.28	0.28	0.24
Female																	
Formal employment (%)	28.3	25.9	24.7	23.6	24.7	26.8	27.7	26.2	26.5	27.7	29.6	33.9	35.1	35.3	35.9	37.8	38.2
CV (inter-provincial)	0.43	0.53	0.54	0.69	0.59	0.58	0.53	0.49	0.45	0.43	0.42	0.37	00.36	00.35	00.33	00.34	00.30
Male/female ratio of formal employment	1.43	1.40	1.36	1.35	1.35	1.23	1.19	1.29	1.24	1.17	1.19	1.19	1.22	1.23	1.21	1.19	1.18

Source: Calculated from Sakernas

Table 6.7 Vulnerable employment (per cent of total employment) and its regional variation (CV), 1996–2016

	1996	*2001*	*2002*	*2003*	*2004*	*2005*	*2006*	*2007*	*2008*	*2009*	*2010*	*2011*	*2012*	*2013*	*2014*	*2015*	*2016*
Total																	
Vulnerable employment (%)	39.4	38.6	37.5	38.5	38.0	36.4	37.4	37.6	37.3	37.4	36.8	34.1	32.8	32.8	32.5	31.0	30.7
CV (inter-provincial)	0.23	0.24	0.20	0.19	0.18	0.20	0.19	0.16	0.15	0.16	0.17	0.21	0.21	0.22	0.22	0.24	0.19
Male																	
Vulnerable employment (%)	30.9	28.6	27.8	28.5	28.7	27.8	29.5	29.3	29.0	29.3	28.2	25.7	24.2	24.1	24.0	22.5	22.7
CV (inter-provincial)	0.25	0.31	0.28	0.21	0.22	0.25	0.25	0.18	0.16	0.15	0.15	0.20	0.23	0.25	0.24	0.25	0.21
Female																	
Vulnerable employment (%)	53.1	55.6	52.7	56.5	55.0	52.7	51.9	52.0	51.2	50.8	51.0	47.9	47.0	47.2	46.7	45.4	43.3
CV (inter-provincial)	0.26	0.23	0.27	0.26	0.27	0.26	0.23	0.21	0.20	0.22	0.23	0.24	0.24	0.24	0.24	0.25	0.22
Female/male ratio of Vulnerable employment	1.72	1.95	1.89	1.99	1.92	1.89	1.76	1.77	1.77	1.73	1.81	1.87	1.94	1.96	1.94	2.02	1.90

Source: Calculated from Sakernas

Table 6.8 Vulnerable employment by provinces (%), 2000, 2010 and 2016

Province	*2001*	*2010*	*2016*
11. Aceh	58.3	38.3	33.8
12. North Sumatera	39.8	40.9	36.2
13. West Sumatera	42.1	38.2	32.7
14. Riau	38.9	38.4	32.6
15. Jambi	43.1	41.5	37.5
16. South Sumatera	44.4	43.9	36.8
17. Bengkulu	43.0	43.0	37.9
18. Lampung	49.3	40.9	37.7
19. Bangka Belitung	36.4	39.5	36.4
21. Riau Islands	26.0	25.8	24.4
31. Jakarta	23.6	27.1	22.3
32. West Java	34.5	32.2	24.5
33. Central Java	37.3	35.2	29.6
34. Yogyakarta	35.5	32.6	27.9
35. East Java	37.0	36.3	28.4
36. Banten	28.7	31.7	19.9
51. Bali	39.4	34.4	28.2
52. West Nusa Tenggara	39.8	37.5	35.3
53. East Nusa Tenggara	48.1	47.9	41.9
61. West Kalimantan	40.3	43.4	38.5
62. Central Kalimantan	43.6	41.5	36.7
63. South Kalimantan	50.1	40.7	37.5
64. East Kalimantan	44.4	33.4	30.5
71. North Sulawesi	35.0	36.4	35.1
72. Central Sulawesi	45.1	43.4	35.3
73. South Sulawesi	43.4	39.1	35.6
74. Southeast Sulawesi	50.5	44.4	40.5
75. Gorontalo	58.4	39.3	35.8
76. West Sulawesi	53.6	47.8	39.4
81. Maluku	58.7	47.5	41.5
82. North Maluku	49.6	46.7	39.0
91. West Papua	57.4	40.3	38.2
94. Papua	60.9	55.3	46.2
Indonesia	38.6	36.8	30.7

Source: Calculated from BPS data

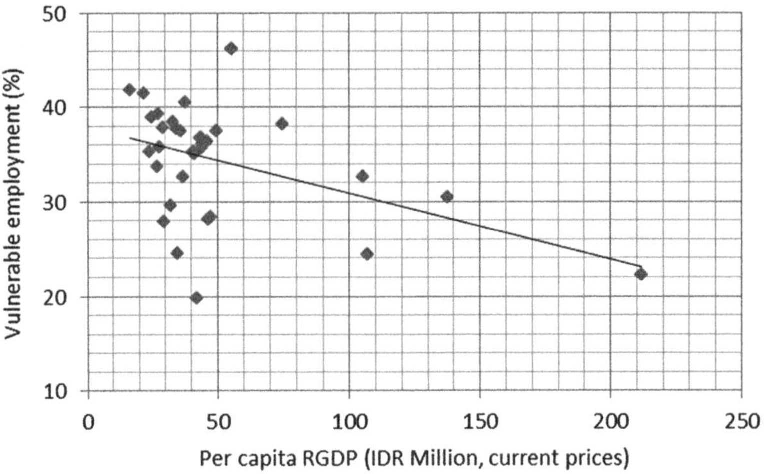

Fig. 6.7 Vulnerable employment (2016) and per capita RGDP (2015). (Source: Calculated from BPS data)

Box 6.2 Employment and Regional Economic Progress

Unlike the unemployment rate data, the formal employment figures provide a more consistent and meaningful picture when they are correlated with other regional macro indicators (see Table 6.9). Formal employment has a strong positive correlation with per capita RGDP, indicating that richer provinces have larger proportions of formal employment as they have a larger modern sector in their economies. Formal employment also displays a strong positive correlation with the share of manufacturing sector in the economy. Furthermore, formal employment is strongly and positively correlated with HDI. This underscores the importance of formal employment and hence re-industrialisation.

There is virtually no correlation between formal employment and RGDP growth indicating that the overall economic growth has no effect on the expansion of the formal employment based on the

(*continued*)

Box 6.2 (continued)

Table 6.9 Correlations of formal and vulnerable employment with regional macroeconomic data (33 provinces, 2001–2011)

	Formal employment (per cent of total employment)	*Vulnerable employment (per cent of total employment)*
Formal employment		−0.775***
Unemployment rate	0.382***	−0.282***
Per capita RGDP	0.747***	−0.528***
Growth of RGDP	0.042	−0.069
Growth of fixed capital formation (investment)	−0.007	0.094*
Human development index (HDI)	0.630***	−0.510***
Share of manufacturing in RGDP	0.584***	−0.585***

Note: *** and * indicate 1 per cent and 10 per cent levels of significance respectively

Source: Calculated from BPS data

observations in the 33 provinces during 2001–2011.[9] Thus, regional economic growth during 2001–2011 was virtually "jobless", when formal employment is considered. On the other hand, correlations between vulnerable employment and other regional macro variables tell a rather consistent story. A possible explanation is that growth in Indonesia lacks quality as it failed to expand the formal (modern) employment. The reduction in unemployment rates since 2005, when there has been no significant association between regional growth and formal employment, implies that most job growth was low-quality informal or vulnerable type.

More interestingly, investment[10] does not show any meaningful correlations with formal employment, implying that investment was concentrated in sectors with high capital intensity, such as mining

(*continued*)

[9] Although this is only a simple descriptive observation, this is quite a major finding that has a merit for further and more rigorous investigation.

[10] Investment refers to the fixed capital formation component of the RGDP.

Box 6.2 (continued)

and telecommunication. Therefore, investment did not significantly expand the overall size of formal employment. The wage effect of investment, if any, seemed to be enjoyed by only a small segment of regular wage employment in those sectors with high capital intensity. Hence, it is not surprising that wage inequality rose in post-crisis Indonesia, as evidenced by the Gini coefficient of wage, which increased from 0.36 to 0.44 during 2001–2011. Thus, the growth Indonesia experienced in the last decade was not a quality growth, at least from an employment perspective.

During 2001–2016, average annual growth of investment was 6.3 per cent higher than the 5.2 per cent average annual GDP growth (Fig. 6.8). More interestingly, during the period, the average real wage grew only at an average of 1.7 per cent annually, far lower than the GDP growth and labour productivity growth, indicating a more unequal distribution of economy's value added between capital and labour.

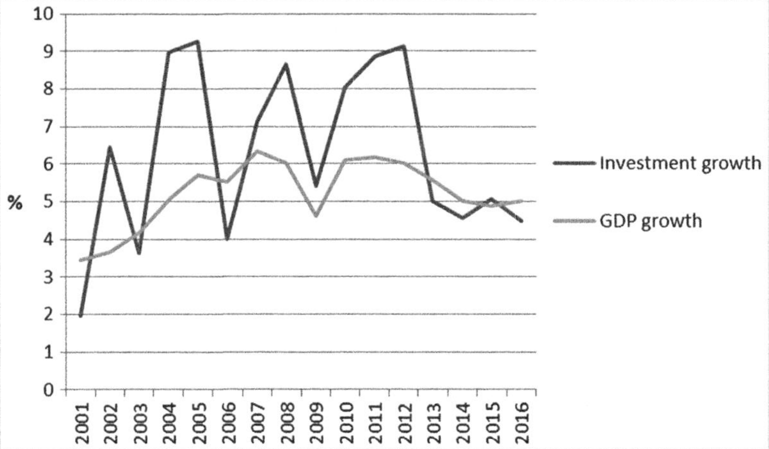

Fig. 6.8 Investment growth exceeds GDP growth (%), 2001–2016 (aggregate Indonesia). (Source: Calculated from BPS data)

6.4 Labour Force and Wage

Table 6.10 presents the trend of inter-provincial variation of wage earnings and gender gap as the ratio of male-female wage earnings. During 2001–2016, inter-provincial variation of wage earnings was quite low but showing a slightly increasing trend. The provincial variation of wage earning among male workers is less than that among female workers. Male workers earned more than female counterparts, but the gap declined. In 2001, male workers earned 49 per cent higher than female workers, while in 2016, the gap declined to 30 per cent.

Figure 6.9 shows that four provinces with the highest level of labour force education are Riau Islands, Jakarta, Banten and East Kalimantan.

Table 6.10 Provincial variation (CV) and gender gap of wage earning, 2001–2016

	2001	*2005*	*2010*	*2016*
Overall	0.238	0.252	0.264	0.264
Male	0.211	0.248	0.257	0.257
Female	0.288	0.262	0.276	0.277
Male/female ratio of wage earning	1.49	1.41	1.31	1.30

Source: Calculated from BPS data

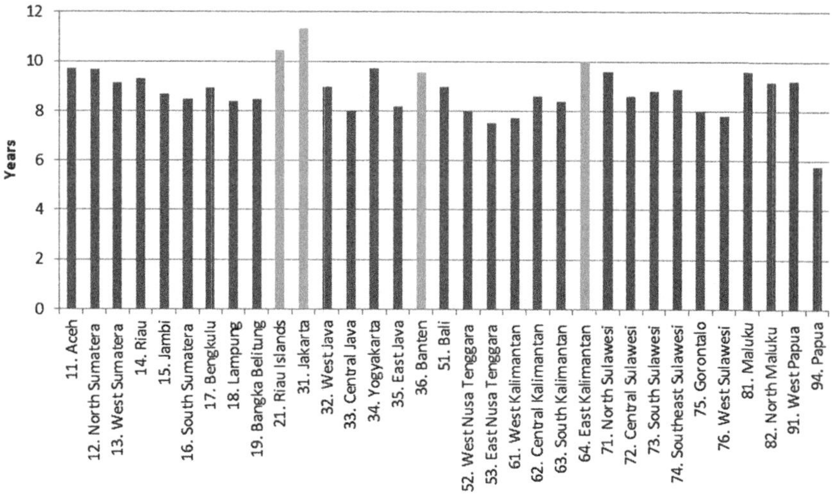

Fig. 6.9 Years of schooling of the labour force by provinces, 2015. (Source: BPS data)

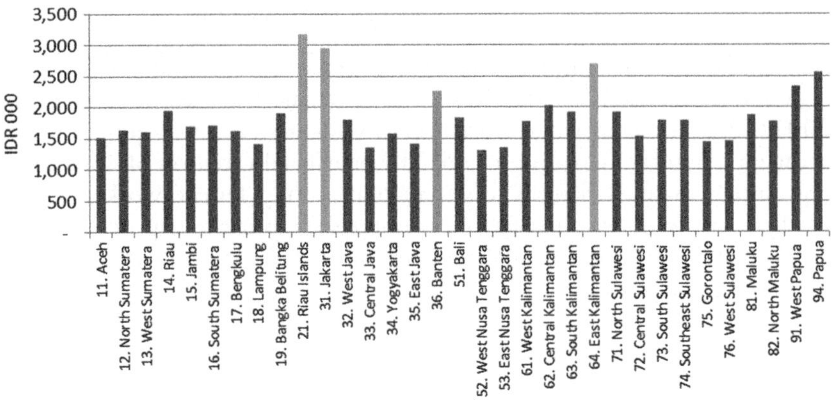

Fig. 6.10 Wage earning across provinces, 2015 (IDR 000/month). (Source: Calculated from BPS data)

They have strength in capital-intensive manufacturing. As can be expected, push for higher wage will be higher in these regions; these provinces have the highest wages across Indonesian provinces (Fig. 6.9).

Push for higher wages would be less in provinces with strength in labour-intensive manufacturing such as West Java, Central Java and East Java, where the level of labour force education is also lower. As depicted in Fig. 6.10, wage levels in these provinces are still relatively lower.

6.5 Correlates of Formal Employment and Real Wage

This section examines relationships among several employment-related indicators disaggregated at the provincial level, such as the size of formal employment (or that of vulnerable employment), wage inequality and trends in real wages and earnings. It presents results of econometric estimation of an empirical model that correlates formal employment and real wage and several key macro variables. The unit of observation is province-year for 33 provinces during 2001–2011. Since the independent variables suffer from multicollinearity, we do not infer any causality. However, correlation estimates derived from the panel data models are more systematic than the simple bivariate correlations presented in the previous section.

The regression results are presented in Table 6.11. Provinces with higher shares of formal employment (as a percentage of total employment)

Table 6.11 Correlates of formal employment and real wage, 2001–2011

	Formal employment	*Real wage*
	(Random effects)	*(Random effects)*
	Standardised coefficient	*Standardised coefficient*
Real wage (IDR 000)	0.042	
	(0.029)	
Formal employment (per cent total employment)		0.13
		(0.093)
Labour productivity (IDR 000)	0.411***	0.07
	(0.086)	(0.123)
Growth of RGDP (per cent)	0.016	−0.01
	(0.020)	(0.037)
Government consumption (per cent RGDP)	−0.009	−0.05
	(0.054)	(0.086)
Investment (capital formation as per cent RGDP)	0.184***	−0.10
	(0.044)	(0.073)
Human Development Index (HDI)	0.373***	−0.55***
	(0.0484)	(0.082)
Real minimum wage (IDR 000)	−0.128***	0.33***
	(0.037)	(0.062)
No. of observations	363	363
No. of provinces	33	33
Prob. > chi2	0.000	0.000
R-sq. (overall)	0.667	0.234

Notes: Standard errors are in parentheses. *** indicates 1 per cent level of significance. Each regression has a constant term. The choice between fixed effects and random effects is based on the Hausman test. For random effects estimation, the valid R square is R-sq. (overall)

tend to have higher shares of physical capital investment (as a percentage of RGDP), higher HDI and higher labour productivity. Without implying any causality, these findings indicate the importance of formal employment and investment in terms of both physical and human capital for labour productivity.

The only important correlate of real wage is the level of real minimum wage. Provinces with higher minimum wage tend to enjoy higher real wage. This means that higher minimum wage tends to push the average wage upward. This explains the persistence of workers in demanding higher minimum wages during the last decade, made possible by democratisation and labour law reforms.

The negative correlation between HDI and real wage is quite unusual as it indicates that provinces with better stock of human capital (represented by HDI) do not enjoy higher real wage. This could be explained by the missing link between real wage and labour productivity, as discussed in Chap. 3. The delinking between real wage and labour productivity is strongly indicated by virtually *no* correlation between real wage and labour productivity across sectors and provinces in Indonesia. The high percentage of low-pay incidence and the rising wage inequality seem to be strongly related to the delinking between wage and productivity, as discussed in previous chapters.

6.6 Provincial Variation of the Manufacturing Sector

Figure 6.11 shows the role of manufacturing in RGDP during the post-AFC period. The manufacturing sector dominates the economy of Riau Islands, Banten and West Java with over 40 per cent contribution to their RGDP. Manufacturing plays an insignificant role with less than 5 per cent share in RGDP in the provinces of Maluku, Bengkulu, West Nusa Tenggara, NTT and Papua. However, as can be seen, during 2000–2015, the significance of manufacturing in provincial economies generally declined, which is consistent with the overall national trend of de-industrialisation. While in Chap. 4, we have seen an overall trend of pre-

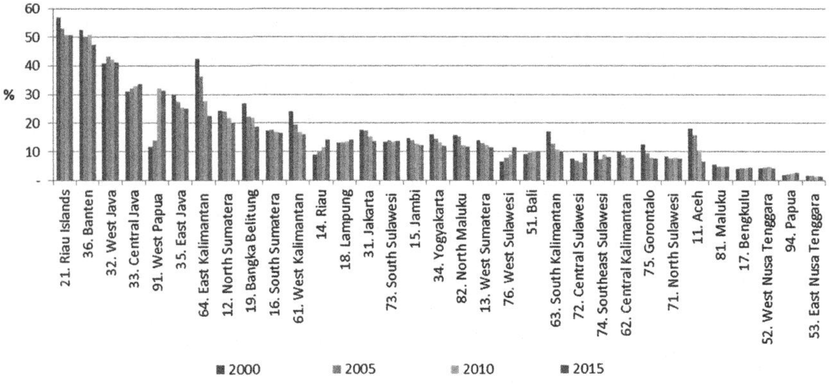

Fig. 6.11 Shares of manufacturing in provincial RGDP, 2000, 2005, 2010 and 2015. (Source: Calculated from BPS data)

mature de-industrialisation in Indonesia, the trends are far from homogeneous across Indonesian provinces. Few of them are worth further discussion.

First, the manufacturing share has clearly declined in the economies of three most industrialised provinces (Riau Islands, Banten and West Java) and East Java, but increased in Central Java. These provinces are key manufacturing areas in the country. In Riau Islands, despite the decline of the whole manufacturing sector in the provincial economy during the post-AFC period, the capital-intensive sub-sectors of basic metals and fabricated metals dominate the manufacturing sector with 65 per cent contribution. These sub-sectors also displayed higher growth, higher than the manufacturing growth and the growth of the province overall economy. During 2010–2015, these two sub-sectors accounted for 75 per cent of overall manufacturing growth. This points to the strength of capital-intensive manufacturing in the economy of Riau Islands Province. In Banten, the growth of labour-intensive manufacturing sub-sectors (textile and leather) is far lower than the growth of capital-intensive sub-sectors (chemicals, basic metals and fabricated metals), indicating that the province is losing competitiveness in labour-intensive manufacturing. In West Java, among four leading manufacturing sub-sectors (food, textile, fabricated metals and transport equipment), fabricated metal manufacturing showed the slowest growth, less than the growth of the manufacturing sector and the overall provincial economy. In Central Java, with increasing share of manufacturing, the growth of food manufacturing sub-sector has been the most impressive. Although, they are located on the same Island, Central Java shows strength in labour-intensive manufacturing relative to Jakarta and Banten.

Second, provinces with substantial oil and gas manufacturing activities, such as Aceh, East Kalimantan and West Papua, experienced sharp fluctuations in the shares of manufacturing in their regional GDP (see Table 6.12). For example, in Aceh, and East Kalimantan, the shares of manufacturing declined from 18.1 per cent to mere 6.6 per cent and from 42.4 per cent to 22.6 per cent, respectively, due to the shrinking oil and gas manufacturing activities. On the other hand, in West Papua (Papua Barat), the share of manufacturing nearly tripled from 11.6 per cent to 31.4 per cent due to the new development of Tangguh LNG field operated by the British Petroleum Company in the Bintuni Bay area of West Papua. Tangguh LNG is the third-largest LNG supply facility in Indonesia and the first fully combined upstream and downstream LNG operation in the country.

Table 6.12 Decreasing and increasing shares of manufacturing, 2000–2015

Declining share of manufacturing	*Magnitude of decrease (percentage points; 2000–2015)*	*Increasing share of manufacturing*	*Magnitude of increase (percentage points; 2000–2015)*
11. Aceh	−11.6	14. Riau	5.4
12. North Sumatera	−4.5	17. Bengkulu	0.4
13. West Sumatera	−2.5	18. Lampung	0.9
15. Jambi	−2.4	33. Central Java	2.5
16. South Sumatera	−0.8	51. Bali	0.8
19. Bangka Belitung	−8.4	52. West Nusa Tenggara	0.2
21. Riau Islands	−6.2	72. Central Sulawesi	1.7
31. Jakarta	−3.8	73. South Sulawesi	0.3
32. West Java	−2.2	76. West Sulawesi	5.1
34. Yogyakarta	−4.0	91. West Papua	19.8
35. East Java	−4.6	94. Papua	0.7
36. Banten	−5.2		
53. East Nusa Tenggara	−0.2		
61. West Kalimantan	−7.9		
62. Central Kalimantan	−2.1		
63. South Kalimantan	−7.4		
64. East Kalimantan	−19.8		
71. North Sulawesi	−0.8		
74. Southeast Sulawesi	−2.1		
75. Gorontalo	−4.8		
81. Maluku	−0.7		
82. North Maluku	−4.1		

Note: West Java is for 2005–2015

Source: Calculated from BPS data

Third, while the de-industrialisation trend is quite common in other provinces, few provinces showed increasing shares of manufacturing sector such as Riau and West Sulawesi. These imply that the trends of declining manufacturing shares or de-industrialisation in post-crisis Indonesia across provinces are not homogeneous. There could be complementarities

Table 6.13 Provinces with a dominant role of manufacturing sector, 2015

	Share of manufacturing to national manufacturing GDP (%)	*Share of manufacturing in provincial RGDP (%)*
32. West Java	25.9	41.2
35. East Java	17.2	25.2
33. Central Java	11.6	33.6
31. Jakarta	10.6	13.9
36. Banten	8.0	47.4
12. North Sumatra	4.6	20.0
21. Riau Islands	4.3	50.8

Source: Calculated from BPS data

among the diverse trends. Table 6.11 details provinces with decreasing and increasing shares of manufacturing in their respective economies during 2000–2015.

In contrast to the mining sector, manufacturing activities are concentrated in Java's provinces and few outer Island provinces: North Sumatra, Riau Islands and East Kalimantan. In those provinces, manufacturing activities play a significant role in their provincial economy (Table 6.13).

Next we examine the structure of manufacturing sector in those provinces as presented in Table 6.14, which shows the distribution of manufacturing sub-sectors in the highly industrialised provinces in Indonesia. Sub-sectors with more than 10 per cent contribution to the province's manufacturing sector are highlighted, and different characteristics of industrial development can be clearly identified across those provinces as follows.

Within Java, manufacturing characteristics are different across provinces. Jakarta's manufacturing is dominated by capital-intensive industry, where wages are expected to be much higher. West Java's manufacturing is more diverse. The province has both capital- and labour-intensive industries. Central Java's strength is in labour-intensive food and tobacco industry. This is in addition to the oil and gas manufacturing due to the existence of oil refinery in the province. Banten also has capital-intensive manufacturing as well as the labour-intensive textile industry.

The following characteristics of manufacturing in the three provinces outside Java are very different from Java's manufacturing. North Sumatra's manufacturing sector is dominated by low-technology food industry and

Table 6.14 Manufacturing by sub-sectors in highly industrialised provinces (manufacturing share >30 per cent), 2015

Sub-sector	*North Sumatra*	*Riau Islands*	*Jakarta*	*West Java*	*Central Java*	*East Java*	*Banten*	*East Kalimantan*
1 Coal and refined petroleum products	0.02	2.73	0.03	4.42	17.46	0.26	0.50	68.14
2 Food products and beverages	71.02	1.77	6.80	10.15	32.89	28.49	9.82	9.63
3 Tobacco products	1.58	0.47	–	0.46	20.68	24.12	0.00	–
4 Textiles and wearing apparel	0.28	2.33	5.50	14.28	8.29	1.55	11.93	0.07
5 Leather and related products and footwear	0.32	0.16	0.13	1.23	0.91	1.19	7.82	0.02
6 Wood and products of wood and cork, and articles of straw and plaiting materials	1.26	1.21	0.18	0.80	4.80	5.90	0.41	3.27
7 Paper and paper products, printing and reproduction of recorded media	1.28	0.63	3.16	2.31	0.87	4.95	8.74	2.51
8 Chemicals and pharmaceuticals and botanical products	2.81	0.62	12.81	5.41	5.90	8.97	20.26	13.41
9 Rubber, rubber products and plastic products	6.86	3.83	1.83	3.17	1.24	5.21	3.41	0.17
10 Other non-metallic mineral products	1.90	0.29	0.85	1.70	1.93	4.41	3.45	0.52
11 Basic metals	10.78	15.18	2.81	3.02	1.05	4.44	9.95	–
12 Fabricated metal products, computer and optical products, and electrical equipment	0.89	50.19	7.37	23.99	1.53	4.90	17.41	0.66
13 Machinery and equipment	0.30	5.60	0.13	8.14	0.32	0.18	1.07	0.12
14 Transport equipment	0.07	7.77	56.45	19.56	0.72	1.26	3.60	0.89
15 Furniture	0.57	2.36	0.88	0.40	1.07	3.11	0.41	0.41
16 Other manufacturing, repair and installation of machinery and equipment	0.07	4.86	1.09	0.98	0.35	1.05	1.23	0.18
All manufacturing	100	100	100	100	100	100	100	100.00

Source: Calculated from BPS data

the capital-intensive basic metal manufacturing. Riau Islands' manufacturing sector is dominated by capital-intensive and technology-intensive manufacturing (basic metals and fabricated metals). High-wage oil-gas and chemical industries dominate in East Kalimantan.

Table 6.15 shows the structure of manufacturing sector in provinces with reasonable level of industrialisation, with manufacturing shares in the provincial economy range between 15 per cent and 30 per cent. The data

Table 6.15 Manufacturing by sub-sectors in reasonably industrialised provinces (manufacturing share 15–30 per cent), 2015

Sub-sector	*South Sumatra*	*Bangka Belitung*	*West Kalimantan*	*West Papua*
1 Coal and refined petroleum products	27.44	–	–	91.27
2 Food products and beverages	32.51	28.29	75.27	2.98
3 Tobacco products	0.00	–	–	–
4 Textiles and wearing apparel	0.16	0.29	0.43	0.04
5 Leather and related products and footwear	0.00	–	0.04	0.08
6 Wood and products of wood and cork, and articles of straw and plaiting materials	1.07	2.08	6.04	4.13
7 Paper and paper products, printing and reproduction of recorded media	7.04	0.36	0.32	0.14
8 Chemicals and pharmaceuticals and botanical products	10.32	0.25	0.04	0.01
9 Rubber, rubber products and plastic products	17.71	3.38	6.33	–
10 Other non-metallic mineral products	1.70	5.32	0.65	0.49
11 Basic metals	0.12	58.29	1.78	–
12 Fabricated metal products, computer and optical products, and electrical equipment	1.05	1.06	4.36	0.07
13 Machinery and equipment	0.03		0.17	–
14 Transport equipment	0.15	0.41	0.80	0.14
15 Furniture	0.24	0.09	2.15	0.62
16 Other manufacturing, repair and installation of machinery and equipment	0.45	0.19	1.62	0.03
All manufacturing	100	100	100	100
Manufacturing share in RGDP (%)	16.6	18.7	16.2	31.4

Source: Calculated from BPS data

reveal that each province has different manufacturing strength. It seems that labour-intensive manufacturing is probably more suitable in provinces with a significant presence of food industry.

6.7 Concluding Remarks: Regional Dimensions Are Critical

In a country as vast and as diverse as Indonesia, regional dimensions are critical for policymaking, especially when growing regional disparity can threaten national progress and create socio-political instability. While regional labour market and socio-economic indicators display more or less similar national trends, there are significant variations across the provinces. Although there are signs of convergence, the policymakers need to focus on the varying speed of convergence across the regions. One of the factors that seem to be driving the regional variations in inequality is the disjoint between labour productivity and real wage.

Unfortunately, however, the national planning documents are deficient in appreciating underlying dynamics causing regional variations. For example, the previous Medium-Term National Development Planning Document (RPJM 2010–2014) did not provide any analysis and policy directive with regard to the regional variation of unemployment rates across provinces, let alone other indicators reflecting the quality of employment, even though it elaborated the national target into disaggregated unemployment targets by provinces. It seems that the provincial targets were laid down without a careful analysis of disaggregated unemployment rates across provinces. For example, while the national unemployment rate was targeted to decline from 7.9 per cent in 2009 to the range of 5–6 per cent in 2014, the unemployment rate in Banten was targeted to reduce to the range of 14.9–16.5 per cent in 2014. In fact, the unemployment rate in Banten in 2009 was already at 15 per cent, slightly down from 15.2 per cent in 2008. Located in the western tip of Java Island and directly bordered with the national capital Jakarta, Banten is a province with the highest unemployment rate among the Indonesian provinces.

The RPJM 2010–2014 also did not have clear and specific targets with regard to other key labour market indicators (such as the expansion of formal employment and reduction of low-pay incidence), let alone policies dealing with regional inequalities or these indicators. Similar deficiencies seem to persist in the current RPJM (2015–2019). The next chapter reflects on policies aimed at re-industrialisation and decent employment creation as well as balanced development of Indonesia.

References

Akita, T. 1988. "Regional development and income disparities in Indonesia." *Asian Economic Journal* 2(2): 165–91.

Akita, T. and R.A. Lukman 1995. "Interregional inequalities in Indonesia: A sectoral decomposition analysis for 1975–92." *Bulletin of Indonesian Economic Studies* 31(2): 61–81.

Akita, T. and R.A. Lukman 1999. "Spatial patterns of expenditure inequalities in Indonesia." *Bulletin of Indonesian Economic Studies* 32(2): 67–90.

Cobham, A. and A. Sumner 2013. "Putting the Gini back in the bottle? 'The Palma' as a policy-relevant measure of Inequality." Available at: https://www.kcl.ac.uk/aboutkings/worldwide/initiatives/global/intdev/people/Sumner/Cobham-Sumner-15March2013.pdf. Accessed on 1 January 2016.

Esmara, H. 1975. "Regional income disparities." *Bulletin of Indonesian Economic Studies* 11(1): 41–57.

Garcia, J.G. and L. Soelistianingsih 1998. "Why do differences in provincial incomes persist in Indonesia?" *Bulletin of Indonesian Economic Studies* 34(1): 95–120.

Hill, H. 2000. *The Indonesian economy*, 2nd edition. Cambridge: Cambridge University Press.

Hill, H. and Y. Vidyattama 2014. "Hares and tortoises: Regional development dynamics in Indonesia." In H. Hill (Ed.), *Regional dynamics in a decentralized Indonesia* (pp. 68–97). Singapore: ISEAS.

Hughes, G.A. and I. Islam 1981. "Inequality in Indonesia: A decomposition analysis." *Bulletin of Indonesian Economic Studies* 17(2): 42–71.

Islam, I. and H. Khan 1986. "Spatial patterns of inequality and poverty in Indonesia." *Bulletin of Indonesian Economic Studies* 22(2): 80–102.

Nazara, S. 2010. *The informal economy in Indonesia: Size, composition and evolution*. Geneva: International Labour Office.

Palma, J.G. 2011. "Homogeneous middles vs. heterogeneous tails, and the end of the 'inverted-U': It's all about the share of the rich." *Development and Change* 42(1): 87–153.

Tadjoeddin, M.Z. 2011. "The economic origins of Indonesia's secessionist conflicts." *Civil Wars* 13(3): 312–32.

Tadjoeddin, M.Z., W. Suharyo and S. Mishra 2001. "Regional disparity and vertical conflicts in Indonesia." *Journal of the Asia Pacific Economy* 6(3): 283–304.

Uppal, J.S. and B.S. Handoko 1986. "Regional income disparities in Indonesia." *Ekonomi Keuangan Indonesia* 34(3): 287–304.

Vidyattama, Y. 2013. "Regional convergence and the role of neighbourhood effects in a decentralised Indonesia." *Bulletin of Indonesian Economic Studies* 49(3): 193–211.

Williamson, J.G. 1965. "Regional inequality and the process of national development: A description of patterns." *Economic Development and Cultural Change* 13(4): 3–45.

Yusuf, A.A. 2014. *Has prosperity been for all? Revisiting the trend of various dimension of inequality in Indonesia*. Jakarta: INFID.

CHAPTER 7

Policy Perspectives

7.1 Introduction

The previous chapters have emphasised the important role of the manufacturing sector as the economy's main engine of growth. In particular, the modern and dynamic segment of large and medium (LM) firms is critical to achieve the goal of turning the country into a high-productivity and high-wage economy. A productivity-driven, rapidly growing, well-balanced economy is crucial to meet Indonesia's constitutional obligations of ensuring social justice (equity) and decent living for its citizens as well as to fulfil its commitment to create decent jobs. Indonesia has done remarkably well in transforming the economy until the close of the last century when it was severely shocked by the Asian financial crisis (AFC) which ushered in a new Indonesia—democratic, decentralised and less clientele. Thus, going forward in the new millennium, a new policy framework is needed. This chapter is aimed at reflecting on this.

The chapter begins with a brief review of industrial, regional development and employment policies prior to the AFC. Then we proceed with an evaluation of changes in economic environment and policy responses after the crisis. Finally, we propose a new policy perspective on industry and employment, where regional minimum wage can play a vital role.

M. Z. Tadjoeddin, A. Chowdhury, *Employment and Re-Industrialisation in Post Soeharto Indonesia*, Critical Studies of the Asia-Pacific, https://doi.org/10.1057/978-1-137-50566-8_7

7.2 Development Strategies to Turn a "Basket Case" to a Miracle Economy[1]

Overall, Indonesia's economic development strategies have been nationalistic even during the Soeharto's New Order era, influenced by constitutional obligations, such as the establishment of a "justice and equal society" as enshrined in the Preamble,[2] and Article 33 (2) of the 1945 Constitution stipulating "Branches of production which are important for the state as well as influencing the needs of public at large are authorized by state." Consequently, the state plays a central role in providing goods and services deemed essential for public interest, and intervention of the state is the priority alternative.

Indonesia began its three decades of journey to development in the mid-1960s from a predominantly peasant economy, fractured by the Cold War-driven political upheavals, when the country was categorised as a basket case with a very dire prospect as in Higgins (1968) and Myrdal (1968). The industrial sector was nearly non-existent during pre-Soeharto's post-independent Indonesia. Indonesia's minuscule modern industrial sector was dominated by a few large state-owned enterprises (SOEs), largely established by Dutch commercial interests before World War II, subsequently taken over by the state as part of the 1957–1958 nationalisation move. The nationalisations only worsened the limited modern manufacturing sector the country had, including its transport infrastructure (Booth 2016). The country lagged behind its Asian counterparts, experiencing neither the state-orchestrated heavy industrialisation of the People's Republic of China and India nor the state-supported export-oriented growth then getting under way in the Asian newly industrialised economies (Aswicahyono et al. 2013).

[1] This section draws on the authoritative work of Hal Hill and Anne Booth, in particular, Hill (2000) and Booth (2016). A good concise review is McCawley (2013).

[2] The Preamble was also influenced by several philosophical thoughts; one of them came from the Utilitarianism thought "The great happiness for the greatest number" of Jeremy Bentham inspired the founding fathers to formulate landmark and energising starting points in meaningful paragraphs of the Preamble. Inspired by the Soviet socialist revolution, like most independence leaders who fought against the colonial powers, the founding fathers of Indonesia were also deeply committed to social justice and equity.

7.2.1 *Industrial Development Strategies*

Development of modern industrial sector in Indonesia began in the late 1960s only after President Soeharto, who took over power through a bloody military coup, managed to put the political house in order and stabilise the economy. The pre-AFC industrial development strategies under the New Order regime of President Soeharto can be divided into three phases: stabilisation (1966–early 1970s), economic nationalism and import substitution (1970s), and adjustment and export orientation (mid-1980s–1996). There was also a period of state activism towards "high-tech" industrialisation since the mid-1980s abruptly punctuated by the AFC.

Under a highly centralised administration of an authoritarian regime of President Soeharto, the national planning agency, *Badan Perencanaan Pembangunan Nasional* (Bappenas) was firmly in charge of designing and implementing national development strategies, such as annual, five-year, and long-term development plans, until the early 1980s. But with the departure of Professor Widjojo from the cabinet in 1983, Bappenas no longer had the same authority, although it still played an important role as a coordinator of aid projects and controlled disbursement of development budget funds. Bappenas also continued to produce multi-volume documents for the fourth and fifth five-year plans (1984/1985–1988/1989 and 1989/1990–1993/1994), containing important insights into government thinking on policies in sectors such as agriculture, transport and education. But the planning process seemed to have become more ritualistic and less important as a guide to government policy (Booth 2005).

The 1980s also saw a stronger role for planning bureaus (*biro perencanaan*) within most line ministries. This coincided with the rise of B.J. Habibie as a Science and Technology Minister—discussed later—who was given the responsibility to drive President Soeharto's vision for industrialisation. Thus, the research and development centres played an important role in planning and implementing development projects.

Stabilisation (1966–Early 1970s)

The hallmark of government policies in this phase was the "balanced budget requirement" and capital account liberalisation with full convertibility of the rupiah. With most capital control measures removed by 1971, the exchange rate was unified and pegged to the dollar. These actions were very bold in an environment when monetised deficit financing, multiple exchange rates and capital control were a norm in developing countries. One can, in fact, say that Indonesia was an early testing ground for the macroeconomic policy framework that has later become a centrepiece of the so-called Washington consensus. The balanced budget requirement essentially removed fiscal dominance over monetary policy, which, thus, attained some independence. As a result, the hyperinflation was quickly brought under control, the annual inflation rate dropping from over 1000 per cent in 1966 to 15.5 per cent in 1969 and to 4.4 per cent in 1971.

The "balanced budget requirement" was defined cleverly as total budgetary expenditures not exceeding revenues from all sources, including foreign aid and government borrowing. Although this definition is not very helpful in analysing the impact of the budget on the economy,[3] it succeeded in changing the mindset of policymakers and politicians to bring budget deficit under control after 1969.[4] This was, of course, helped by Western donor countries underwriting Indonesia's aid demand, seen as vital for a country willing to act as a bulwark against communist advances in the region. The oil boom in the 1970s also contributed to the maintenance of the balanced budget requirement. However, the guaranteeing of aid flows and oil revenue boom also made the government "lazy"; it had "little incentive to implement reforms of the domestic tax system" (Booth 2016, p. 71). This severely impaired government's ability to respond to shocks when oil prices collapsed in the early 1980s, which saw drastic cuts in government expenditures.

Economic Nationalism and Import Substitution (1970s–Early 1980s)

Developments during this period were shaped by three five-year plans. The first plan (1969–1973/1974) placed considerable emphasis on improving output and productivity in the agricultural sector, with around 40 per cent of planned development expenditure devoted to agriculture and irrigation. The second and third plans were more ambitious, but many of the macroeconomic and sectoral targets were overtaken by fast-changing domestic and foreign economic events, such as two oil price shocks and the Pertamina (state oil company) crisis.

[3] The concept of budget deficit as a difference between domestic revenues and domestic expenditures is more useful in analysing the impact of the budget on the domestic economy.

[4] See Booth (2016).

However, what is not commonly recognised is the influence of the nationalist student riot against Japan's perceived economic hegemony, which erupted in Jakarta on 15 January (1974) during the visit of then Japanese Prime Minister Kakuei Tanaka, on this interventionist phase. Japan was largely seen by Indonesian students as an "economic imperialist" and "exploiter", and the Japanese companies were blamed to have put much of the local textile industry out of business. The anti-Japanese reaction was driven more by political and psychological factors than economic issues.[5] The anti-Japanese riot was also significant for Indonesia's evolution as an economy that displayed elements of pro-poor growth and "shared" prosperity. As the *New York Times* reported, "Not all of the protests were aimed solely at the Japanese. Some of the complaints were against the ruling establishment in each country with which the Japanese do business—and thus help the rich leave the poor farther and farther behind."[6]

Ironically, the policy orientation of this phase was also inspired by Japan's Ministry of International Trade and Industry (MITI) and the emerging newly industrialising economies of East Asia which followed the Japanese state-led development model. Thus, Indonesia's trade and industrial policy was largely set by the then Ministry of Trade and Industry during the 1970s. Fiscal incentives, such as tax concessions and subsidies, as well as non-tariff measures were used to promote sectors or industries deemed to be of strategic importance, such as base metals, petrochemicals and auto parts. Restrictive and discretionary investment procedures were also used, such as complex investment approval and licensing processes. Thus, this period saw a proliferation of regulations and restrictions. Sectors were either open or close for investment and received import facilities based on the status of firms—foreign, domestic or small-scale enterprises—and whether they were on the priority list being regarded as "right". Domestic upstream industries received protection through stringent local content requirements known as "the deletion programme".[7] The

[5] An Indonesian economist summed up the reasons that the Japanese often are disliked here. Asked whether they are guilty of all they have been charged with, he said: "Of intent, no. Of being oblivious, insensitive, unthinking, short-sighted, excessively competitive, yes. They do not look at whose garden they are trampling on." "Tanaka's Explosive Trip" by Richard Halloranjan, *The New York Times*, 21 January 1974.

[6] Ibid.

[7] This involved deleting the product from the list of components that can be imported once domestic suppliers were identified.

nationalist orientation of this phase remained entrenched even in the later export orientation phase as extensive regulations on foreign investments continued well into the 1990s.

The SOEs were also an important industrial policy tool for the Government of Indonesia (GOI). They played an important role in industrial deepening and high-technology investment, contributing a quarter of non-oil manufacturing value added during 1974–1975.[8] At the height of the boom, the oil sector contributed up to 70 per cent of total revenue, and massive amounts of revenues from oil windfall were channelled through existing or newly created SOEs, including those in oil refinery, petrochemicals, fertilisers and steel. The primary goal was to meet production targets and create backward linkages. "SOEs also often had to be concerned with non-economic objectives, such as regional development and price stabilisation" (Tijaja and Faisal 2014, p. 7).

Preferential allocation of lucrative import and distribution licences to support nationalistic development provided a fertile ground for a patrimonial network to grow between the state (or high-ranking government officials) and the Indo-Chinese business community known as *cukongism*. While many observers saw the dominance of SOEs and few Indo-Chinese conglomerates facilitated by business-government relation as catalysts for Indonesia's economic transformation, many others later attributed Indonesia's vulnerability to the AFC, its inability to effectively respond to inefficient SOEs and the "unholy" business-state alliance.

Adjustment and Export Orientation (Mid-1980s–1996)

Indonesia entered the 1980s with a favourable macroeconomic situation. A pre-emptive devaluation in 1978 when its balance of payments was not under severe pressure helped Indonesia avoid classic Dutch disease from oil price booms. Thus, Indonesia's industrial growth during this period should have been unhindered by loss of competitiveness due to real appreciation from the oil windfall. But the boom did not last long, and oil price began falling in the early 1980s and accelerated in 1986 during which the price dropped by two-thirds in just six months. Indonesia was unable to escape from the consequences of its excessive dependence on oil.

Therefore, Indonesia undertook a series of structural adjustments during 1983 and 1984, including the rationalisation of a public investment programme and drastic cuts in public expenditures. A comprehensive tax

[8] The share would be even greater if the oil sector was taken into account (Lewis 1994).

reform was also introduced, including the introduction of value-added tax, which saw revenues from tax rise rapidly. Towards the late 1980s, the proportion of tax revenues from corporations increased to 35 per cent, compared with 27 per cent from SOEs and 38 per cent from individuals (Booth 2016, p. 72). On the macroeconomic front, Indonesia also devalued its currency in 1983 and 1986 and subsequently allowed the exchange rate to float downwards relative to the dollar.

Indonesia's domestic macroeconomic adjustment efforts were aided by sharp appreciation of Japanese Yen following the Plaza Accord in 1985. Although the Yen appreciation in 1985–1986 resulted in a rapid rise of the debt-servicing obligations for Yen-denominated public debts, the Japanese corporate sector found Indonesia, together with other Southeast Asian economies, as attractive to shift their labour-intensive production lines. The appreciation of Korean and Taiwanese currencies during that period also encouraged export producers of these countries to relocate their labour-intensive manufacturing to Indonesia and other Southeast Asian countries (Booth 2016).

The most fundamental change was the realisation that protection from import competition alone could not drive industrial development, and there was a need to ensure simultaneously the emergence of competitive firms. Thus, the mid-1980s saw a series of trade and tariff policy reforms. Among the key reforms was the customs reform in 1985, followed by the adoption of the first deregulation package in May 1986, which included the Agency for Import Duty Exemption and Restitution (*Pusat Pengelolaan Pembebasan dan Pengembalian Bea Masuk* or P4BM). While custom reform significantly reduced clearing time and import costs, the P4BM put in place duty drawback facilities and tariff exemption to replace the General Agreement on Tariffs and Trade (GATT) incompliant export subsidy scheme. The duty drawback facilities and tariff exemption scheme allowed firms to gain access to internationally competitive inputs. Unconditional ex-ante tax exemption or ex-post rebate replaced complex licensing, significantly reducing business costs and uncertainties. Management of the scheme was placed under the Ministry of Finance, deemed more insulated from vested interests, instead of the Ministry of Trade and Industry. These reforms significantly contributed to boosting export competitiveness.

The May 1986 reform package was followed by sector-oriented packages which substantially reduced non-tariff restrictions in terms of both coverage and degree. For instance, the percentage of imports covered by quantitative restrictions dropped from 43 per cent to 3 per cent, as the average nominal tariff declined from 22 per cent to 9 per cent between 1985 and 1992 (Tijaja and Faisal 2014, p. 8).

The investment regime reformed by replacing the investment priority list with the investment negative list and undertaking further deregulation. The reforms resulted in a prolonged investment boom, with the value of investment projects approved by the Indonesia Investment Coordination Board (*Badan Koordinasi Penanaman Modal* or BKPM) peaking at $12.5 billion in 1991 from $1.7 billion in 1986 (Tijaja and Faisal 2014, p. 9).

As a result of the interplay of these reform efforts since the mid-1980s, Indonesia underwent a period of rapid structural change. Starting from a rapid growth in labour-intensive exports, it diversified from simple consumer goods and basic resource processing to a wider range of manufactures with increasing technological sophistication, and instead of SOEs, manufacturing exports became the engine of economic growth (Aswicahyono et al. 2013; Booth 2016).

Leapfrogging to High-Tech Manufacturing

While the adjustment process was in progress in the 1980s, Indonesia was also dreaming of technological leapfrogging. The driver of the vision for a high-technology future was B.J. Habibie, an aeronautical engineer, who was recruited by Soeharto in 1974 in the team guiding Indonesia's industrialisation and development. He quickly rose in the rank and was appointed as Minister of Research and Technology in 1978. Under his leadership, Indonesia began manufacturing a 44-seat commuter plane in 1986 and became the only nation in Southeast Asia to make aircraft of this size. By 1991, Habibie oversaw ten state-owned industries engaged in helicopter manufacturing, ship and train building, steel, arms, communications satellites and energy, and was planning to build several nuclear power plants.

The government invested billions of dollars in advanced industries to allow Indonesia to leapfrog into the ranks of industrialised nations. The government also expanded education and training programmes, especially in science and technology to meet the demand of a high-tech economy.

The rise of Habibie basically sidelined a group of policymakers popularly known as the Berkeley Mafia, named for the California university campus where many received their higher degrees. They engineered Indonesia's economic boom and tended to believe that the nation's immediate economic future rested in low-tech manufacturing employing semi-skilled labourers, like garments and shoes.

Critics have charged that Habibie was intoxicated with his own dreams of technological success and that his schemes were too expensive for a developing economy. However, given the short stint, abruptly punctuated by the AFC, it is difficult to judge whether Indonesia would have been successful in accelerating its exit from low-wage, low-productivity industrial activities. Similar attempts in the Republic of Korea (South Korea) referred to as heavy and chemical industries (HCI) drive during 1972–1979 were also criticised, but despite initial difficulties, South Korea succeeded in becoming an industrial giant.

7.2.2 *Regional Development Strategies*

With the aim of accelerating regional development and balancing economic progress, there was an attempt to build up regional planning capacity, especially at the provincial level beginning in the 1970s. Thus, a presidential decree established regional planning boards (*Badan Perencanaan Pembangunan Daerah* or Bappeda) in each province just before the beginning of Repelita 2 (second five-year plan 1974–1979). Although at the beginning they were just administrative offices, since the late 1970s they gradually began to play a more important role in initiating and implementing development projects, funded by the government through the central development budget, including *Inpres* (*Instruksi Presiden* or Presidential Instruction) grants, and also by provinces themselves using their own revenues (Booth 2005). Planning boards at the district level were also established. The government spent considerable resources to train officials in these agencies, and they are an important resource for planning, implementation and auditing of government expenditures in the regions.

Regional development featured prominently in the government's equalisation scheme, particularly emphasised in the third five-year plan (1979–1984) under the so-called development trilogy. It consisted of dynamic *stability* of national security, high economic *growth* and *equalisation* of development and its results across regions.[9]

[9] The equalisation component of the trilogy was specified in the "eight paths of equalisation". They are equalisations of (1) basic needs, (2) access to educations, (3) income distribution especially through labour-intensive economic activities, (4) employment opportunities though regional development, (5) entrepreneurship opportunities through credit access to economically disadvantage groups, (6) participation especially for youths and women, (7) population distribution through government-sponsored transmigration and (8) access to justice.

The main vehicle for equalisation has been *Inpres*, an instrument for inter-governmental fiscal transfer. The *Inpres* was introduced in the early 1970s. The most important rationale for the programme was to enhance the financial capacity of regional governments to achieve socio-economic development. The scaling up of the programme was made possible mainly by the surplus of oil revenue following oil price surges in the mid-1970s and by the flow of foreign aid (Azis 1990). Throughout its existence, there were seven types of *Inpres*, which were divided into block types for province, district and village, and categorical types for elementary school, health development, environmental development and reforestation and road development. In addition, public spending on rural agricultural infrastructure, especially irrigation system, also featured prominently leading the country to achieve rice (staple food) self-sufficiency in 1984.

The government was also aware of the critical importance of communications and transport infrastructures in a large archipelago country, especially when little new infrastructure was built since independence and colonial rudimentary infrastructure was not well maintained. Therefore, the Soeharto government gave a very high priority to infrastructures, even when the oil revenues were declining, and the government was forced to a regime of fiscal austerity (Booth 2016). In addition to rehabilitation and expansion of existing road and irrigation networks, rapid expansion of electricity production and improvements of ports and airports, the government's infrastructure programme included construction of healthcare facilities and provision of clean drinking water to both urban and rural areas. To cite a few examples of achievements, the length of asphalt roads increased over 8-fold, while production of electricity increased 33-fold during 1968–1995 (Booth 2016). Inter-city bus and inter-island ferry services also improved many-fold.

There was a more deliberate skewing of allocations of public investment and *Inpres* funds during the fifth five-year plan (1989–1994), more sharply towards the country's relatively neglected eastern regions. Six provinces—West Kalimantan, West and East Nusa Tenggara, East Timur, Maluku and Irian Jaya—with the highest incidence of poverty received a high share of *Inpres* allocations per capita. This reflected a growing concern about a widening development gap, including in the level of industrialisation, between more prosperous Java/Bali and Sumatra on the one hand and the rest of the country on the other as highlighted in Chap. 1.

Another important instrument for equalisation has been the transmigration programme. Under one of the largest resettlement programmes in the world, people were relocated from the densely populated Java and Bali to the sparsely inhabited outer islands. It was aimed at alleviating pressure on land in Java and Bali and at the same time contributing significantly to the development of outer Islands. Massive financial support from the World Bank, Asian Development Bank (ADB) and bilateral donors helped boost the programme in the 1980s. At its peak between the mid-1970s and late 1980s, around 3.5 million people were resettled in the outer Islands at the government expenses (Adhiati and Bobsien 2001). The transmigration was followed by an even larger number of voluntary migrations.

These efforts certainly had positive impacts, and there has been some convergence among regions. However, increased allocations of development funds were not sufficient to close the development gap and make up for decades of neglect of infrastructure in eastern regions of Indonesia. Moreover, the forced transmigration programme also had political and security agenda of relocating nationalistic Javanese to remote outer Islands. This created resentments among local/indigenous population against the migrants, which were kept under the lid during Soeharto's authoritarian regime. As the Indonesian society was fracturing with ethnic violence and separatist movements immediately following the fall of Soeharto, an unfortunate corollary was the "aspiration to inequality" against the converging development trend due to Soeharto's equalisation programme (Tadjoeddin et al. 2001). That is, the resource-rich regions felt that their socio-economic development was not in line with their resource endowments and were unwilling to subsidise socio-economic development of poorer regions.

In an attempt to face these challenges of separatism and the aspiration to inequality, the new post-Soeharto government of B.J. Habibie undertook a radical decentralisation scheme and abandoned the forced transmigration programme. The successive governments also have been very careful in designing and revising the fiscal transfer formula. It is hoped that the far-reaching decentralisation move would result in more balanced regional development and defuse the threat to Indonesia's unity in diversity.

7.2.3 Employment, Industrial Relations and Manpower Policy

Indonesia never had a stand-alone national employment policy or a white paper on employment policy at the national level. A section on employment was part of the overall national development planning documents consisting of long-term and medium-term plans. That is, employment was mainly seen as an outcome of economic growth.

However, government's transmigration and infrastructure programmes can be regarded as indirectly related to employment. Although their main aim was primarily balancing regional development, they helped to some extent in relieving pressure to create jobs in urban centres. They also boosted economic activities in depressed remote areas and hence created employment opportunities.

In line with his leading agenda on economic development and putting aside politics through the jargon of "growth with stability", Soeharto's moves gradually and firmly disciplined labour by "consolidating" existing labour unions into a single government-controlled union called All Indonesian Workers' Union (*Serikat Pekerja Seluruh Indonesia* or SPSI). Soeharto government's industrial relations policies that suppressed labour activism were seen as vital for business, especially for foreign investors. The relocating Japanese, South Korean and Taiwanese labour-intensive firms found Indonesia attractive for low-wage and largely disciplined labour. At the peak of the industrialisation phase during 1986–1997, growth of workers' real earnings at 4 per cent was well below non-oil and gas workers' productivity growth at 5.3 per cent (Dhanani et al. 2009). During the period, there was "industrial peace" resulting from the suppression of labour activism through the merging of previously active labour unions into a single government-controlled union.

In the same vein, government's education and training programmes were also geared to make Indonesia attractive for investment. Between the early 1970s and mid-1980s, educational expenditure as a proportion of development expenditure increased from 5 per cent to 14 per cent (UNDP 2001). Basic education featured prominently in the *Inpres* programme. During 1974–1978, the government constructed more than 61,000 primary schools throughout the country, making it as one of the largest school construction programmes on record. Duflo (2001) found that this programme led to an increase in years of educational attainment of children ranging from 0.12 to 0.19 for each additional school built per 1000 children. In short, the focus was predominantly on the supply side of the labour market. It was understandable during a period when investment in labour-intensive activities was driving growth and employment.

However, employment got explicit attention in the 1990s. For example, in its opening paragraph, the chapter on manpower of the last medium-term development plan of Soeharto's the New Order administration (adopted in 1994) made a specific reference to the 1945 Constitution, Article 27, Clause 2: "*Setiap warga negara berhak atas pekerjaan dan penghidupan yang layak bagi kemanusiaan*" (every citizen has the right to have *decent work* and decent life for humanity). This was a reminder of a very visionary goal of the nation set by its founding fathers when the country was founded. But the chapter did not elaborate on what it actually meant by decent work, nor did it articulate the steps required to achieve the grand vision. The chapter's sections on employment objectives and targets made no specific reference to decent work, although they touched on some elements of it. The reference, however, has never been made in subsequent development plans.

7.3 Post-AFC Strategies to Transform Indonesia into an Industrialised Economy

Indonesia was the worst crisis-hit economy in the region. The crisis response and economic recovery were not helped by political and administrative changes, triggered by the crisis itself. It took nearly a decade to attain a growth rate close to the pre-crisis level. Until about 2005, the government was focused on economic recovery, and there was no clear plan in place in terms of its medium- to long-term economic development.

The government turned its focus to long-term development in 2007, with the introduction of Law No. 27 on Long-Term National Development Plan (*Rencana Pembangunan Jangka Panjang Nasional* or RPJPN) for the period 2005–2025. The document formulated eight long-term development missions, one of which was to make the nation competitive. This centred on developing quality human resources through the advancements of education and health as well as acquisition of science and technology, which in turn will strengthen the economy. Within this framework, the RPJPN placed the industrial sector as the engine of growth for strengthening the economic structure, supported by agriculture activities in its broad term, the mining sector and effective services provision. The law also included a commitment to apply industry and management best practices for robust economic security. It committed to transform the economy from relying on comparative advantage of resource endowments into competitive advantage of acquiring more sophisticated technology.

Implementation of the RPJPN is operationalised through the five-yearly RPJMN, which serves as a basis for ministries and government agencies in formulating their strategic and budget allocation plans. So far there have been three RPJMN—the first one covered 2005–2009, the second covered 2010–2014 and the third covers 2015–2019.

Regional governments are also required to take RPJMN into account when formulating and adjusting their Regional Medium-Term Development Plans (*Rencana Pembangunan Jangka Menengah Daerah* or RPJMD) in order to ensure better central-regional coordination. The RPJMN is further expanded in the annual Government Work Plan (*Rencana Kerja Pemerintah* or RKP) to ensure the timely and effective implementation of the RPJPN. RKP becomes the basis for formulating the Draft Government Budget (*Rencana Anggaran Pendapatan dan Belanja Negara* or RAPBN).

7.3.1 Industry and Regional Development Policies

As highlighted in Chap. 1, the manufacturing sector contracted roughly by the same magnitude as the economy-wide contraction during the AFC, but the manufacturing recovered much more slowly than the economy-wide recovery. While the early post-crisis period placed more attention on macro stabilisation, RPJPN 2005–2025 adopted in 2007 was a shift towards more active industrial policy. As mentioned earlier, the RPJPN placed the industrial sector as the engine of growth for strengthening the economic structure. The timing of the RPJPN launching coincided with the resource-boom era which was rather unfavourable for industrial development. Thus, the emphasis was placed on improving efficiency, modernisation and value addition in the primary sector, including mining, to promote local and international competitiveness and strengthen the national industrial base.

Balanced re-industrialisation is also seen as an instrument for addressing uneven regional socio-economic development. Thus, in the following year, in 2008, the government issued the Presidential Regulation on National Industrial Policy setting up a long-term industrial development vision for Indonesia to be a strong industrialised nation by 2025, similar with the RPJPN timeline. In 2011, the government also launched Master Plan for Acceleration and Expansion of Indonesia Economic Development (MP3EI) to encourage rapid, balanced, equitable and sustainable economic growth. Balanced re-industrialisation is also seen as an instrument for addressing uneven regional socio-economic development. With the aim of creating complementary and balanced regional development, six economic corridors are planned across the regions with focus on eight main programmes, one of which is industry (see Box 7.1).

The more nationalistic government of President Joko Widodo has rekindled the vision for an industrialised Indonesia. The implementation of this vision has been articulated in Government Regulation No. 14/2015 concerning Master Plan of National Industry Development (*Rencana*

Box 7.1 Six Economic Corridors of MP3EI

In the Master Plan for Acceleration and Expansion of Indonesia Economic Development (MP3EI), regional development takes a centre stage. The plan for six economic corridors articulated in different development themes is as follows (see Fig. 7.1): (1) Sumatra Economic Corridor as a centre for production and processing of natural resources and as nation's energy reserves, (2) Java Economic Corridor as a driver for national industry and service provision, (3) Kalimantan Economic Corridor as a centre for production and processing of national mining and energy reserves, (4) Sulawesi Economic Corridor as a centre for production and processing of national agricultural, plantation, fishery, oil-gas and mining, (5) Bali-Nusa Tenggara Economic Corridor as a gateway for tourism and national food support and (6) Papua-Maluku Islands Economic Corridor as a centre for development of food, fisheries, energy and national mining.

The plan for six economic corridors is based on the comparative advantage of the different regions of Indonesia to promote connectivity within Indonesia and the ASEAN region, as well as to improve human resources and science and technology. The economic corridors are basically a strategy to integrate sectoral and regional development approaches. New growth centres are aimed at optimising agglomeration advantages, exploring regional strengths and reducing spatial imbalance of economic development throughout the country. The MP3EI is a very ambitious plan. It aims to propel Indonesia into the top ten economies and raise per capita from US$3000 to US$15,000 by 2025. See Strategic Asia (2012) for an assessment of MP3EI and its implementation challenges.

(*continued*)

Box 7.1 (continued)

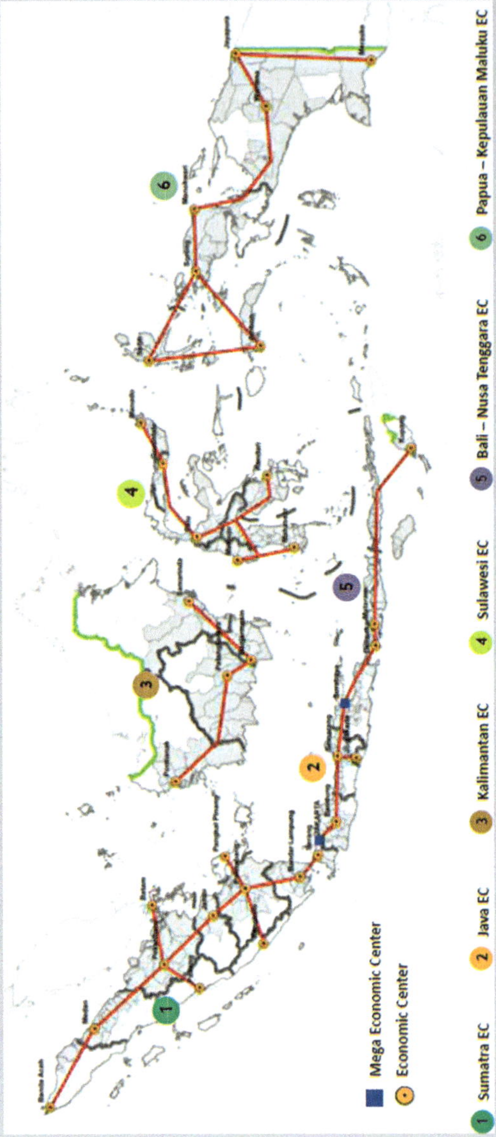

Fig. 7.1 Map of MP3EI six economic corridors. (Source: GOI 2011, p. 46)

Induk Pembangunan Industri Nasional or RIPIN) 2015–2035. It further strengthened government's priority to re-industrialise the economy. The vision is to elevate Indonesia as a strong internationally competitive industrial country with a deep industrial structure, based on innovation and technology. It is aimed at placing the industrial sector as the engine of national economic growth and the main vehicle for regional development by deepening and strengthening the industrial structure throughout the country. Prescribed industrial development strategies include developing upstream and intermediate industries based on natural resources by controlling exports of raw materials and energy resources in the medium term, and developing strategic industries in the longer term by improving the mastery of industrial technology and the quality of industrial human resources. One of the key strategies is the establishment of complementary industrial zones in line with Indonesia's regional diversity.

To achieve this vision, Bappenas has been empowered again, and since October 2014, it is no longer under the Coordinating Minister for the Economy. In addition to the Secretariat of State and Head of the Presidential Office, the Bappenas is now directly under the president. The change is aimed to make an easier coordination workflow with the president. In announcing the change, President Joko Widodo said that Bappenas would translate the programmes he conveyed during his presidential campaign into actual policies: "The planning of the president's vision and mission must be guarded."[10]

The current medium-term development plan, RPJMN (2015–2019), is in essence an elaboration of the President Joko Widodo's campaign promises of a national development agenda called *Nawa Cita*, consisting of nine development priorities. The third development priority of Joko Widodo's *Nawa Cita*, namely "development of peripheral areas", basically concerns regional development. Spreading development beyond Java, especially to the eastern part of the country, is a top priority. The key strategy is accelerating growth centres in each island (outside Java) following respective island's potentials and characteristics, through the development of special economic zones and industrial estates. The RPJMN 2015–2019 set a target of increasing the existing 8 special economic zones to 15 by 2019, where additional zones were planned in the outer Islands. In addition, 14 new industrial estates are also planned, all located in the

[10] https://en.tempo.co/read/news/2014/10/29/056617961/Bappenas-to-Serve-as-Jokowis-Think-Tank

outer Island.[11] The special economic zones are designated areas that offer both foreign and local investors preferential regulatory and tax regimes, as well as the availability of key physical infrastructure such as harbours and power plants that should attract foreign investment in these zones.

This plan is well integrated with a plan on key infrastructure development across the regions. The regions are set to be locally integrated and internationally connected. This is also in line with the plan to spread development of modern industries beyond Java and Batam, with different emphases in each area mainly depending on local resource characteristics such as petrochemical, mining resources and agriculture commodities. While industrial development plan in outer Islands largely follows resource distributions, within Java, the regional development section of the current RPJMN has recognised different manufacturing strengths of provinces in Java. For example, while capital- and technology-intensive manufacturing is more suitable in Jakarta and its surrounding areas, labour-intensive manufacturing has been directed to other areas in West and Central Java, where wage pressures are much less.

7.3.2 Employment and Manpower Policies

In line with policies to revitalise the manufacturing sector, the RPJMN 2014–2019 places a target of increasing formal employment (as the percentage of total employment) from 40.5 per cent in 2014 to 50 per cent in 2019. Previous RPJMNs never had such a bold development target related to achieving quality employment as they only outlined the targeted unemployment reductions. The target of expanding formal employment seems to resonate well with the positive association between manufacturing's GDP share and the size of formal employment implying that the industrial development should contribute to the improvement of employment quality. In fact, the current RPJMN outlines employment creation in the industrial sector as the first vehicle to achieve the target of expanding quality employment (decent jobs).

[11] The 14 new industrial estates are (1) Bintuni, West Papua; (2) Buli, Halmahera Timur, North Maluku; (3) Bitung, North Sulawesi; (4) Palu, Central Sulawesi; (5) Morowali, Central Sulawesi; (6) Konawe, Southeast Sulawesi; (7) Bantaeng, South Sulawesi; (8) Batulicin, South Kalimantan; (9) Jorong, South Kalimantan; (10) Ketapang, West Kalimantan; (11) Landak, West Kalimantan, (12) Kuala Tanjung, North Sumatra, (13) Sei Mangee, North Sumatra; and (14) Tanggamus, Lampung.

National employment policy can be located in two places. First, it is related to employment-related regulations in the forms of laws, government regulations, presidential decrees and so on. Second, it is related to the macro-sectoral employment policy component of the medium-term national planning documents.

Employment and Industrial Relations Regulations

During the early years of the democratic transition after the collapse of the New Order regime, five major pieces of labour-related regulations were enacted: the law on manpower (Law no. 13/2003), the law on trade union (Law no. 21/2000), the law on industrial disputes settlement (Law no. 2/2004), the law on placement and protection of overseas migrant worker (Law no. 39/2004) and the law on national social security system (Law no. 40/2004).

The law on manpower has been the most controversial one. The law puts more emphasis on industrial relations in the formal sector. Hence, it cannot be seen as a law on national employment as such, although industrial relations have important bearings on hiring and firing, as well as employment conditions. This law is seen to be very protective of labour (in the formal sector), especially in terms of regulations related to severance pay rates and dismissals, short-term contract and outsourcing and minimum wages.

Due to this law, Indonesia has been viewed to have the most rigid labour market regulation in the region (World Bank 2010). At the same time, labour market rigidity has been blamed for the dismal employment performance, especially pertaining to the stagnant growth of formal sector employment due to its effect on the business climate (World Bank 2010; Manning and Roesad 2007). Despite having an average economic growth of nearly 5 per cent during 2001–2005,[12] the unemployment rate was on the rise and the share of formal employment declined. Politically this trend was an unfavourable starting point for President Soesilo Bambang Yudhoyono (SBY) in 2005, who set halving the unemployment rate as a key objective of his administration.

Against this background, the first SBY administration had an agenda of rewriting the manpower law to create a more flexible labour market. It was

[12] However, the 4.5 per cent average annual GDP growth during the period was lower than both high-performing Asian economies such as China, India and Vietnam and the pre-crisis years.

clearly stated in the RPJMN 2004–2009 that manpower development was aimed at expanding formal sector employment through improving labour market flexibility, and the revision of the 2003 manpower law was high on the political agenda. In early 2006, the government announced its intention to revise the Manpower Law in the Presidential Instruction No. 3/2006, "Investment Climate Recovery Policy Package". It contained a list of proposed revisions, mainly focusing on the severance pay, fixed-term contracting, minimum wages and outsourcing issues. But the severance pay provisions are seen by the workers as a social protection measure when facing job termination or unemployment in the absence of unemployment benefits schemes. Therefore, the union movement resisted these changes and initiated large-scale demonstrations, culminating in a protest involving around 100,000 workers on 1 May 2006 in Jakarta. This prompted the government to abandon its reform attempt.

The plan to revise the manpower law was dropped from the 2011 national legislation programme (*Program Legislasi Nasional* or PROLEGNAS). The focus in that year was to pass the law on Social Security Implementing Agency (*Badan Penyelenggara Jaminan Sosial* or BPJS) as mandated by the 2004 law on national social security system. The 2004 national social security system law provides a framework for integration of various social security schemes that already existed and new social security schemes, as well as the expansion of social security coverage to the entire population as mandated by the Constitution. This law provided only a framework that needed a derivative law on its implementation. After some delay, the Parliament passed Law No. 24/2011 on BPJS at the end of 2011. The new law created two social security implementing agencies: BPJS Health, which began operation in January 2014, and BPJS Employment, which began operation in July 2015 (Suryahadi et al. 2014; Maftuchan and Fanggidae 2015).

It seemed that the manpower law could only be reformed to make it more flexible in the presence of clear provisions of social security. Therefore, with the passing of Law No. 24/2011 on BPJS, it was hoped that there would be less workers' resistance to the revisions of the Manpower law. Thus, in early 2015, the new administration of President Joko Widodo proposed the revision of the 2003 Manpower Law to be included in the 2015 parliamentary agenda (PROLEGNAS). But the move faced strong resistance by the labour unions and was finally rejected by the parliament. The revision is still out of the agenda. With the slowdown in the Indonesian economy accompanied by workers' dismissals in several factories, in

February 2016, the Indonesian Employers' Association (*Asosiasi Pengusaha Indonesia* or APINDO) renewed their call for the urgency of revising the 2003 Manpower Law to create a more flexible labour market.[13] As of mid-2016, 17 judicial reviews regarding the 2003 Manpower Law have been submitted to the Constitutional Court; 9 were accepted, 2 are still being processed and the remaining were either withdrawn or rejected.

On the other hand, there are arguments for supporting the regulations in current Manpower Law 13/2003 as they are necessary to protect labour rights and safeguard against workplace risks. They could also promote productivity and growth in the long run (Dhanani et al. 2009). Furthermore, ILO (2010) argues that the claim of labour market rigidity resulting in a poor investment climate that reduces employment creation is often not supported by empirical evidence. The declining unemployment rate during 2005–2010 despite lack of improvement in the quality of employment indicates that the Manpower Law did not have adverse consequences on labour market outcomes.[14] The World Bank's "Doing Business" survey listed labour market regulations as only one of the ten factors affecting the overall index of "ease of doing business" in which Indonesia ranked 122 out of 183 economies in 2010. More importantly, the values of rigidity indices related to different components of employing workers were virtually constant during 2003–2007. Furthermore, according to an executive opinion survey by the World Economic Forum, labour rigidity was not among the top five obstacles to operating a business in Indonesia.[15] An investment climate survey in 2007 by the University of Indonesia listed macroeconomic instability, transport and corruption as the top three constraints while labour regulation ranked 11th (LPEM-FEUI 2007). In a follow-up survey in 2009, labour regulation was not listed even in the top 20 obstacles in doing business for manufacturing (LPEM-FEUI 2011).

Yet, the current status quo of labour market regulations in Indonesia, especially regarding the severance pay, is being viewed as a stalemate that traps workers and employers in a lose-lose situation, constraining job creation and leaving employees inadequately protected (World Bank 2010).

[13] See http://ekbis.sindonews.com/read/1083502/34/diguncang-phk-pemerintah-didesak-revisi-uu-ketenagakerjaan-1454845310, accessed on 29 February 2016.

[14] Dhanani et al. (2009) also make a similar point based on their analysis of labour market outcomes during 2000–2007.

[15] World Economic Forum, *The Global Competitiveness Report 2009–2010.*

It is often argued that Indonesia's high *de jure* severance rates deter foreign investment and discourage entrepreneurs from creating new businesses. However, in reality, the high *de jure* severance rates have not been effective in protecting workers. According to 2008 data, only 34 per cent of all eligible workers who separated from a job actually received severance pay. Of those workers who actually received severance pay, 78 per cent collected less than the amount to which they were legally entitled (World Bank 2010). On paper, the regulations will only benefit workers with a permanent contract (less than 3 per cent of the workforce) and unionised employees (11 per cent of wage employees). Regulations, thus, are largely irrelevant for the 92 per cent of all workers who either are employed without a contract or work in the informal sector.

Macro-sectoral Employment Policy

Since 2004, elements of macro-sectoral employment policy at the national level can be found in RPJMN. By default, the national medium-term development planning documents always contain chapters on employment. The RPJMN 2004–2009's priority on improvement of the manpower climate was focused on (1) expanding the formal (modern) sector of the economy and (2) enhancing workers' productivity. The employment component was also found in the priority on poverty reduction. The key intervention on expanding the formal sector of the economy, among others, was creation of a flexible labour market. But the manpower section of the RPJMN 2004–2009 made no reference to decent work agenda.

The RPJMN 2010–2014 stressed the triple-track strategy of *pro-growth*, *pro-poor* and *pro-job*. The manpower section of the RPJMN (2010–2014) in the economics chapter recognised that the main problem of employment was the limited opportunities for the labour force to obtain decent work (*terbatasnya kesempatan untuk memperoleh pekerjaan yang baik*). This is due to the segmented nature of the Indonesian labour market, where around 70 per cent of employment is still in the informal sector, and relatively low education level of the workforce, where around 70 per cent of workforce is only equipped with junior secondary education or less. Therefore, the first directive of the manpower development was to "enhance the creation of decent work, which is productive employment with the adequate protection and social security" (*Mendorong terciptanya kesempatan kerja yang baik (decent work), yaitu lapangan kerja produktif serta adanya perlindungan dan jaminan sosial yang memadai*). In fact, as mentioned earlier, the vision of having decent work and decent life for each and every Indonesian is enshrined in Indonesia's 1945 Constitution.

Thus, it has to be recognised that the RPJM 2010–2014's adoption of the "decent work" phrase literally in English is a major indicator of progress towards fulfilling government's constitutional obligation.

In the current RPJMN (2015–2019), open unemployment rate is targeted to reach 4–5 per cent by 2019, with the creation of ten million new employments during the five-year period. Although no reference to decent work is made in the current RPJMN, it has a specified target of improving the quality of employment through increased share of formal employment by 2019. It also includes the protection of Indonesia's migrant workers abroad among its first development priority list.

Improving labour competitiveness is listed in the sixth development priority. This agenda concerns with the overall improvements of the quality and skills of Indonesian workforces. The vision for re-industrialisation seems to be supported by policies to improve skills and education of the labour force and investment in research and development, which in turn are expected to enhance labour productivity. As part of President Joko Widodo's *Nawa Cita*, key education policies include the introduction of 12-year compulsory education, improved access and quality of higher education through research and higher education infrastructure, and ensuring links between higher education and industry needs.

The current RPJMN's treatment of industrial relations is largely similar to the previous RPJMNs. As in the two previous RPJMNs, this RPJMN also views the current labour regulations as rigid. Therefore, the RPJMN highlights the need to revise the 2003 Manpower Law No. 13/2003.

7.3.3 Minimum Wage Policy

In line with the regime's consistent effort to suppress labour movement, the authoritarian New Order government was never serious about implementing minimum wage policy. It was only in the late 1980s that a first attempt at implementing minimum wage regulation was made as part of response to internal pressures emanating from the rise in labour unrests and external pressures from international labour rights activists demanding better condition for Indonesian workers. In 1989, a regulation issued by the Minister of Manpower introduced *Kebutuhan Fisik Minimum* (KFM or minimum physical needs) as the benchmark for minimum wages. In 1995, another regulation from the ministry upgraded KFM into the more decent *Kebutuhan Hidup Minimum* (KHM or minimum living needs) as a new benchmark for minimum wages.

The fall of Soeharto and the transition to democracy saw a sudden burst of union activities and the passing of Law No. 21/2000 on trade union. Since then, there has been a push for higher minimum wages and social security provisions. Thus, the minimum wage benchmark was further upgraded to *Kebutuhan Hidup Layak* (KHL or decent living needs) by the 2003 Manpower Law. It also introduced Wage Councils at national, provincial and district levels, where representatives from employees, employer and government, including academics/experts, negotiate the level of minimum wage.[16] However, Indonesia does not have a uniform national minimum wage (see Box 7.2). It is at the provincial/district-level Wage Councils where the real negotiations take place in determining regional minimum wages in their respective regions, while the National Wage Council functions primarily on policy monitoring. Until the end of 2000, provincial governors recommended the provincial minimum wages for their respective provinces, and then to be issued as a decree by the Ministry of Manpower, which indicated the executive-heavy nature of the minimum wage setting (Tjandra 2015).

Decentralised minimum wage setting was essentially a follow-up of the decentralisation reform which began in 2001, where the task was delegated to provincial governors and, in some cases, was further passed on to

Box 7.2 Provincial Minimum Wages

Figure 7.2 shows the variation in regional minimum wages. While the highest provincial minimum wage is found in the national capital Jakarta, other provinces in Java have much lower minimum wages, all far below the national average (red line). While Banten is the province with the second highest minimum wage in Java, other Javanese provinces have the lowest minimum wages in the country. That is, the most industrialised Island of Java has the maximum variation, with both the highest and lowest provincial minimum wages.

Interestingly minimum wages in less industrialised and outer Islands display less variations and are close to the national average. This can be a disincentive for labour-intensive manufacturing firms

(*continued*)

[16]The 2013 Manpower Law is the main legal basis for the Wage Council. However, its origin can be traced back to the establishments of *Dewan Penelitian Pengupahan Nasional* (DPPN or National Wage Research Council) in 1969, followed by *Dewan Penelitian Pengupahan Daerah* (DPPD or Regional Wage Research Council).

Box 7.2 (continued)

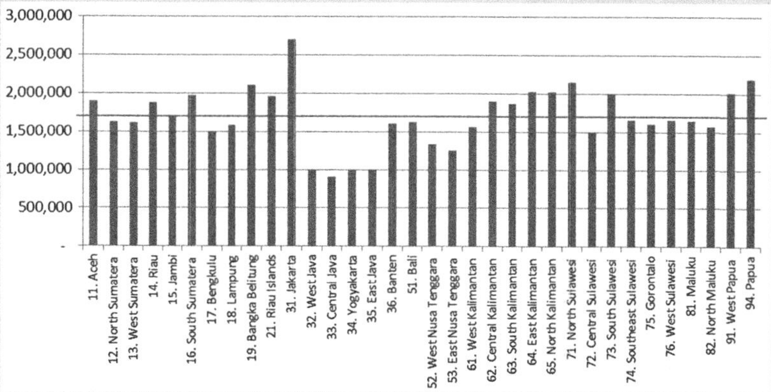

Fig. 7.2 Provincial minimum wage (IDR per month), 2015. (Source: BPS data)

wanting to relocate out of high-wage Jakarta and Banten. On the other hand, Javanese provinces (Central Java, East Java, West Java and Yogyakarta) seem to be racing to the bottom to compete with less industrialised and outer Island provinces. Instead, they should be raising minimum wages to accelerate upgrading of their industries, as experienced in Singapore (see Chowdhury 2008). These Javanese provinces should be aiming at downstream industries with high linkages with the advanced industrial activities in Jakarta and Banten rather than trying to attract low-productivity activities. Such policies will bring their per capita income closer to Jakarta and hence reduce inequality within Java.

Therefore, variations in regional minimum wages in accordance with region's level of industrial development are crucial. Therefore, policymakers and other stakeholders, including labour unions, should consider this factor in negotiating provincial minimum wages. Variations in regional minimum wages can effectively create labour market flexibility to encourage industrial relocation within Indonesia. Of course, minimum wage is only one policy instrument; it has to be complemented with other policies, such as those regarding human resource development and infrastructure.

heads of districts. A district-level minimum wage must be higher than the provincial minimum wage, and a sectoral provincial/district minimum wage must be at least 5 per cent higher than the respective provincial/ district minimum wage.

Periodic adjustments of minimum wage have been a hotly contested industrial relations issue for the provinces. The proponents of labour market flexibility, in particular the business community, see faster adjustments of minimum as problematic, especially for small and medium enterprises (SMEs) and hence an impediment for job creation. Workers, on the other hand, regard upward minimum wage adjustments as essential for marinating a decent living. Thus, two unfavourable scenarios may emerge, depending on the relative bargaining power of the two sides. First, if the business community is stronger and the government sides with it, there could be a race to the bottom in an attempt to woo business from other provinces. Second, if the unions are stronger, then there is a risk of wage-price spirals, resulting in accelerating inflation.

In order to prevent these potentially debilitating outcomes and prolonged widespread disputes in the process of minimum wage setting, the central government introduced a new simplified formula for adjusting minimum wage in late 2015. The new formula stipulates that the percentage increase in minimum wage equals to the national inflation rate plus the national GDP growth rate. Provinces need to arrange gradual adjustments within four years if their current levels of minimum wages are lower than respective "decent living needs" (KHL).[17] The KHL across provinces are scheduled to be reviewed every five years.

The new method has been praised for its simplicity and for taking politics out of the wage determination process. In 2016 and 2017, regional minimum wages increased by 11.5 per cent and 8.25 per cent respectively based on the newly introduced formula. The new formula is largely accepted by employer associations for making minimum wage increases more predictable, but strongly rejected by trade unions since the minimum wage increase is limited to inflation and economic growth. Nevertheless, the new regulation seems to have effectively ended the previously rather volatile movements of minimum wage. During 2010–2015, minimum wages went up by around 20 per cent (or 15 per cent after adjusting for inflation) in main industrial regions in and around Jakarta

[17] Government Regulation (*Peraturan Pemerintah* or PP) no. 78/2015.

and Surabaya. The following examples from Jakarta and Sukabumi are illustrative of increased labour activism in influencing minimum wage setting. The 2013 minimum wage in Jakarta was increased by 44 per cent from the previous year, by far the highest regional minimum wage increase in the country's history.[18] Significant minimum wage increases in 2013 were also experienced by key industrial districts in Banten and West Java. In Sukabumi, the district's minimum wage was nearly doubled in the space of only three years between 2010 and 2013 (Tjandra 2015). The 2013 minimum wage increase was, in fact, the outcome of the largest industrial action in Jakarta on 3 October 2012 attracting around two million workers from across at least 14 industrial cities in Indonesia.

7.4 Concluding Remarks: Creating Internal Flying Geese and Avoiding Race to the Bottom

Despite undergoing a systemic transition after the demise of the Soeharto regime, the successive governments remained focused on advancing Indonesia's progress towards an industrialised country. Of course, however, the approach has shifted from centralised planning to decentralised decision-making. Within the broad guidelines set by the central government, regions are pursuing policies to take advantage of their local conditions. The decentralisation reform has been largely successful in defusing separatist tendencies by empowering local governments. A more consultative approach to fiscal equalisation and the strategy of spreading industrial activities based on local resource endowments and characteristics also seem to have succeeded in reversing resource-rich regions' aspiration to inequality.

Government's various long-term and medium-term plans have, in fact, anticipated the findings of this study, especially on the issue of balanced re-industrialisation and regional development. The strategy of creating economic corridors, regional growth centres and industrial complementarity, including value addition in natural resource sectors, should strengthen backward and forward linkages not only within the industrial sector but also among the regions.

[18] *The Jakarta Post*, 21 November 2012, http://www.thejakartapost.com/news/2012/11/21/jokowi-sets-jakarta-s-2013-minimum-wage-rp-22m.html, accessed on 19 March 2016.

Regional minimum wages can play a vital role in this regard, especially in creating an internal "flying-geese" formation of industrial activities or internal division of labour. Variations in regional minimum wages are critical. Higher minimum wages in developed industrial regions, such Jakarta and its surrounding areas as well as Batam, can effectively force relocation of labour-intensive activities to outer regions with lower minimum wages. The developed industrial regions, thus, can upgrade to more skill- and technology-intensive higher value-added activities to compete at the high end of the global market. Such development strategies can also address the issue of growing inequality by ensuring wages growth in line with overall productivity growth as well as creating productive employment in outer regions.

In facilitating such balanced development, the governments at both the centre and regions need to ensure the provision of good and reliable infrastructure and well-trained labour force. More importantly, they have to guard against fragmenting the national economy and the race to the bottom, especially in labour and environmental standards. In this regard, national-level coordination and strict compliance of regulations such as provincial minimum wages are critical.

References

Adhiati, M.A.S. and A. Bobsien. 2001. "Indonesia's transmigration programme – An update." *A Report Prepared for Down to Earth.* London: International Campaign for Ecological Justice in Indonesia.

Aswicahyono, H., H. Hill and D. Narjoko. 2013. "Industrialization: Patterns, issues, and constraints." In H. Hill, M.E. Khan and J. Zhuang (eds.). *Diagnosing the Indonesian economy: Toward inclusive and green growth.* Manila: Asian Development Bank.

Azis, Iwan Jaya. 1990. "Inpres' role in the reduction of interregional disparity." *Asian Economic Journal* 4 (2):1–27.

Booth, Anne 2005. "The evolving role of the central government in economic planning and policy making in Indonesia." *Bulletin of Indonesian Economic Studies* 41(2): 197–219.

Booth, Anne. 2016. *Economic change in modern Indonesia: Colonial and post-colonial comparisons.* Cambridge: Cambridge University Press.

Chowdhury, A. 2008. "Labour market policies as instruments of industry policy: What can Europe learn from Southeast Asia?" *American Journal of Economics and Sociology* 67(4): 661–81.

Dhanani, S., I. Islam and A. Chowdhury. 2009. *The Indonesia labour market: Challenge and changes*. London: Routledge.

Duflo, Esther 2001. "Schooling and labor market consequences of school construction in Indonesia: Evidence from an unusual policy experiment." *American Economic Review* 91(4): 795–813.

GOI. 2011. *Master plan for acceleration and expansion of Indonesia economic development*. Jakarta: Government of Indonesia.

Higgins, B. 1968. Economic development principles, problems, and policies. London: Constable.

Hill, H. 2000. *The Indonesian economy, 2nd edition*. Cambridge: Cambridge University Press.

ILO. 2010. *Accelerating a job-rich recovery in G20 countries: Building on experience*. Geneva: International Labour Office.

Lewis, J.D. 1994. "Indonesia's industrial and trade policy during and after the oil boom." *Development Discussion Papers* No. 491. Cambridge, MA: Harvard Institute for International Development.

LPEM-FEUI. 2007. *Investment climate monitoring. Round IV*. Jakarta: Institute for Economic and Social Research, University of Indonesia.

LPEM-FEUI. 2011. *Final report: Survey of the impact of the global economic crisis in Indonesia's investment climate*. Jakarta.

Maftuchan A. and V. Fanggidae. 2015. "Social security for all workers." *The Jakarta Post*, July 7.

Manning, C. and K. Roesad. 2007. "The manpower law of 2003 and its implementing regulations: Genesis, key articles and potential impact." *Bulletin of Indonesian Economic Studies* 43(1): 59–86.

McCawley, Peter. 2013. "The Indonesian economy during the Soeharto era: A review." *Masyarakat Indonesia* 39(2): 269–88.

Myrdal, G. 1968. *Asian drama – An inquiry into the poverty of nations*. Harmondsworth: Penguin Books.

Strategic Asia. 2012. "Implementing Indonesia's Economic Master Plan (MP3EI): Challenges, limitations and corridor specific differences." *Report for the UK Foreign and Commonwealth Office in Jakarta*.

Suryahadi, A, V. Febriany and A. Yumna. 2014. "Expanding social security in Indonesia: The processes and challenges." *UNRISD Working Paper* 2014–14.

Tadjoeddin, M.Z., W. Suharyo and S. Mishra. 2001. "Regional disparity and vertical conflicts in Indonesia." *Journal of the Asia Pacific Economy* 6(3): 283–304.

Tijaja, J. and M. Faisal. 2014. "Industrial policy in Indonesia: A global value chain perspective." *Asian Development Bank Economics Working Paper Series* No. 411.

Tjandra, S. 2015. *Labour law and development in Indonesia*. PhD Thesis at University of Leiden.

UNDP. 2001. *Indonesia National Human Development Report (NHDR): Towards a new consensus, democracy and human development in Indonesia.* Jakarta: UNDP.

World Bank. 2010. *Indonesia jobs report: Towards better jobs and security for all.* Jakarta: World Bank.

Index[1]

A
Active industry policy, 5, 145
ASEAN economic community (AEC), v, 11
Asian Financial Crisis (AFC), 1, 2, 8, 14, 15, 17, 19–22, 25, 43, 53, 54, 61–63, 73, 103, 126, 145, 153, 168, 189, 191, 194, 197, 202
Average real wage, 107, 176

B
Backward linkages, 5, 194
Balanced regional development, v, 10, 199, 203

C
Capital intensive, 8, 14, 14n8, 53, 94, 109, 111, 114, 115, 117, 125, 128, 142, 178, 181, 183, 185
Casual-employment, 40, 50, 52, 53, 62, 96, 105, 106
Commodity price boom, 2

D
Decent life for humanity, 10, 201
Decentralisation, 21, 22, 25–34, 39, 160, 199, 212, 215
Decomposition analysis, 9
Deindustrialisation, 2, 3, 8, 17–19, 17n9, 103, 104, 109, 145, 180–182
De-linking between wages and productivity, 7, 141
Democratisation, 21, 22, 25, 33, 160, 179
Division of labour, v, 5, 9, 216
Dutch disease, 3, 19, 194
Dynamic panel data (DPD), 125, 138

[1] Note: Page numbers followed by 'n' refer to notes

M. Z. Tadjoeddin, A. Chowdhury, *Employment and Re-Industrialisation in Post Soeharto Indonesia*, Critical Studies of the Asia-Pacific, https://doi.org/10.1057/978-1-137-50566-8

E

Efficiency wage theory, 81, 82
Employment functions, 92, 123, 134–149
Employment quality, 10, 21, 48, 50–70, 73, 77, 206
Employment rate, 6, 40–45, 168
Employment status, 21n10, 50–55, 62, 66, 67, 74–76, 74n2, 166, 166n6, 167
Exchange rates, 3, 5, 19, 22, 191, 192, 195
Export promotion, 127
Export-oriented industrialisation, 12

F

Factor intensity, 7, 8, 107, 111–119, 124–126, 128, 142, 143, 145
Flying-geese, v, 5, 9, 215, 216
Formal sector, 3, 49, 53, 56–58, 66, 70, 78, 96, 100, 207, 208, 210
Forward linkages, v, 6, 10, 215
Functional distribution of income, 86

G

Gini index, 23, 23n12, 25, 62, 63, 64n9, 92n7, 94, 96–99, 153, 154, 156–159
Global Financial crisis (GFC), v, 2, 19, 39, 44, 86, 126, 163

H

Human development index (HDI), 9, 27–29, 161, 174, 175, 179, 180
Human resource development (HRD), 5, 10, 213

I

Import substitution, 13, 34, 127, 191–194
Incidence of low pay, 6, 39, 60–66, 70, 73
Industrial relations, 10, 159, 199–201, 207–211, 214
Industrial relocations, 9–11, 213
Inequality, v, 1, 39, 73–100, 103, 123, 153–186, 199
Input-Output (I-O), 86, 87
Internal dynamics, 10

J

Jobless growth, 3, 20–22, 106, 161, 165

L

Labour intensive, 2, 5, 8, 14, 14n7, 15, 17, 20, 22, 34, 53, 109, 111, 112, 114, 115, 119, 127, 178, 181, 183, 186, 195, 200, 206, 216
Labour market flexibility, 10, 95, 136, 208, 213, 214
Labour market rigidity, 106, 207, 209
Labour shares of income, 11, 94
Large-medium firms, 113, 124–129, 140–145

M

Marginal productivity theory, 81, 82
Median real wage, 6
Micro-small firms, 117, 120
Minimum wage, v, xix, xxiii, 4, 5, 7, 10, 11, 26, 64, 75, 76, 76n5, 85, 95–100, 118, 120, 136, 179, 189, 207, 208, 211–216

P

Palma ratio, 25
Post Keynesian paradigm, 83
Poverty line, 1, 23, 45, 46, 49, 58–60
Productivity, 3, 43, 73–100, 103–120, 123–149, 153, 192

Q

Quality of employment, 3, 6, 39, 45, 48, 50, 60, 66, 68, 70, 166, 168, 186, 209, 211

R

Race to the bottom, 6, 10, 11, 145, 214–216
Reindustrialisation, v, 3, 4, 8, 9, 119, 120, 145, 153, 174, 186, 202, 211, 215
Research and development (R & D), 5, 191, 211
Resource intensive, 8, 111, 112, 114, 115, 117, 126, 128, 143

S

Self-employment, 48, 53
Severance pay, 4, 118, 207–210
Social security, 39, 45, 46, 55–57, 69, 207, 208, 210, 212
Soeharto, 1, 10, 29, 39, 42, 127, 190, 196, 198–201, 212, 215
Spatial inequalities, 9, 29, 153–176, 163n4
Structural transformation, 2, 12–20

T

Trade unions, 11, 207, 212, 214

U

Under-employment, 6, 39, 50, 51, 57, 58, 60
Unemployment rate, 6, 20, 40–51, 53, 60, 66, 69, 161–166, 174, 175, 186, 207, 209, 211
Unity in diversity, 33, 33n18, 199

V

Vulnerable employment, 6, 54–55, 66, 161, 166–176, 178

W

Wage-earnings, 6–8, 11, 61, 73–79, 86, 88, 92–99, 92n7, 103, 106, 107, 138–140, 177, 178
Wage-productivity ratio, 7–9, 73, 83, 86, 87, 92–94, 106, 108–111, 113–116, 140, 142
Working poor, 4, 6, 43–46, 43n1, 48, 136

Y

Youth NEET (neither in employment or education and training), 6, 39, 68–69

The manufacturer's authorised representative in the EU is Springer Nature Customer Service Centre GmbH, Europaplatz 3, 69115 Heidelberg, Germany. If you have any concerns regarding our products, please contact ProductSafety@springernature.com

Printed and bound by CPI Group (UK) Ltd, Croydon, CR0 4YY
13/10/2026
02232352-0002